PREMIER EDITION

TRADITIONAL *Family* HOME PLANS

— PUBLISHER: JAMES D. MCNAIR III —

EDITORAL STAFF: Debra Cochran, Sue Barile

COVERS & INTERIOR LAYOUTS: Laura Scott

Submit all Canadian plan orders to:
The Garlinghouse Company
60 Baffin Place, Unit #5
Waterloo, Ontario N2V 1Z7
Canadians Order only: 1-800-561-4169
Fax#: 1-800-719-3291
Customer Service#: 1-519-746-4169

GARLINGHOUSE

Library of Congress No.: 99-71537/ISBN: 0-938708-88-0

DESIGN 94928

The Great room views the rear yard through a terrific bay window with transoms above. The sunny dinette, also enhanced by a bay window, features a built-in planning desk. The kitchen is roomy and efficient. A built in pantry, two lazy Susans, a snack bar and a cozy see through fireplace shared with the Great room, highlight the kitchen. A wet bar/servery is located between the dinette and the Great room. The large master suite encompasses the arched window at the front of the home. The master bath has a walk-in closet, his and her vanities and a corner whirlpool tub with windows above. The secondary bedrooms have private access to a full double vanity bath. The photographed home may have been modified to suit individual tastes.

GRACIOUS FOYER

Main Floor	1,808 sq. ft.
Basement	1,808 sq. ft.
Garage	551 sq. ft.
Bedrooms	3
Bathrooms	2 full, 1 half
Foundation	Basement
Width...64'-0"	Depth...44'-0"
Price Code	C

TOTAL LIVING AREA:
1,808 sq. ft.

© design basics, inc.

main floor

DESIGN 99456

Stucco accents and graceful window treatments enhance this home. The double doors open to the private den with bright bayed windows. The French doors open to a spacious screened-in veranda ideal for outdoor entertaining. The open living room and handsome curved staircase add drama to the entry area. The gourmet kitchen, bayed dinette and volume family room flow together nicely. The

bayed master bedroom, with a ten foot vaulted ceiling, is situated for privacy. Two walk-in closets, his'n'her vanities, corner whirlpool and compartment shower and stool highlights the master dressing area. The three additional bedrooms have private access to baths. The photographed home may have been modified to suit individual tastes.

First Floor............1,631 sq. ft.
Second Floor.........1,426 sq. ft.
Basement.............1,631 sq. ft.
Garage...................681 sq. ft.
Bedrooms.............................4
Bathrooms...........3 full, 1 half
Foundation............Basement,
Width....60'-0" Depth...58'-0"
Price Code..............................E

TOTAL LIVING AREA:
3,057 sq. ft.

HIGH IMPACT HOME

DESIGN 94942

A covered porch invites you into this country style home. Handsome bookcases frame the fireplace in the family room. Double doors provide the family room with added privacy. The kitchen features an island, a lazy Susan and easy access to the walk-in laundry. The master bedroom features a boxed ceiling and separate entries into the walk-in closet and master bath. The master bath is spacious and includes a double vanity, whirlpool tub and a shower. The photographed home may have been modified to suit individual tastes.

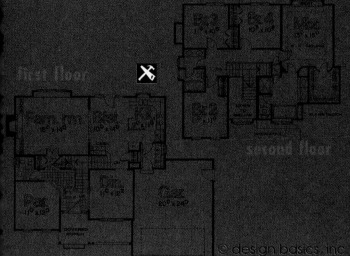

DESIGN 99477

Gables lend impact to this home, while the covered front porch is supported by columns. The dining room has an angled entry and bay windowed front. The Great room has a fireplace and transom windows in the front and back walls. Enjoy meals in the breakfast nook with its 10' ceiling. The kitchen has a center island and a a snack bar. The secluded master bedroom has a whirlpool tub in the bath. The photographed home may have been modified to suit individual tastes.

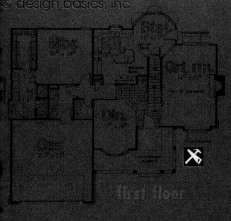

DESIGN 93090

Twin arches add to the symmetry of this European influenced design. Inside, the floor plan provides all the elements demanded by a ninety's lifestyle including dual areas for entertaining in the living room and family room. The functional kitchen design with angled eating bar opens the area to the family room and the breakfast room. The dining room is located off the foyer and is visible through a series of elegant arches. Upstairs, three bedrooms, two baths and a game room complete the plan. This plan is available with a basement, crawl space, or slab foundation. Please specify when ordering. No materials list is available for this plan. The photographed home may have been modified to suit individual tastes.

First Floor............1,919 sq. ft.
Second Floor........1,190 sq. ft.
Bonus Room...........286 sq. ft.
Garage...................561 sq. ft.
Bedrooms........5   Baths...3.5
Foundation............Basement,
            Slab, Crawl Space
Width...64'-6" Depth...55'-10"
Price Code...........................E

TOTAL LIVING AREA:
3,109 sq. ft.

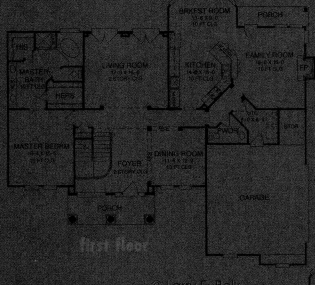

first floor

© Larry E. Belk

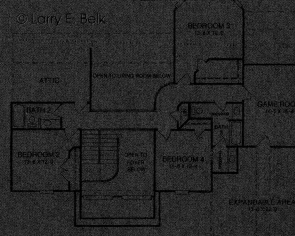

second floor

ELEGANCE

...race and elegance are found around every

...orner and in every columned entryway.

5

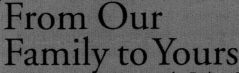

From Our Family to Yours

by Debra Cochran

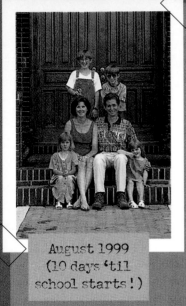

Congratulations! You're ready for that all-important family home. While you are thinking of all the amenities you would like in this home, it is only natural to remember growing up in your parent's home. Memories of childhood always seem to revolve around your neighborhood, your house, the backdrop of your life at the time. Your room was your domain. Or, maybe, you shared a room with a sibling. In your room, you pursued hobbies, had posters on the walls, and the treasures you had collected were on display. Your room was your personal niche. You may remember fighting over your privacy with your sister or wanting to throttle your brother for finding your diary in your secret hiding place. Fondly, you think of those sleepovers with friends and family celebrations around the dining table. You may remember mom cooking dinner in the kitchen or dad down in the basement working at his workbench. There were summer nights of catching fireflies in the back yard and putting them into a jar. You can visualize the family dog curled up in front of the fireplace or the cat on the front stoop. There was rollerskating with the neighborhood kids, jump rope, hop scotch, basketball, baseball and cookouts. There were snowball fights and sledding...Why you could go on and on. Seems that those memories of ours get rosier with time. But, some of what we remember we do want for our children. We want our children to have wonderful memories of growing up in a home full of love. That backdrop we remember, our home, is more than shelter from the elements. It becomes part of our personal history.

We want a home that is efficient and convenient, one that has a homey and welcoming feeling. If we are just starting out, we want room to grow. If we are slowly becoming empty nesters, we want the home arranged so that when those "chicks" come back for a visit, there is room for family dinner and accommodations for overnight stays.

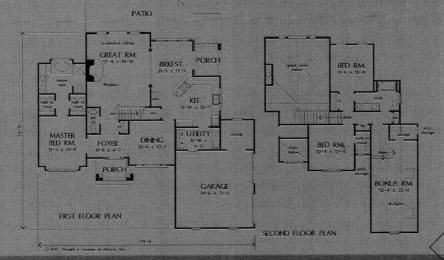

Celebrating
2 years in their
new home...now
expecting!

Today's architects and designers have taken all of this into account. Thee is a mixture of traditional styles combining into the family home today. Great open spaces, kitchens blending with eating areas and flowing into family rooms enabling interaction of family members between the living spaces. These living spaces are also perfect for family celebrations. First floor master suites have become very popular, giving the owners a private retreat. The master bath includes whirlpool tubs, separate showers and dual vanities. Another popular feature is secondary bedrooms with private access to secondary baths. These baths with dual vanities, eliminate arguments over the sink and the mirror. The traditional family in our modern age is busy, active, growing towards their goals for the future.

The Garlinghouse Company is pleased to present a splendid collection of Traditional Family Home Plans. Our award winning network of designers have developed homes that are innovative and unique in caring for the needs of the modern family. The Garlinghouse Company has been helping families just like yours move into their dream homes since 1907. Our longevity and success comes from staying up-to-date with our customer's needs without losing sight of the values and quality we have come to stand for. As you page through our assortment of home plans, keep in mind that you are creating the backdrop of your families memories. Our "family" at The Garlinghouse Company wishes your family happiness in creating those precious memories in your new home.

Back from
vacation,
before pizza
arrives

2 weeks before
Halloween,
Fall '98

Just moved in!

Frequently Asked Questions

Can I make changes to the plans?
Your builder can make simple non-structural changes. The Garlinghouse Company Design Staff can make significant structural changes after the purchase of the erasable, reproducible vellum. Or if you prefer, you may have the changes done locally after the purchase of an erasable reproducible vellum. For details see page 249.

What does the materials list Include?
A materials list will include quantities, dimensions and specifications of major materials needed to build your home and are available for most plans at a modest additional charge. You will get faster, more accurate bids and avoid paying for unused materials and waste. Due to differences in regional requirements electrical, plumbing and heating/air conditioning equipment specifications are not designed specifically for each plan.

What do I get with my plans?
Exterior Elevations
Foundation Plan
Typical Wall Section
Cabinet details (most plans)
Fireplace details (if available)
Information necessary to construct Roof
Typical Cross Section
Detailed Floor Plans
Stair Information (if available)

Will these plans meet my local building codes? All plans are drawn to conform to one or more of the industry's national building standards. However, your plan may need to be modified to meet your local code.

What benefit is there in buying stock blueprints as opposed to starting from scratch with an architect? First of all you save in time. You start out with a drawn "idea" of what you want and can customize the home from that point. Second, you save money; in fact in many instances you can save thousands of dollars.

How can I find out if I can afford to build a home?
The Garlinghouse Company offers Zip-Quote just for this purpose. By purchasing Zip-Quote you can find out the building cost for your new home without waiting for a contractor to compile the bids. We offer Zip-Quote in two options, Itemized Zip-Quote and Bottom Line Zip-Quote. For a detailed explanation of this product please see order page 250 at the back of the book.

DESIGN 99457

The spacious two-story entry surveys the formal dining room, enhanced by built-in hutch space. The Great room certainly lives up to its name. A built-in entertainment center, a see-through fireplace and an elegant bayed window highlight the room. The kitchen/breakfast hearth room areas feature gazebo dining, wrapping counters, and numerous amenities. On the second floor the luxurious master suite is topped by a decorative ceiling and enjoys a lavish bath featuring a whirlpool tub, his-n-her vanity and a walk-in closet. The three additional bedrooms share the compartmented bath in the hall. The photographed home may have been modified to suit individual tastes.

© design basics, inc.

First Floor.............1,150 sq. ft.
Second Floor........1,120 sq. ft.
Basement..............1,150 sq. ft.
Garage.....................457 sq. ft.
Bedrooms...........................4
Bathrooms...........2 full, 1 half
Foundation................Basement
Width...46'-0"   Depth...48'-0"
Price Code............................D

TOTAL LIVING AREA:
2,270 sq. ft.

first floor   second floor

TWO-STORY ENTRY

DESIGN 99813

Square columns with chamfered corners adorn the front porch. Inside, the vaulted ceiling in the Great room gracefully arches to receive a center dormer that bathes the room in light. The dining room, front bedroom, and master suite feature tray ceilings. The private master bath includes a separate shower, a garden tub, a skylight, dual vanity, and an enclosed toilet. This plan is available with a basement or crawl space foundation. Please specify when ordering.

Donald. A. Gardner Architects, Inc.

© 1995 Donald A. Gardner Architects, Inc.

Main Floor	1,959 sq. ft.
Bonus Room	385 sq. ft.
Garage	484 sq. ft.
Bedrooms	3 Baths 2
Foundation	Bsmnt,Crawl
Width	65'-8" Depth 55'-2"
Price Code	D

TOTAL LIVING AREA:
1,959 sq. ft.

DESIGN 99809

This handsome, efficient house contains many popular innovations. It's designed for easy, affordable construction. A spacious cathedral ceiling expands the open Great room, kitchen and dining area. The bedroom/study features a cathedral ceiling that emphasizes double windows with a circle top. The master bedroom is highlighted by a cathedral ceiling for extra volume and light. The private bath includes a double bowl vanity, garden tub, and linen closet. A walk-in closet next to the bedroom completes the suite.

Donald A. Gardner Architects, Inc.

Main Floor	1,417 sq. ft.
Garage	441 sq. ft.
Bedrooms	3 Baths 2
Foundation	Crawl
Width	69'-0" Depth 39'-0"
Price Code	C

TOTAL LIVING AREA:
1,417 sq. ft.

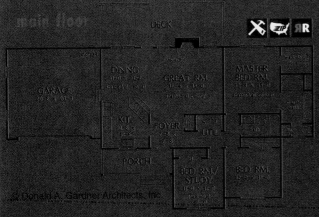

© 1995 Donald A. Gardner Architects, Inc.

DESIGN 32146

If you are looking for style and scale, look no further. This plan has two bedrooms on the first floor and three on the second floor. The first floor guest room has a full bath. The dining room is accented by columns and is across the hall from the Great room. The kitchen, breakfast area and the family room flow into each other for a spacious informal living area. The master suite enjoys a secluded location and a private porch. Access the rear deck from several rooms of this home. The photographed home may have been modified to suit individual tastes.

First Floor............2,727 sq. ft.
Second Floor.........1,168 sq. ft.
Basement.............2,250 sq. ft.
Garage....................984 sq. ft.
Bonus......................213 sq. ft.
Bedrooms.....4   Baths...4.5
Foundation..............Basement
Width...73'-8" Depth...72'-2"
Price Code.............................F

TOTAL LIVING AREA:
3,895 sq. ft.

first floor

second floor

GRANDEUR

Each room exudes the style and panache you'd expect from a home of this scale.

DESIGN 99830

This compact plan with rear garage offers plenty of room for families just starting out and empty-nester scaling down. The Great room's cathedral ceiling, combines with the openness of the adjoining dining room and kitchen to create spaciousness. The dining room has a bay window while a palladian window allows ample light into the Great room. The master suite features ample closet space and a skylit bath which boasts a dual vanity and separate tub and shower.

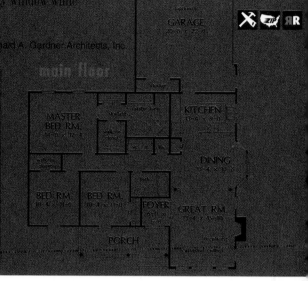

© Donald A. Gardner Architects, Inc.

© Donald A. Gardner Architects, Inc.

DESIGN 96484

Spacious home in just 1,246 square feet? Yes, by opening up the living spaces to flow into one another and vaulting the ceilings in key rooms for added volume. A cathedral ceiling maximizes space in the open Great room and dining room. The kitchen features a center skylight, breakfast bar, and access to a garage via the screened porch. Two bedrooms share a bath up front, while the master suite with cathedral ceiling, walk-in closet, and well-equipped bath maintains privacy in back.

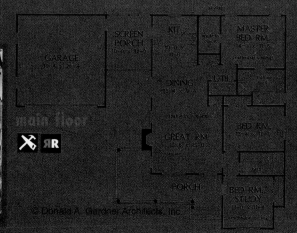

© Donald A. Gardner Architects, Inc.

14

DESIGN 99490

Design Basics, Inc.

The cozy front porch of this home gives an attractive country appearance to the home. Inside, the tiled foyer leads into the Great room which is accented by a fireplace with transom windows to either side. The kitchen includes a snack bar/island, a pantry and is open to the breakfast room. A bright bay window highlights the breakfast room with natural illumination. The master suite includes a five-piece, whirlpool bath and a walk-in closet. The photographed home may have been modified to suit individual tastes.

Main Floor............1,479 sq. ft.
Bedrooms............................3
Bathrooms......................2 full
Foundation.....Basement, Slab
Width...48'-0"   Depth...50'-0"
Price Code..........................A

TOTAL LIVING AREA:
1,479 sq. ft.

Main Floor	1,782 sq. ft.
Basement	1,782 sq. ft.
Garage	466 sq. ft.
Bedrooms	3 Baths 2
Foundation	Bsmnt
Width	52'-0" Depth 59'-4"
Price Code	B

TOTAL LIVING AREA:
1,782 sq. ft.

DESIGN 94917

The arched windows and volume ceiling in the dining room capture the eye upon entry. The hearth area has bayed windows and shares a three-sided fireplace. The breakfast area is enhanced with light through the picture awning windows. The kitchen is equipped with a snack bar peninsula, large pantry and a Lazy Susan. The master suite is enhanced by a nine foot ceiling, large walk-in closet and a whirlpool tub. The photographed home may have been modified to suit individual tastes.

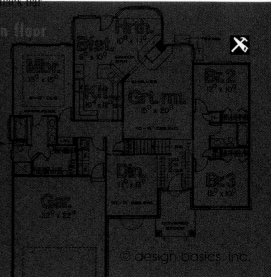

Main Floor	1,508 sq. ft.
Basement	1,429 sq. ft.
Garage	440 sq. ft.
Bedrooms	3 Baths 2
Foundation	Bsmnt, Slab, Crawl
Width	60'-0" Depth 47'-0"
Price Code	B

TOTAL LIVING AREA:
1,508 sq. ft.

DESIGN 92649

An enchanting one-level home with grand openings between rooms creates a spacious effect. The functional kitchen provides an abundance of counter space. Additional room for quick meals or serving an oversized crowd is provided at the breakfast bar. Double hung windows and angles add light and dimension to the dining area. The Great room with a sloped ceiling and a wood burning fireplace opens to the dining area and the foyer, making this three bedroom ranch look and feel much larger than its actual size. No materials list is available for this plan.

DESIGN 99406

Design Basics, Inc.

The entry leads into the formal dining room with a built-in hutch space. The Kitchen boasts a central island, efficient cabinet space, a pantry and Lazy Susans. The breakfast area shares a see through fireplace with the Great room. The prominent windows and the thirteen foot ceiling illuminates and enhances the Great room. The master bedroom presents a vaulted ceiling and a generous walk-in closet. Secondary bedrooms share a convenient hall bath. The bonus room is available for storage or expansion. The photographed home may have been modified to suit individual tastes.

First Floor............1,597 sq. ft.
Second Floor............685 sq. ft.
Basement.............1,597 sq. ft.
Garage...................711 sq. ft.
Bedrooms..............................4
Bathrooms...........2 full, 1 half
Foundation...............Basement
Width....65'-4" Depth....48'-8"
Price Code............................D

TOTAL LIVING AREA:
2,282 sq. ft.

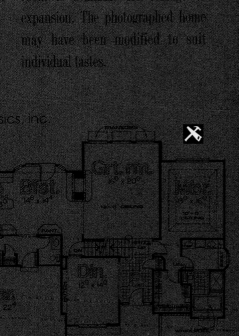

© design basics, inc.

COMFY ATMOSPHERE

The Garlinghouse Company

DESIGN 24701

This home features a well designed floor plan, offering convenience and style. The roomy living room includes a two-sided fireplace shared with the dining room. An efficient U-shaped kitchen, equipped with a peninsula counter/breakfast bar, is open to the dining room. An entrance from the garage into the kitchen eliminates tracked in dirt and affords step-saving convenience when unloading groceries. The private master suite includes a whirlpool tub, a double vanity and a step-in shower.

Main Floor............1,625 sq. ft.
Basement.............1,625 sq. ft.
Garage...................455 sq. ft.
Bedrooms.............................3
Bathrooms...................2 full
Foundation.............Basement,
Slab, Crawl Space
Width....54'-0" Depth....48'-4"
Price Code............................B

TOTAL LIVING AREA:
1,738 sq. ft.

main floor

found. option

CAREFREE RANCH

DESIGN 92557

This home exudes elegance and style, using detailing and a covered front porch accented by gracious columns. The den is enhanced by a corner fireplace and adjoins with the dining room. The efficient kitchen is well-appointed and has easy access to the utility room/laundry. The master bedroom is topped by a vaulted ceiling and pampered by a private bath and a walk-in closet. The two secondary bedrooms are located at the opposite end of the home from the master suite and share a full bath located between the rooms. This plan is available with a crawl space or slab foundation. Please specify when ordering.

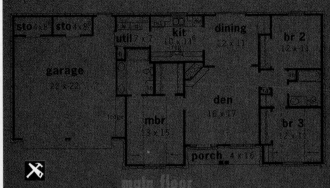

DESIGN 99806

A one-story design with lots of appeal and many extras. From the front wrap porch, enter an open, volume space that takes in the Great room with fireplace, dining room, and kitchen. The kitchen has a pantry, a skylight, and a peninsula counter. The master suite boasts a cathedral ceiling, both walk-in and linen closets, and a garden tub. The front swing room is topped by a cathedral ceiling.

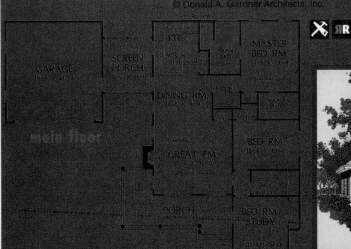

© Donald A. Gardner Architects, Inc.

19

DESIGN 24700

Notice the palladian window with a fan light above at the front of the home. The entrance porch includes a turned post entry. Once inside, the living room is topped by an impressive vaulted ceiling. A fireplace accents the room. A decorative ceiling enhances both the master bedroom and the dining room. Efficiently designed, the kitchen includes a peninsula counter and serves the dining room with ease. A private bath and double closet highlight the master suite.

Main Floor............1,312 sq. ft.
Basement.............1,293 sq. ft.
Garage...................459 sq. ft.
Bedrooms............................3
Bathrooms.......................2 full
Foundation.............Basement,
　　　　Slab, Crawl Space
Width....0'-0"　　Depth....0'-0"
Price Code..............................A

TOTAL LIVING AREA:
1,312 sq. ft.

SPACIOUS LIVING

DESIGN 92625

Studer Residential Design, Inc.

A classic design and spacious interior make this home attractive to the discriminating buyer. Brick and wood trim, multiple gables, and wing walls enhance the outside. Sloped ceilings, a corner fireplace, windows across the rear of the Great room and a boxed window in the dining room area are visible as you enter the open foyer. The kitchen has a pantry, and the breakfast area is surrounded by windows. The master suite boasts a whirlpool tub, a double sink, a shower and a walk-in closet. No materials list available for this plan.

Main Floor	1,710 sq. ft.
Basement	1,560 sq. ft.
Garage	455 sq. ft.
Bedrooms	3
Bathrooms	2 full
Foundation	Basement
Width...65'-10"	Depth...56'-0"
Price Code	B

TOTAL LIVING AREA:
1,710 sq. ft.

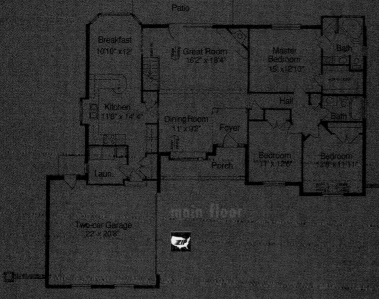

CLASSIC DESIGN

First Floor.....................891 sq. ft.
Second Floor..................894 sq. ft.
Basement.......................891 sq. ft.
Garage..........................534 sq. ft.
Bedrooms.......2   Baths.......2.5
Foundation....Bsmnt,Slab,Crawl
Width......46'-8" Depth......35'-8"
Price Code............................B

TOTAL LIVING AREA:
1,785 sq. ft.

DESIGN 24610

The Great room of this home has a two story fireplace. A multi-paned, arched window illuminates the room. The well-designed kitchen includes a central island, a built-in pantry, double sinks, not to mention the ample storage and counter space. The second floor overlooks the Great room. The master bedroom has a private bath and a walk-in closet. The two additional bedrooms share a full hall bath.

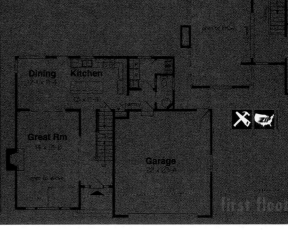

Main Floor................1,699 sq. ft.
Bonus Room.................386 sq. ft.
Garage & Storage.........637 sq. ft.
Bedrooms.......3   Baths..........2
Foundation........................Crawl
Width......63'-8" Depth......55'-2"
Price Code............................D

TOTAL LIVING AREA:
1,699 sq. ft.

DESIGN 99831

Keystone arches, gables, and stucco give European sophistication to this plan. A large Great room has a cathedral ceiling and a fireplace. An octagonal tray ceiling dresses up the dining room. Tray ceiling treatments in both the master and front bedrooms add impact. An indulgent master bath features a separate toilet area, garden tub, shower, and dual vanity. A bonus room over the garage adds flexibility to this one-level plan.

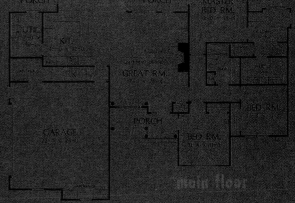

© Donald A. Gardner Architects, Inc.

© Donald A. Gardner Architects, Inc.

DESIGN 99807

Donald. A. Gardner Architects, Inc.

Dormers cast light into the foyer for a grand first impression. The Great room is articulated by columns and features a cathedral ceiling. Tray ceilings and picture windows with circle tops accent the front bedroom and dining room. A secluded master suite boasts a tray ceiling, and includes a skylight garden tub, separate shower, dual vanity and a spacious walk-in closet. Plan includes a crawl space foundation and a basement option is available.

Main Floor	1,879 sq. ft.
Bonus Room	360 sq. ft.
Garage	485 sq. ft.
Bedrooms	3
Bathrooms	2 full
Foundation	Basement, Crawl Space
Width	66'-4" Depth...55'-2"
Price Code	D

TOTAL LIVING AREA:
1,879 sq. ft.

SOLID IMPRESSION

DESIGN 20164

Here's a pretty, one-level home designed for carefree living. The central foyer divides active and quiet areas. Step back to a fireplaced living room with dramatic, towering ceilings and a panoramic view of the backyard. The adjoining dining room features a sloping ceiling crowned by a plant shelf, and sliders to a deck. A handy, U-shaped kitchen features a window over the sink, and a walk-in pantry. You'll find three bedrooms tucked off the foyer. Front bedrooms share a handy full bath. The master suite boasts its own private bath with both shower and tub, a room-sized walk-in closet, and a bump-out window that adds light and space.

Main Floor.............1,456 sq. ft.
Basement.............1,448 sq. ft.
Garage....................452 sq. ft.
Bedrooms.............................3
Bathrooms......................2 full
Foundation.......Basement, Slab,
Crawl Space
Width...50'-0"   Depth...45'-4"
Price Code..............................A

TOTAL LIVING AREA:
1,456 sq. ft.

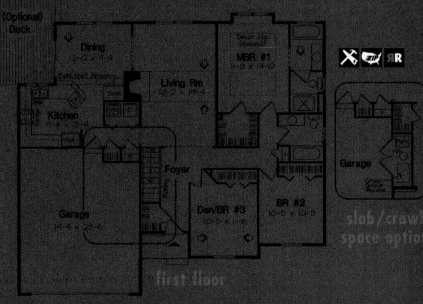

COMPACT CHARM

To Order, please call 1.800.235.5700

DESIGN 99803

Donald. A. Gardner
Architects, Inc.

This three bedroom executive home makes both everyday life and entertaining a breeze. A palladian window floods the foyer with light for a dramatic entrance alluding to an open floor plan. Whip up meals in the well-planned kitchen, while chatting with family and friends in the large Great room with cathedral ceiling, fireplace, and built-in cabinets. The screened porch, breakfast area, and master suite access the deck with optional spa. The private master suite features a skylit bath with a separate shower, and a corner whirlpool tub. A skylit bonus room above the garage adds space when needed. This plan is available with a basement or crawl space foundation. Please specify when ordering.

Main Floor............1,977 sq. ft.
Bonus.....................430 sq. ft.
Garage...................610 sq. ft.
Bedrooms................................3
Bathrooms.......................2 full
Foundation..............Basement,
                              Crawl Space
Width...69'-8" Depth...63'-10"
Price Code..............................D

TOTAL LIVING AREA:
1,977 sq. ft.

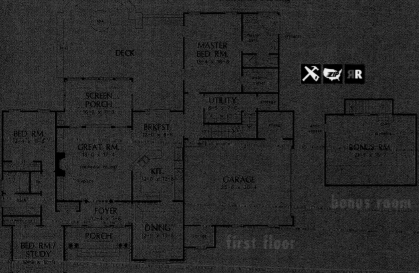

© Donald A. Gardner Architects, Inc.

EXECUTIVE RANCH

© Donald A. Gardner Architects, Inc.

DESIGN 99812

A dormer brightens the foyer. This cozy home is full of today's comforts yet cost-effective to construct. The open Great room, dining, and kitchen feature a cathedral ceiling. The front bedroom is expanded by a cathedral ceiling, and a double window with a circle top. The master suite has a cathedral ceiling and a garden tub. A skylit bonus room above the garage offers flexibility.

Main Floor............1,386 sq. ft.
Bonus.....................314 sq. ft.
Garage....................517 sq. ft.
Bedrooms............................3
Bathrooms.....................2 full
Foundation........Crawl Space
Width....54'-10" Depth...48'-0"
Price Code.............................C

TOTAL LIVING AREA:
1,386 sq. ft.

DELIGHTFUL DORMER

DESIGN 99835

High ceilings, and an open floor plan create spaciousness in this delightful home. The Great room and kitchen share a vaulted ceiling. Clerestory dormers pour light into the Great room which sports a fireplace and rear patio access. Tray ceilings add to the dining room and master bedroom. The master suite is positioned for privacy. Two bedrooms and a bath complete the plan. The skylit bonus space over the garage features built-ins for a multitude of uses. This plan includes a crawl space foundation.

Donald. A. Gardner Architects, Inc.

Main Floor	1,515 sq. ft.
Bonus	288 sq. ft.
Garage	476 sq. ft.
Bedrooms.......3	Baths.........2
Foundation	Crawl
Width......51'-10"	Depth.....55'-4"
Price Code	D

TOTAL LIVING AREA:
1,515 sq. ft.

© Donald A. Gardner Architects, Inc.

DESIGN 34150

Consider this plan if you work at home and would enjoy a well-lit office or den. The huge, arched window floods the front room with light. This house offers a lot of other practical details for the two-career family. Compact and efficient use of space means less to clean and organize. The open plan keeps the home from feeling too small and cramped. Plenty of closet space, step-saving laundry facilities and a window wall in the living room make this a delightful plan.

The Garlinghouse Company

Main Floor	1,492 sq. ft.
Basement	1,486 sq. ft.
Garage	462 sq. ft.
Bedrooms.......3	Baths.........2
Foundation....Bsmnt, Slab, Crawl	
Width......56'-0"	Depth.......48'-0"
Price Code	A

TOTAL LIVING AREA:
1,492 sq. ft.

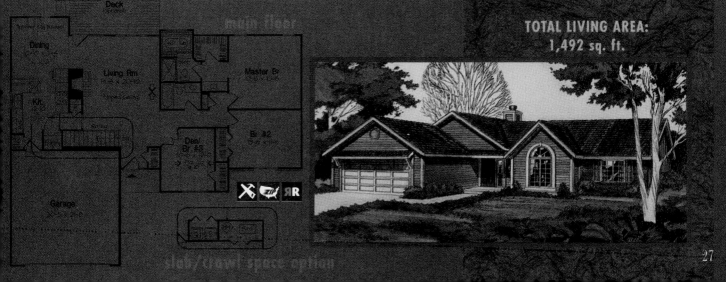

DESIGN 20100

Stacked windows fill the wall in the front bedroom of this one-level home, creating an attractive facade and a sunny atmosphere inside. Around the corner, two more bedrooms and two full baths complete the private bedroom wing. Notice the elegant vaulted ceiling in the master bedroom, the master tub and shower illuminated by a skylight, and the double vanities in both baths. Active areas enjoy a spacious feeling. High, sloping ceilings impact the fireplaced living room. Sliders unite the breakfast room and kitchen with a deck.

Main Floor............1,737 sq. ft.
Basement.............1,727 sq. ft.
Garage...................484 sq. ft.
Bedrooms......................3
Bathrooms.................2 full
Foundation.......Basement, Slab, Crawl Space
Width....72'-4" Depth...43'-0"
Price Code............................B

TOTAL LIVING AREA:
1,737 sq. ft.

CONVENIENCE

DESIGN 96458

Country charm and ranch convenience combine in this three bedroom home. The open Great room, kitchen, and breakfast bay merge into one common area. Cathedral ceilings add spaciousness. The master suite is elegantly appointed with a cathedral ceiling, walk-in closet, and bath with a whirlpool tub, a shower, and a dual vanity. Two additional bedrooms, one with a cathedral ceiling and arched window, share a full bath at the front of the house.

Donald. A. Gardner Architects, Inc.

Main Floor..................1,512 sq. ft.
Garage & Storage.........455 sq. ft.
Bedrooms........3   Baths..........2
Foundation....Bsmnt,Slab,Crawl
Width......64'-4" Depth......44'-4"
Price Code..................................D

**TOTAL LIVING AREA:
1,512 sq. ft.**

DESIGN 99811

Two dormers add volume to the foyer, while a cathedral ceiling enlarges the open great room. The foyer, Great room, kitchen, and breakfast area are defined by accent columns. The private master suite features a tray ceiling in the bedroom. The master bath includes a garden tub, separate shower, and two skylights over a double bowl vanity. The front bedroom also doubles as a study. It boasts a tray ceiling and a picture window topped off by a half-round window.

Donald. A. Gardner Architects, Inc.

Main Floor..................1,699 sq. ft.
Bonus Room.................336 sq. ft.
Garage..........................498 sq. ft.
Bedrooms.......3   Baths..........2
Foundation..........................Crawl
Width......64'-6" Depth......49'-8"
Price Code..................................D

**TOTAL LIVING AREA:
1,699 sq. ft.**

29

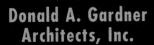
DESIGN 99802

This smaller, traditional beauty features large arched windows, round columns, covered porch, brick veneer, and an open floor plan. Clerestory dormers above the covered porch cast natural light into the foyer. The Great room, with cathedral ceiling and fireplace, opens to the island kitchen with a breakfast area. Columns define the spaces. Tray ceilings create an out-of-the-ordinary master bedroom, dining room and bedroom/study. The master bath features double vanity, separate shower, and whirlpool tub.

© Donald A. Gardner Architects, Inc.

DESIGN 34029

Keep dry during the rainy season under the covered porch entry way of this gorgeous home. The living room features a vaulted beamed ceiling and a fireplace. The master bedroom has a decorative ceiling and is located for privacy. A skylight is located above the entrance of the master bath. An optional deck is offered, accessible through sliding glass doors off of this wonderful master bedroom.

DESIGN 10839

The Garlinghouse Company

This Ranch home features a large sunken Great room, centralized with a cozy fireplace. The master bedroom has a private bathroom with a skylight. The huge three-car plus garage can include a work area for the family carpenter. In the center of this home, the kitchen has a roomy eating nook. The porch at the rear of the house has easy access from the dining room. One other bedroom and a den, which can easily be converted to a bedroom, are on the opposite side of the house from the master bedroom.

Main Floor	1,738 sq. ft.
Basement	1,083 sq. ft.
Garage	796 sq. ft.
Bedrooms	2
Bathrooms	2 full
Foundation	Basement, Slab, Crawl Space
Width....66'-0"	Depth...52'-0"
Price Code	B

TOTAL LIVING AREA:
1,738 sq. ft.

slab/crawl space option

Optional Deck

Master Br

Great Rm

Screened Porch

Kitchen

Dining Rm

Foyer

Br

Breakfast

Garage

Porch

Den

Main floor

SPACIOUS RANCH

DESIGN 20161

The exciting, spacious living room, is complete with high sloping ceilings and a fireplace flanked by windows. The master bedroom shows off a full wall of closet space, a private bath, and an extraordinary decorative ceiling. The dining room boasts decorative ceiling details, and a full slider out to the deck. Along with great counter space, the kitchen includes a double sink and an attractive bump-out window. The adjacent laundry room, optional expanded pantry, and a two-car garage make this Ranch a charmer. The photograph may have been modified to suit individual tastes.

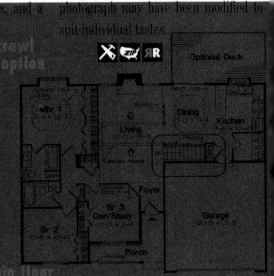

DESIGN 99851

Flanked by columns, the barrel vaulted entrance of this home is echoed in its arched windows and gables. Interior columns add elegance while dividing the living areas. The Great room has a cathedral ceiling and an arched clerestory window. The kitchen features an angled center island with a breakfast counter for the busy family. The secluded master suite, boasts his-n-her closets and a garden tub with a skylight. Two bedrooms upstairs share another skylit bath. This plan is available with a basement or crawlspace foundation. Please specify when ordering.

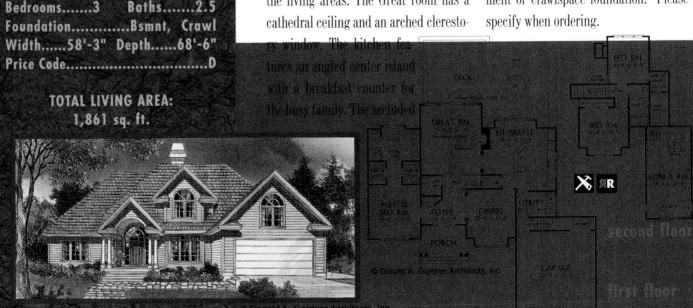

© Donald A. Gardner Architects, Inc.

Design by
The Garlinghouse Company

Br 2
11-8 x 12-4

Br 3
11-8 x 12-5

optional skylight

DN   railing

linen

Mstr. Suite
18-4 x 13-4

DN

open to below

Common
9-5 x 13-8

Bonus
11-4 x 15-8

Second Floor

TOTAL LIVING AREA:
2,578 SQ. FT.

w/h
furn.

crawl access

**Crawl Space/
Slab Option**
No. 24653

Dignified Family Home

■ This plan features:

— Three bedrooms

— Two full and one half baths

■ A beautiful elevation with multi-paned windows and an arched entrance

■ A two-story Foyer

■ The Living Room adjoins the Dining Room

■ A U-shaped Kitchen is equipped with a built-in Pantry and an island

■ The Family Room with a focal point fireplace

■ The Master Suite has a lavish Bath

■ A bonus room for future needs

■ No materials list is available for this plan

FIRST FLOOR — 1,245 SQ. FT.
SECOND FLOOR — 1,333 SQ. FT.
BASEMENT — 1,245 SQ. FT.
BONUS ROOM — 192 SQ. FT.
GARAGE — 614 SQ. FT.

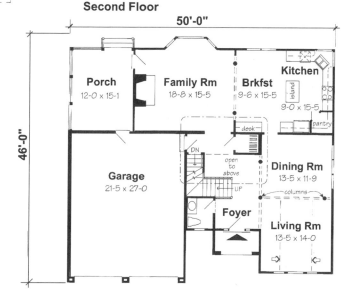

50'-0"

46'-0"

Porch
12-0 x 15-1

Family Rm
18-8 x 15-5

Brkfst
9-6 x 15-5

Kitchen

island
9-0 x 15-5

pantry

desk

DN

Garage
21-5 x 27-0

open to above

UP

Dining Rm
13-5 x 11-9

columns

Foyer

Living Rm
13-5 x 14-0

First Floor

Design by
Larry E. Belk

Refer to **Pricing Schedule C** on the order form for pricing information

Double Arches Add Elegance

■ This plan features:

— Three bedrooms

— Two full baths

■ Double arches form the entrance to this elegantly styled home

■ Two palladian windows add distinction to the elevation

■ Ten-foot ceilings in all major living areas give the home an expansive feeling

■ The Kitchen features an angled eating bar and opens to the Breakfast Room

■ The Master Suite includes a Bath with all the amenities

■ No materials list is available for this plan

MAIN FLOOR — 1,932 SQ. FT.
GARAGE — 552 SQ. FT.

TOTAL LIVING AREA:
1,932 SQ. FT.

© Larry E. Belk

MAIN FLOOR
No. 93098

53–5

To order your Blueprints, call 1-800-235-5700

Design by
Frank Betz Associates, Inc.

PLAN NO. 97257

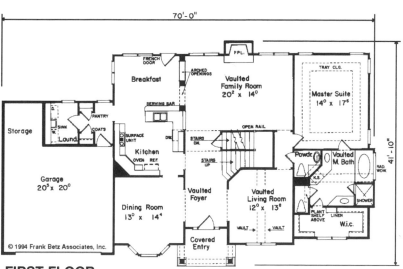

70'-0"

FIRST FLOOR

No. 97257

© 1994 Frank Betz Associates, Inc.

Storage

Garage
20⁹ x 20⁰

Laund.

Pantry

Sink

Coats

Surface Unit

Kitchen

Oven Ref

Dining Room
13⁰ x 14⁴

Breakfast

French Door

Arched Openings

Serving Bar

Vaulted Family Room
20² x 14⁰

FPL.

Tray Clg.

Master Suite
14⁰ x 17⁶

Open Rail

Stairs Dn.

Stairs Up

Vaulted Foyer

Vaulted Living Room
12⁰ x 13⁸

Powdr.

Vaulted M. Bath

Shower

Plant Shelf Above

Linen

W.i.c.

Covered Entry

Vault

41'-10"

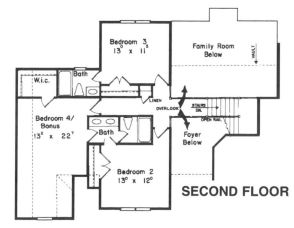

Bedroom 3
13⁰ x 11⁵

W.i.c.

Bath

Family Room Below

Vault

Bedroom 4/ Bonus
13² x 22⁷

Bath

Linen

Overlook

Stairs Dn.

Open Rail

Foyer Below

Bedroom 2
13⁰ x 12⁰

SECOND FLOOR

Modern Elegance

■ This plan features:

— Three bedrooms

— Two full baths

■ Vaulted ceilings in the Living Room and the Family Room add volume to the living space

■ The Family Room is highlighted by a fireplace

■ The Kitchen flows into the Breakfast Area with a serving bar and French doors to the rear yard

■ The Master Suite is topped by a tray ceiling in the Bedroom and a vaulted ceiling in the Bath

■ An optional basement or crawl space foundation — please specify when ordering

■ No materials list is available for this plan

FIRST FLOOR — 1,809 SQ. FT.
SECOND FLOOR — 922 SQ. FT.
BASEMENT — 1,809 SQ. FT.
GARAGE — 483 SQ. FT.

TOTAL LIVING AREA:
2,731 SQ. FT.

Design by
Jannis Vann & Associates, Inc.

Refer to **Pricing Schedule B** on the order form for pricing information

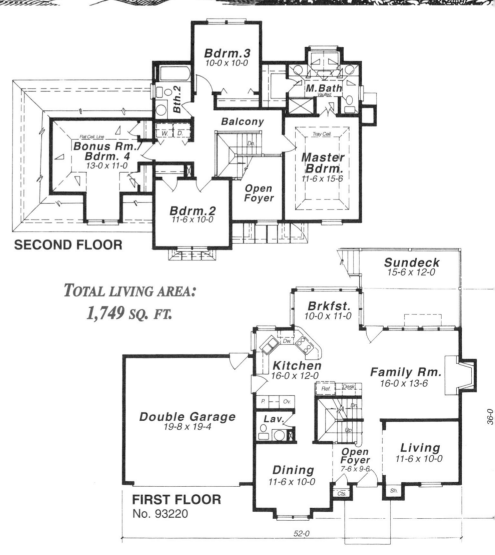

Spacious Family Areas

■ This plan features:

— Three bedrooms

— Two full and one half baths

■ Two-story Foyer with landing staircase leads to formal Living and Dining rooms

■ Open layout for Kitchen/Breakfast Area and Family Room

■ Family Room with a focal point fireplace and a wall of windows

■ Master Bedroom has a decorative ceiling and French doors into private Bath and walk-in closet

■ Two bedrooms, full Bath, laundry closet and Bonus Room complete second floor

■ An optional basement, slab or crawl space foundation — please specify when ordering

FIRST FLOOR — 902 SQ. FT.
SECOND FLOOR — 819 SQ. FT.
FINISHED STAIRCASE — 28 SQ. FT.
BONUS ROOM — 210 SQ. FT.
BASEMENT — 874 SQ. FT.
GARAGE — 400 SQ. FT.

SECOND FLOOR

Bdrm. 3
10-0 x 10-0

Bth. 2

M. Bath
Vaulted

Balcony

Bonus Rm./
Bdrm. 4
13-0 x 11-0

Flat Ceil. Line

W. D.

Tray Ceil.

Master
Bdrm.
11-6 x 15-6

Open
Foyer

Bdrm. 2
11-6 x 10-0

TOTAL LIVING AREA:
1,749 SQ. FT.

Sundeck
15-6 x 12-0

Brkfst.
10-0 x 11-0

Kitchen
16-0 x 12-0

Family Rm.
16-0 x 13-6

Dw.

Ref.

Desk

Dn.

Up

Double Garage
19-8 x 19-4

P.

Ov.

Lav.

Open
Foyer
7-6 x 9-6

Living
11-6 x 10-0

Dining
11-6 x 10-0

Cts.

Sh.

36-0

52-0

FIRST FLOOR
No. 93220

To order your Blueprints, call 1-800-235-5700

Refer to **Pricing Schedule E** on the order form for pricing information

Design by
Ahmann Design, Inc.

PLAN NO. 97128

BR. #2
11'0"x12'4"

MBR.
13'4"x17'6"

DOWN

BR. #3
11'6"x15'0"

OPEN TO
E.

BR. #4
11'6"x12'6"

PLANT LEDGE

SECOND FLOOR

FIRST FLOOR
No. 97128

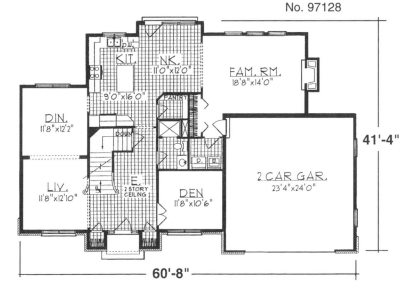

KIT.

NK.
11'0"x12'0"

FAM. RM.
18'8"x14'0"

9'0"x16'0"

PANTRY

DIN.
11'8"x12'2"

DOWN

LIV.
11'8"x12'10"

E.
2 STORY
CEILING

DEN
11'8"x10'6"

2 CAR GAR.
23'4"x24'0"

41'-4"

60'-8"

Family Togetherness

■ This plan features:

— Four bedrooms

— Three full and one half baths

■ The airy Family Room has a cozy fireplace

■ The Kitchen has a center island and a walk-in Pantry

■ Formal Dining and Living rooms provide an elegant atmosphere for entertaining

■ Upstairs, the Master Bedroom has a generous walk-in closet, and spa tub in the Bath

■ Two additional Bedrooms share a full Bath with separate vanities

■ No materials list is available for this plan

FIRST FLOOR — 1,492 SQ. FT.
SECOND FLOOR — 1,306 SQ. FT.

TOTAL LIVING AREA:
2,798 SQ. FT.

Design by
Donald A. Gardner Architects, Inc.

Refer to **Pricing Schedule D** on
the order form for pricing information

©1996 Donald A. Gardner Architect

Offering an Inviting Welcome

- This plan features:
— Three bedrooms
— Two full and one half baths

- Triple gables and a wrapping front Porch

- Cathedral ceiling impacts the Great Room which alsohas defining columns and a cozy fireplace

- Octagonal Dining Room has a tray ceiling and access to the Porch for dining outdoors

- Kitchen equipped with a pantry and a work island

- Two bedrooms share a full bath and access a skylit bonus room

FIRST FLOOR — 1,512 SQ. FT.
SECOND FLOOR — 477 SQ. FT.
BONUS ROOM — 347 SQ. FT.
GARAGE & STORAGE — 636 SQ. FT.

TOTAL LIVING AREA:
1,989 SQ. FT.

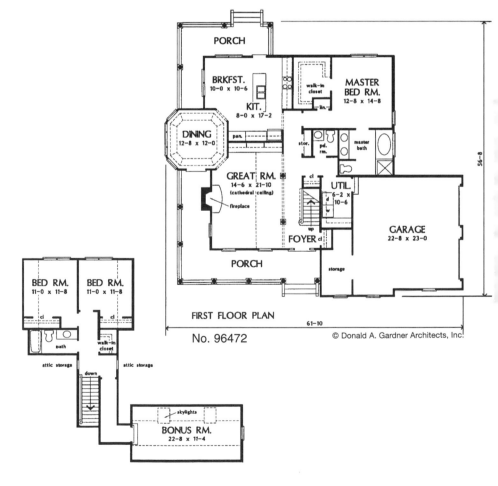

FIRST FLOOR PLAN

No. 96472

© Donald A. Gardner Architects, Inc.

SECOND FLOOR PLAN

To order your Blueprints, call 1-800-235-5700

Design by
Studer Residential Design, Inc.

TOTAL LIVING AREA:
1,782 SQ. FT.

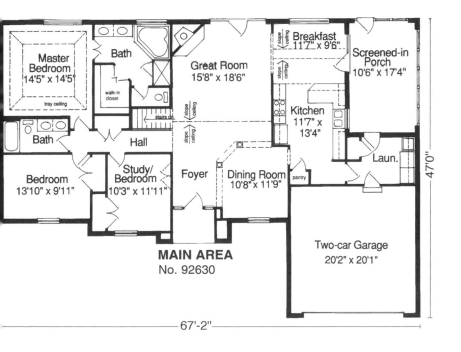

MAIN AREA
No. 92630

67'-2"

Charming Brick Ranch

■ This plan features:

— Three bedrooms

— Two full baths

■ Sheltered entrance leads into open Foyer and Dining Room defined by columns

■ Vaulted ceiling spans Foyer, Dining Room, and Great Room with corner fireplace and atrium door to rear yard

■ Central Kitchen with separate Laundry and Pantry easily serves Dining Room, Breakfast Area and Screened Porch

■ Luxurious Master Bedroom offers tray ceiling and French doors to Bath

■ Two additional Bedrooms, one easily converted to a Study, share a full Bath

■ No materials list available for this plan

MAIN AREA —1,782 SQ. FT.
GARAGE — 407 SQ. FT.
BASEMENT — 1,735 SQ. FT.

Design by
Patrick J. Morabito A.I.A.

Refer to **Pricing Schedule C** on
the order form for pricing information

Home for Today & Tomorrow

■ This plan features:

— Three bedrooms

— Two full and one half baths

■ The Foyer is flanked by the Dining and Living rooms

■ The rear of the home has an open layout for family interaction

■ A cozy fireplace in the Family Room adds warmth

■ The Master Suite includes a walk-in closet, whirlpool tub, separate shower and double vanity

■ No materials list is available for this plan

FIRST FLOOR — 1,004 SQ. FT.
SECOND FLOOR — 946 SQ. FT.
BASEMENT — 1,004 SQ. FT.
GARAGE — 450 SQ. FT.

TOTAL LIVING AREA:
1,950 SQ. FT.

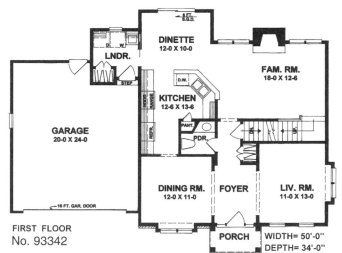

FIRST FLOOR
No. 93342

WIDTH = 50'-0"
DEPTH = 34'-0"

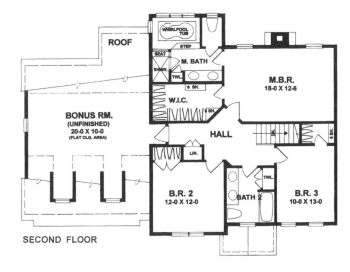

SECOND FLOOR

To order your Blueprints, call 1-800-235-5700

Design by
Design Basics, Inc.

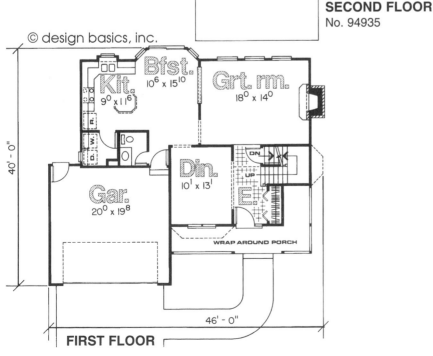

SECOND FLOOR
No. 94935

© design basics, inc.

FIRST FLOOR

Appealing Front Porch

■ This plan features:

— Four bedrooms

— Two full and one half baths

■ Appealing wrap-around Porch graces this home

■ Light and airy two-story entrance with a side-light, plant shelf and a closet

■ Wall of windows and fireplace featured in the Great Room

■ Open Kitchen with easy access to the Breakfast area, Dining Room and the Garage

■ Lovely Master Suite with tiered ceiling, two walk-in closets and a deluxe Bath

FIRST FLOOR — 919 SQ. FT.
SECOND FLOOR — 923 SQ. FT.
BASEMENT — 919 SQ. FT.
GARAGE — 414 SQ. FT.

TOTAL LIVING AREA:
1,842 SQ. FT.

Design by
The Garlinghouse Company ⚒

Refer to **Pricing Schedule B** on the order form for pricing information

Abundance of Closet Space

■ This plan features:

— Three bedrooms

— Two full baths

■ Roomy walk-in closets in all the Bedrooms

■ The Master Bedroom has a decorative ceiling and a private full Bath

■ The fireplaced Living Room has sloped ceilings and sliders to the Deck

■ An efficient Kitchen, has plenty of cupboard space and a Pantry

MAIN AREA — 1,532 SQ. FT.
GARAGE — 484 SQ. FT.

TOTAL LIVING AREA:
1,532 SQ. FT.

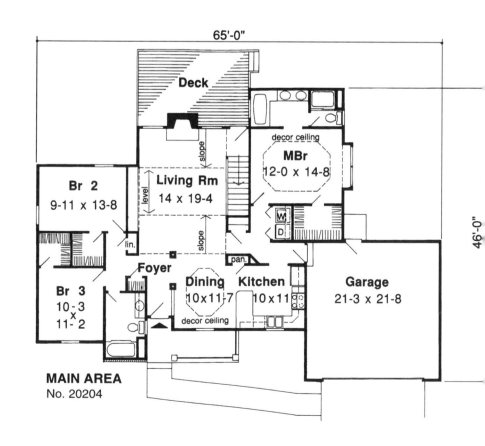

MAIN AREA
No. 20204

Design by
Studer Residential Design, Inc.

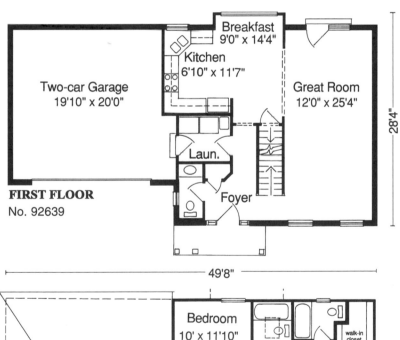

FIRST FLOOR
No. 92639

Two-car Garage
19'10" x 20'0"

Breakfast
9'0" x 14'4"

Kitchen
6'10" x 11'7"

Great Room
12'0" x 25'4"

Laun.

Foyer

28'4"

49'8"

SECOND FLOOR

Bedroom
10' x 11'10"

Bath

Bath

walk-in
closet

Hall

Master
Bedroom
12'4" x 16'11"

Bedroom
10'7" x 11'2"

Comfortable and Relaxed Environment

■ This plan features:

— Three bedrooms

— Two full and one half baths

■ A covered Porch and boxed window enhancing the exterior

■ An easy flowing traffic pattern creates step saving convenience

■ An open stairway adds elegance to the Foyer

■ A spacious Great Room and Breakfast Area form an area large enough for real family enjoyment

■ A U-shaped Kitchen highlighted by a corner sink and ample counter and storage space

■ No materials list is available for this plan

FIRST FLOOR — 748 SQ. FT.
SECOND FLOOR — 705 SQ. FT.
BASEMENT — 744 SQ. FT.

TOTAL LIVING AREA:
1,453 SQ. FT.

Design by
Donald A. Gardner Architects, Inc.

Refer to **Pricing Schedule C** on the order form for pricing information

© 1993 Donald A. Gardner Architects, Inc.

Economical Three Bedroom

■ This plan features:
— Three bedrooms
— Two full baths

■ Dormers above the covered porch casts light into the Foyer

■ Columns punctuate the entrance to the Great Room/ Dining Room Area with a shared cathedral ceiling and a bank of operable skylights

■ Kitchen with a Breakfast Counter, open to the Dining Area

■ Private Master Bedroom with a tray ceiling and luxurious Bath featuring a double vanity, separate shower, and skylights over the whirlpool tub

MAIN FLOOR — 1,322 SQ. FT.
GARAGE & STORAGE — 413 SQ. FT.

TOTAL LIVING AREA:
1,322 SQ. FT.

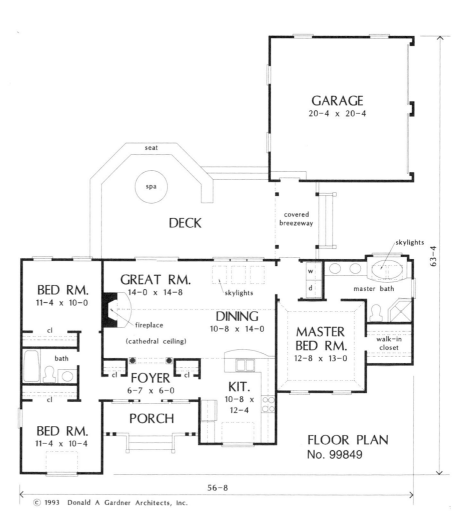

FLOOR PLAN
No. 99849

© 1993   Donald A Gardner Architects, Inc.

To order your Blueprints, call 1-800-235-5700

Design by
The Garlinghouse Company

PLAN NO. 34851

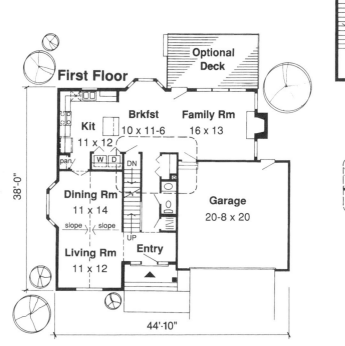

Second Floor
No. 34851

Br 2
10 x 12-8

Br 3
10 x 11

MBr 1
14-4 x 15

DN

slope

slope

open to below

First Floor

Optional Deck

Kit
11 x 12

Brkfst
10 x 11-6

Family Rm
16 x 13

pan

W D

DN

Dining Rm
11 x 14

slope

slope

Garage
20-8 x 20

Living Rm
11 x 12

UP

Entry

38'-0"

44'-10"

Slab/Crawlspace Option

Traditional Gem With Bay Windows

■ This plan features:

— Three bedrooms

— Two full and one half baths

■ A sloped-ceiling Living/Dining Room combination is brightened by windows

■ The Family Room has a cozy fireplace and direct access to the Deck

■ An efficient, well-appointed island Kitchen has a built-in Pantry

■ The Master Suite has a sloped ceiling, a private Master Bath and a walk-in closet

FIRST FLOOR — 1,056 SQ. FT.
SECOND FLOOR — 874 SQ. FT.
BASEMENT — 1,023 SQ. FT.
GARAGE — 430 SQ. FT.

TOTAL LIVING AREA:
1,930 SQ. FT.

Design by
Ahmann Design, Inc.

Refer to **Pricing Schedule C** on
the order form for pricing information

Open Great Room

■ This plan features:

— Four bedrooms

— Two full and one half baths

■ The open Great Room has a cozy
fireplace

■ The unique layout of the Kitchen
adds ease to busy mornings with
ample counter space, an eating
bar, and plenty of room for family dining in the sunny Breakfast
Nook

■ The Master Suite provides a
walk-in closet and a full Bath

■ Other amenities include a main
floor Laundry Room, Powder
Room and attached two-car
Garage

■ No materials list is available for
this plan

MAIN FLOOR — 1,365 SQ. FT.
SECOND FLOOR — 679 SQ. FT.

TOTAL LIVING AREA:
2,044 SQ. FT.

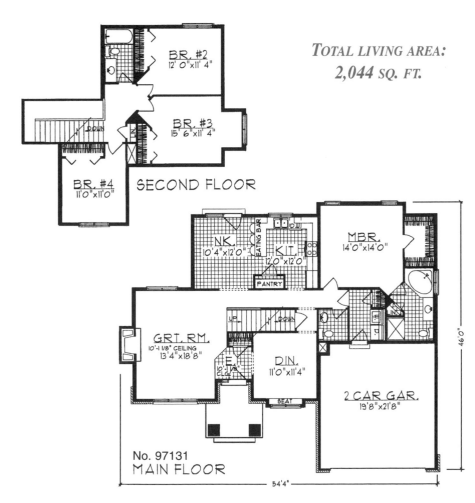

BR. #2
12'0"x11'4"

BR. #3
15'6"x11'4"

BR. #4
11'0"x11'0"

SECOND FLOOR

NK.
10'4"x12'0"

EATING BAR

KIT.
12'0"x12'0"

PANTRY

MBR.
14'0"x14'0"

GRT. RM.
10'-1 1/8" CEILING
13'4"x18'8"

DIN.
11'0"x11'4"

SEAT

2 CAR GAR.
19'8"x21'8"

46'0"

No. 97131
MAIN FLOOR

54'4"

Design by
Studer Residential Design, Inc.

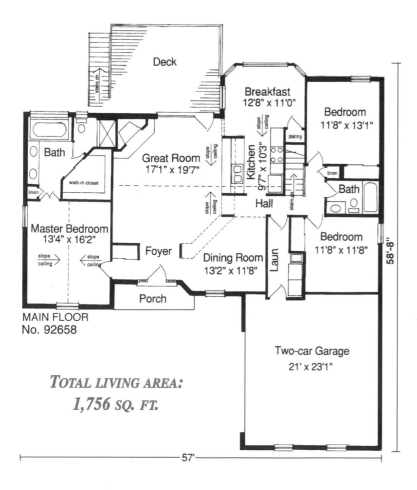

Deck

Breakfast
12'8" x 11'0"

Bedroom
11'8" x 13'1"

pantry

Bath

Great Room
17'1" x 19'7"

Kitchen
9'7" x 10'3"

slope ceiling

linen

walk-in closet

Bath

linen

Hall

Master Bedroom
13'4" x 16'2"

slope ceiling

slope ceiling

Foyer

Dining Room
13'2" x 11'8"

Laun

Bedroom
11'8" x 11'8"

Porch

58'-8"

MAIN FLOOR
No. 92658

Two-car Garage
21' x 23'1"

TOTAL LIVING AREA:
1,756 SQ. FT.

57'

Appealing Arches

■ This plan features:

— Three bedrooms

— Two full baths

■ Brick exterior accented by quoins and arched windows

■ Foyer opens to formal Dining Room and spacious Great Room

■ Sloped ceiling, corner fireplace and atrium door to Deck enhance Great Room

■ Efficient Kitchen has a serving counter with bright Breakfast Area and pantry

■ Secluded Master Bedroom offers a sloped ceiling above arched window, a large walk-in closet and lavish bath

■ Two additional Bedrooms with ample closets, share a full Bath

■ No materials list is available for this plan

MAIN FLOOR — 1,756 SQ. FT.
GARAGE — 485 SQ. FT.
BASEMENT — 1,669 SQ. FT.

Design by
Studer Residential Design, Inc.

Refer to **Pricing Schedule F** on the order form for pricing information

Warm and Charming Showplace

■ This plan features:

— Four bedrooms

— Three full and one half baths

■ An imposing stone and brick exterior hides a warm and charming interior

■ The Great Room has a fireplace and a rear wall of illuminating windows

■ The Kitchen has a convenient center island

■ A three-car Garage with extra storage space finishes off the plan

■ No materials list is available for this plan

FIRST FLOOR — 2,479 SQ. FT.
SECOND FLOOR — 956 SQ. FT.
BASEMENT — 2,479 SQ. FT.

TOTAL LIVING AREA:
3,435 SQ. FT.

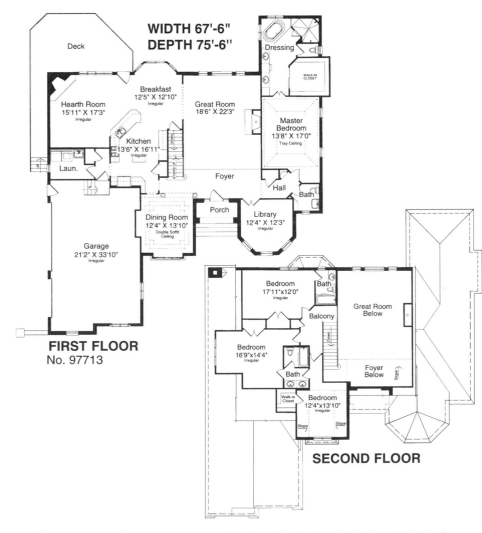

WIDTH 67'-6"
DEPTH 75'-6"

Deck

Dressing

WALK-IN CLOSET

Hearth Room
15'11" X 17'3"
Irregular

Breakfast
12'5" X 12'10"
Irregular

Great Room
18'6" X 22'3"

Kitchen
13'6" X 16'11"
Irregular

Master Bedroom
13'8" X 17'0"
Tray Ceiling

Laun.

Foyer

Hall

Bath

Dining Room
12'4" X 13'10"
Double Soffit Ceiling

Porch

Library
12'4" X 12'3"
Irregular

Garage
21'2" X 33'10"
Irregular

FIRST FLOOR
No. 97713

Bedroom
17'11"x12'0"
Irregular

Bath

Great Room Below

Balcony

Bedroom
16'9"x14'4"
Irregular

Bath

Foyer Below

Walk-in Closet

Bedroom
12'4"x13'10"
Irregular

Slope

SECOND FLOOR

To order your Blueprints, call 1-800-235-5700

Design by
Donald A. Gardner Architects, Inc.

© 1996 Donald A. Gardner Architects, Inc.

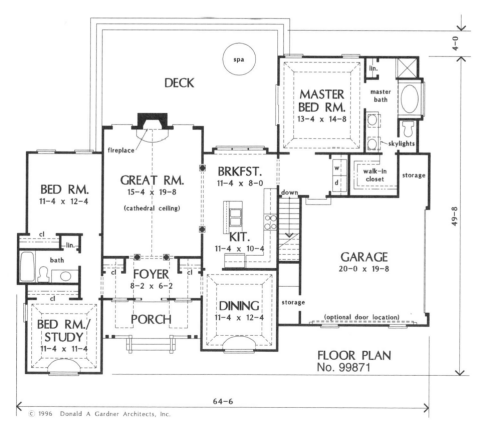

FLOOR PLAN
No. 99871

© 1996 Donald A Gardner Architects, Inc.

TOTAL LIVING AREA:
1,655 SQ. FT.

Charm and Personality

■ This plan features:

— Three bedrooms

— Two full baths

■ Charm and personality radiate through this Country home

■ Interior columns dramatically open the Foyer and Kitchen to the spacious Great Room

■ Drama is heightened by the Great Room cathedral ceiling and fireplace

■ Master Suite with a tray ceiling combines privacy with access to the rear Deck with spa

■ Tray ceilings with round-top picture windows bring a special elegance to the Dining Room and the front Swing Room

■ An optional basement or crawl space foundation — please specify when ordering

MAIN FLOOR — 1,655 SQ. FT.
GARAGE — 434 SQ. FT.

Design by
Lifestyles Home Design

Refer to **Pricing Schedule B** on
the order form for pricing information

Single-Level Living

■ This plan features:

— Three bedrooms

— Two full baths

■ A fireplace forms the focus of the Living Room

■ The angled Kitchen has a sunny Breakfast Room, built-in Pantry and ample storage and counter space

■ A vaulted ceiling in the Master Suite plus a sky lit Bath and walk-in closet

■ Two additional bedrooms are served by a full hall bath

MAIN FLOOR — 1,642 SQ. FT.
BASEMENT — 1,642 SQ. FT.
GARAGE — 448 SQ. FT.

TOTAL LIVING AREA:
1,642 SQ. FT.

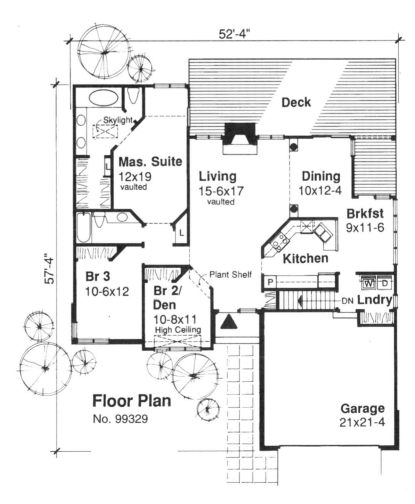

Floor Plan
No. 99329

To order your Blueprints, call 1-800-235-5700

Design by
Fillmore Design Group

Especially Unique

■ This plan features:

— Four bedrooms

— Three full and one half baths

■ From the 11-foot entry turn left into the Study/Media Room

■ The formal Dining Room is open to the Gallery, and the Living Room beyond

■ The Family Room has a built-in entertainment center, a fireplace and access to the rear Patio

■ The private Master Bedroom has a fireplace, a private Bath and a walk-in closet

■ Three spacious Bedrooms off the Family room share two full Baths

■ A three-car Garage

■ No materials list is available for this plan

MAIN FLOOR — 2,748 SQ. FT.
GARAGE — 660 SQ. FT.

TOTAL LIVING AREA:
2,748 SQ. FT.

WIDTH 75'-0"
DEPTH 64'-5"

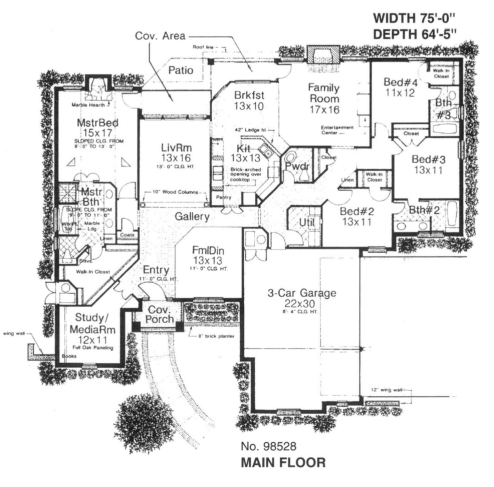

No. 98528
MAIN FLOOR

Design by
Larry E. Belk

Refer to **Pricing Schedule A** on the order form for pricing information

For Today's Sophisticated Homeowner

■ This plan features:

— Three bedrooms

— Two full baths

■ The formal Dining Room opens off the foyer and has a classic bay window

■ The Kitchen is notable for it's angled eating bar that opens to the Living Room

■ A cozy fireplace in the Living Room can be seen from the Kitchen

■ The Master Suite includes a whirlpool tub/shower combination and a walk-in closet

■ Ten foot ceilings in the major living areas, including the Master Bedroom

■ No materials list is available for this plan

MAIN AREA — 1,500 SQ. FT.
GARAGE — 437 SQ. FT.

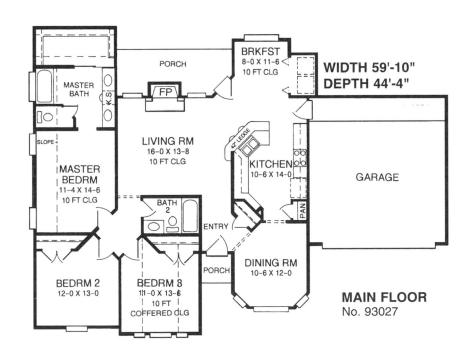

PORCH

BRKFST
8-0 X 11-6
10 FT CLG

WIDTH 59'-10"
DEPTH 44'-4"

MASTER BATH

FP

LIVING RM
16-0 X 13-8
10 FT CLG

KITCHEN
10-6 X 14-0

GARAGE

SLOPE

MASTER BEDRM
11-4 X 14-6
10 FT CLG

BATH 2

PAN

ENTRY

BEDRM 2
12-0 X 13-0

BEDRM 8
11-0 X 13-6
10 FT COFFERED CLG

PORCH

DINING RM
10-6 X 12-0

MAIN FLOOR
No. 93027

TOTAL LIVING AREA:
1,500 SQ. FT.

Design by
Alan Mascord Design Associates

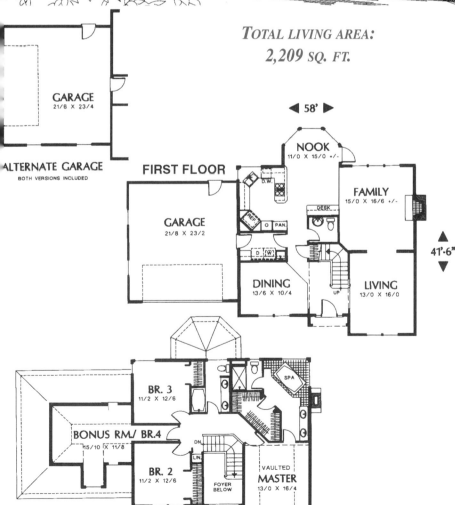

TOTAL LIVING AREA:
2,209 SQ. FT.

GARAGE
21/6 X 23/4

ALTERNATE GARAGE
BOTH VERSIONS INCLUDED

FIRST FLOOR

◄ 58' ►

NOOK
11/0 X 15/0 +/-

GARAGE
21/8 X 23/2

D.W.

REF.   O   PAN.

DESK

FAMILY
15/0 X 16/6 +/-

41'-6"

DINING
13/6 X 10/4

UP

LIVING
13/0 X 16/0

BR. 3
11/2 X 12/6

SPA

BONUS RM./ BR.4
15/0 X 11/8

DN.

LIN.

BR. 2
11/2 X 12/6

VAULTED
MASTER
13/0 X 16/4

FOYER
BELOW

SECOND FLOOR
No. 91534

Charming and Convenient

■ This plan features:

— Three bedrooms

— Two full and one half baths

■ Central entrance opens to formal Dining and Living Areas

■ Spacious Family Room offers an inviting fireplace and back yard view

■ Convenient Kitchen with peninsula counter/snackbar, Pantry, built-in desk, glass eating Nook and nearby Laundry/Garage entry

■ Corner Master suite offers an arched window below vaulted ceiling and a pampering Bath with a walk-in closet and spa tub

■ Two additional Bedrooms with ample closets, share a double vanity Bath and Bonus Room

FIRST FLOOR — 1,214 SQ. FT.
SECOND FLOOR — 995 SQ. FT.
BONUS ROOM — 261 SQ. FT.

Design by
Ahmann Design, Inc.

Charming Two-Story

- ■ This plan features:
- — Three bedrooms
- — Two full and one half baths
- ■ There are built-in cabinets around the fireplace in the Great Room
- ■ The Kitchen has ample counter space and an island
- ■ The sunny Nook provides access to the screen Porch
- ■ The formal Dining Room and Living Room offer elegance while entertaining
- ■ The Master Bedroom has two closets and a large Bath
- ■ An optional room upstairs can serve as a fourth Bedroom or a Game Room
- ■ No materials list is available for this plan

FIRST FLOOR — 2,172 SQ. FT.
SECOND FLOOR — 690 SQ. FT.
BONUS — 450 SQ. FT.

TOTAL LIVING AREA:
2,862 SQ. FT.

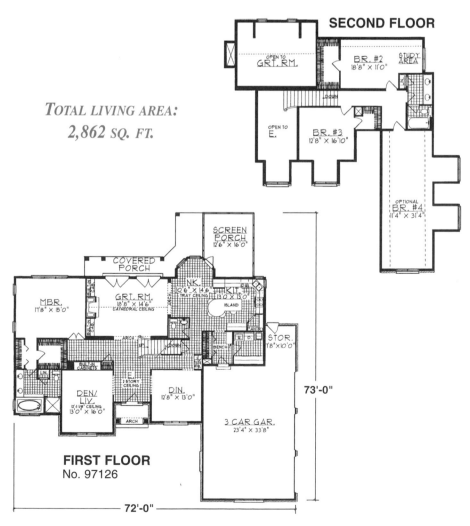

SECOND FLOOR

FIRST FLOOR
No. 97126

To order your Blueprints, call 1-800-235-5700

Design by
Ahmann Design, Inc.

TOTAL LIVING AREA:
2,196 SQ. FT.

MAIN FLOOR PLAN
No. 93190

Luxury on One Level

■ This plan features:

— Three bedrooms

— Two full and one half baths

■ Covered front Porch leads into entry and Great Room with vaulted ceiling

■ Huge Great Room perfect for entertaining or family gatherings with a cozy fireplace

■ Arched soffits and columns impact the formal Dining Room

■ Country-size Kitchen with a Pantry, work island, eating Nook with Screen Porch beyond, and nearby Laundry/Garage entry

■ Master Bedroom offers a walk-in closet and a luxurious Bath

■ Two Bedrooms with over-sized closets share a full Bath

■ No materials list is available for this plan

MAIN FLOOR — 2,196 SQ. FT.
BASEMENT — 2,196 SQ. FT.

Design by
Larry E. Belk

Refer to **Pricing Schedule E** on the order form for pricing informatio

COPYRIGHT LARRY E. BELK

Just Past the Garden Gate

■ This plan features:

— Four bedrooms

— Two full and one half baths

■ From the covered front Porch step through double doors into the Foyer with a 10-foot ceiling

■ There is an arched entry from the Foyer into the Dining Room

■ The Family Room and Breakfast Room are warmed by a fireplace

■ The Living Room has French doors that open to the rear Porch

■ All the bedrooms, including the Master Suite, are located in one wing

■ The Kitchen is located in the rear of the home

■ No materials list is available for this plan

MAIN FLOOR — 2,757 SQ. FT.
GARAGE — 484 SQ. FT.

TOTAL LIVING AREA:
2,757 SQ. FT.

MAIN FLOOR
No. 93097

GARAGE

COPYRIGHT LARRY E. BELK

UTIL

PAN

KITCHEN
15-4 X 13-8
10 FT CLG

42" LEDGE

DEPTH 68-8

BRKFST ROOM
15-4 X 9-4
14 FT CLG

SLOPE→   ←SLOPE

FAMILY ROOM
15-4 X 14-0
14 FT CLG

FP

PORCH

LIVING ROOM
17-0 X 16-4
12 FT CLG

BEDRM 4/STUDY
13-4 X 15-0
10 FT CLG

MASTER
BATH
10 FT
CLG
K.S.

MASTER BEDROOM
15-6 X 15-0
12 FT TRAY CLG

UP→   ←DOWN

DINING ROOM
12-4 X 14-4
12 FT CLG

ARCH

FOYER
10 FT CLG

PWDR

BATH 2

PORCH

BEDROOM 3
12-4 X 12-8
10 FT CLG

BEDROOM 2
12-6 X 12-8
10 FT CLG

© Larry E. Belk

WIDTH 69–6

To order your Blueprints, call 1-800-235-5700

Design by
Donald A. Gardner Architects, Inc.

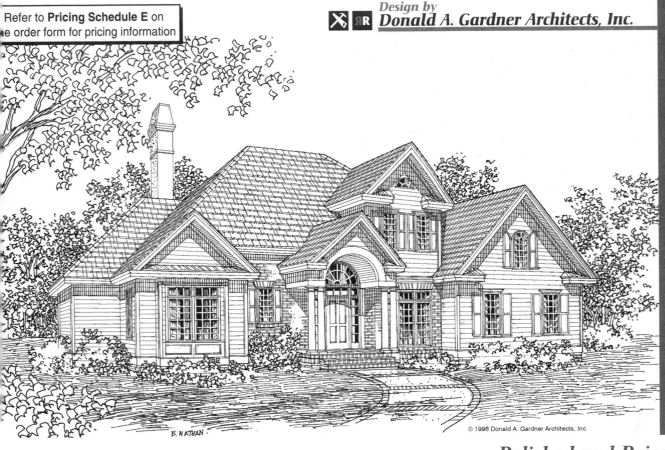

B. NATHAN

© 1996 Donald A. Gardner Architects, Inc.

Polished and Poised

■ This plan features:

— Three bedrooms

— Two full and one half baths

■ Hip roof, gables and brick accents add poise and polish to this traditional home

■ Curved transom window and sidelights illuminate the Foyer

■ A curved balcony overlooks the Great Room which has a cathedral ceiling, fireplace and a wall of windows

■ Hub Kitchen easily serves the Dining Room, Breakfast Area and the Patio beyond

■ Master Bedroom is enhanced by a tray ceiling, walk-in closet and a deluxe Bath

FIRST FLOOR — 1,577 SQ. FT.
SECOND FLOOR — 613 SQ. FT.
BONUS ROOM — 390 SQ. FT.
GARAGE & STORAGE — 634 SQ. FT.

TOTAL LIVING AREA:
2,190 SQ. FT.

Second Floor Plan

SECOND FLOOR PLAN
No. 96471

great room below

BED RM.
11-4 x 12-4

attic storage

attic storage

railing

down

lin.

bath

cl

foyer below

BED RM.
11-4 x 14-0

(cathedral ceiling)

attic storage

skylights

BONUS RM.
12-2 x 27-4

First Floor Plan

FIRST FLOOR PLAN

PATIO

GREAT RM.
18-2 x 21-4
(cathedral ceiling)

fireplace

BRKFST.
11-4 x 8-10

UTIL.
8-6 x 9-0

storage

KIT.
11-4 x 12-6

MASTER BED RM.
13-0 x 14-4

balcony above

walk-in closet

cl

lin.

pd. rm.

master bath

cl

FOYER
10-7 x 5-2
up

DINING
11-4 x 12-10

GARAGE
21-0 x 23-8

PORCH

65-2

© 1996 Donald A Gardner Architects, Inc.

Design by
Ahmann Design. Inc.

Refer to **Pricing Schedule C** on the order form for pricing information

Perfect for Corner Lots

■ This plan features:

— Three bedrooms

— Two full and one half baths

■ Pillars and decorative windows highlight front entrance

■ Spacious Living Room enhanced by a central fireplace and decorative window

■ Convenient Kitchen with a work island

■ Corner Master Suite offers access to the backyard, a large walk-in closet and a pampering bath

■ No materials list is available for this plan

MAIN FLOOR — 1,868 SQ. FT.
BASEMENT — 1,868 SQ. FT.

TOTAL LIVING AREA:
1,868 SQ. FT.

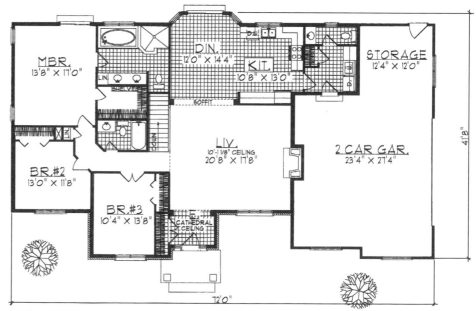

No. 93192
MAIN FLOOR

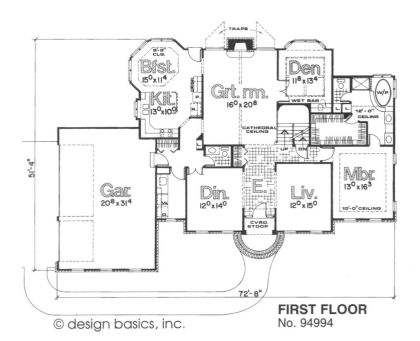

SECOND FLOOR

TRAPS
OPEN TO BELOW
DISPLAY
Br.2 13⁰x12⁸
BOOKS
LIN.
DN
LIN.
Br.3 12⁰x13⁰
OPEN TO BELOW
Br.4 12⁰x13⁰

51'-4"

Bfst. 15⁰x11⁴
Kit. 13⁰x10⁹
DESK
P
TRAPS
Grt. rm. 16⁰x20⁸
Den 11⁸x13⁴
WET BAR
w/p
12'-0" CEILING
CATHEDRAL CEILING
UP DN
Gar. 20⁸x31⁴
Din. 12⁰x14⁰
E.
Liv. 12⁰x15⁰
Mbr. 13⁰x16³
10'-0" CEILING
CVRD. STOOP
72'-8"

© design basics, inc.

FIRST FLOOR
No. 94994

Timeless Beauty

■ This plan features:

— Four bedrooms

— Two full, two three-quarter and one half baths

■ Two-story Entry hall accesses formal Dining and Living room

■ Spacious Great Room with cathedral ceiling and fireplace

■ Ideal Kitchen with built-in desk and Pantry

■ Master Bedroom wing offers a decorative ceiling, and luxurious Dressing/Bath Area with a large walk-in closet and whirlpool tub

FIRST FLOOR — 2,063 SQ. FT.
SECOND FLOOR — 894 SQ. FT.
BASEMENT — 2,063 SQ. FT.
GARAGE — 666 SQ. FT.

TOTAL LIVING AREA:
2,957 SQ. FT.

Design by
Garrell Associates, Inc.

Refer to **Pricing Schedule E** on the order form for pricing information

Old World Styling

■ This plan features:

— Four bedrooms

— Two full and one half baths

■ Stairs lead to the covered Porch, which reveals a transom above the door

■ Inside you are welcomed into a two-story Foyer

■ Columns delineate the Dining Room

■ A two-sided fireplace warms the Gallery and the Grand Room

■ A uniquely shaped island in the center of the Kitchen

■ The first floor Master Bedroom has a decorative ceiling

■ Upstairs, a Loft overlooks the Grand Room

■ No materials list is available for this plan

FIRST FLOOR — 2,062 SQ. FT.
SECOND FLOOR — 802 SQ. FT.
GARAGE — 400 SQ. FT.

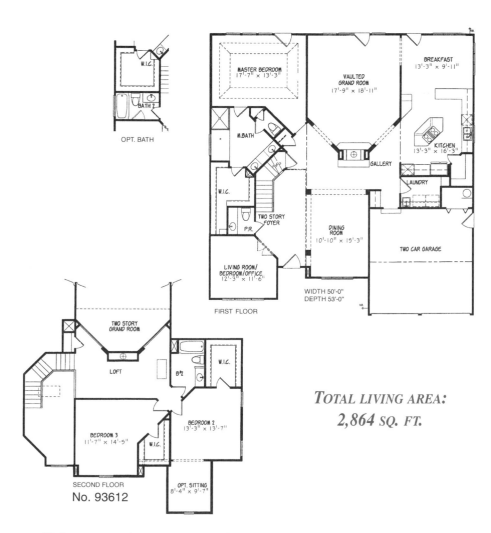

OPT. BATH

FIRST FLOOR

WIDTH 50'-0"
DEPTH 53'-0"

SECOND FLOOR
No. 93612

TOTAL LIVING AREA:
2,864 SQ. FT.

To order your Blueprints, call 1-800-235-5700

Refer to **Pricing Schedule D** on e order form for pricing information

Design by
Patrick Morabito A.I.A.

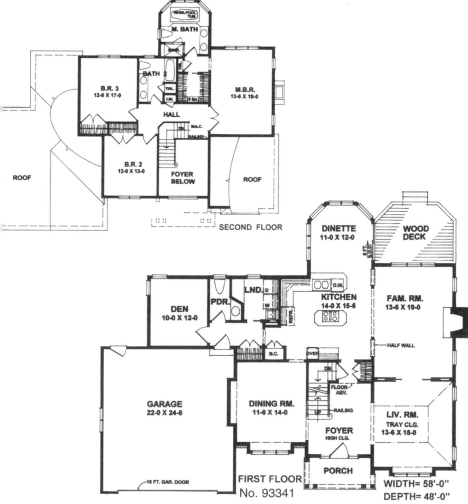

Multiple Roof Lines and Siding

- This plan features:
- — Three bedrooms
- — Two full and one half baths
- The Foyer is framed by the staircase and the Dining and Living rooms
- Living Room accented by tray ceiling, boxed window and pocket doors to Family Room
- Comfortable Family Room has a cozy fireplace
- The open Kitchen has a cooktop island
- No materials list is available for this plan

FIRST FLOOR — 1,430 SQ. FT.
SECOND FLOOR — 1,027 SQ. FT.
GARAGE — 528 SQ. FT.

TOTAL LIVING AREA:
2,457 SQ. FT.

Design by
Design Basics, Inc.

Refer to **Pricing Schedule F** on
the order form for pricing information

Grand Entrance

■ This plan features:

— Four bedrooms

— Two full, two three-quarter and
  one half baths

■ One and a half story, glass Entry
  accesses dramatic staircase, formal
  Dining Room and a Den

■ Expansive Great Room features a
  lovely bow window, raised hearth
  fireplace and wetbar

■ Convenient Kitchen with a bright
  Breakfast Bay, work island/snack bar,

■ Sumptuous Master Bedroom offers a
  bow window, two spacious walk-in
  closets and vanities

■ Three comfortable secondary Bedrooms
  with walk-in closets and private Bath
  access

MAIN FLOOR — 1,871 SQ. FT.
SECOND FLOOR — 1,677 SQ. FT.
BASEMENT — 1,871 SQ. FT.
GARAGE — 779 SQ. FT.

TOTAL LIVING AREA:
3,548 SQ. FT.

© design basics, inc.

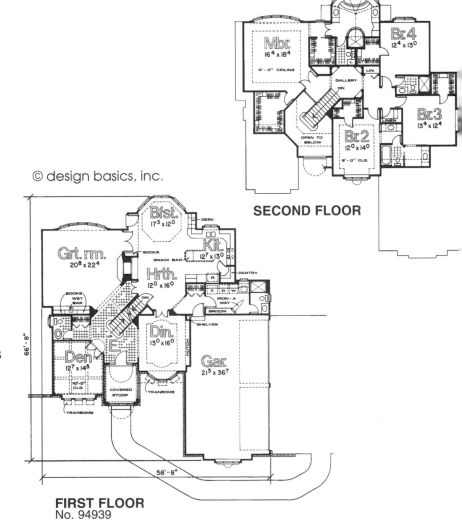

SECOND FLOOR

FIRST FLOOR
No. 94939

To order your Blueprints, call 1-800-235-5700

Refer to **Pricing Schedule E** on
the order form for pricing information

Design by
Design Basics, Inc.

PLAN NO. 99450

© design basics, inc.

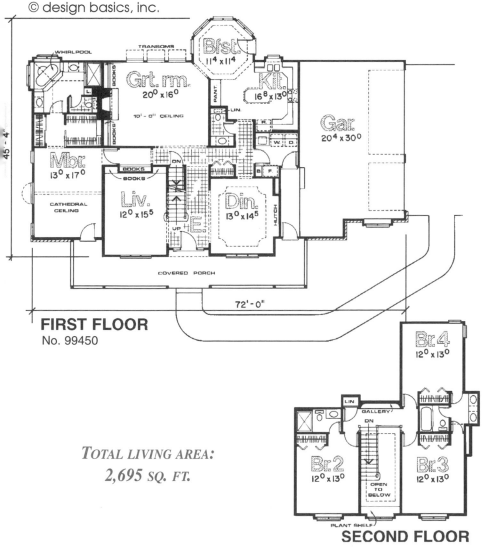

FIRST FLOOR
No. 99450

TOTAL LIVING AREA:
2,695 SQ. FT.

SECOND FLOOR

Fashionable Country Style

■ This plan features:

— Four bedrooms

— Two full, one three quarter and one half baths

■ The large covered front Porch adds old fashioned appeal

■ The Dining Room features a decorative ceiling and a built-in hutch

■ The Kitchen has a center island and is adjacent to the Nook

■ The Great Room is accented by transom windows and a fireplace

■ The Master Bedroom has a cathedral ceiling and a Bath with a whirlpool tub

■ Upstairs are three additional Bedrooms and two full Baths

■ An optional basement or a slab foundation — please specify when ordering this plan

FIRST FLOOR — 1,881 SQ. FT.
SECOND FLOOR — 814 SQ. FT.
GARAGE — 534 SQ. FT.
BASEMENT — 1,020 SQ. FT.

Design by
Ahmann Design, Inc.

Refer to **Pricing Schedule D** on
the order form for pricing information

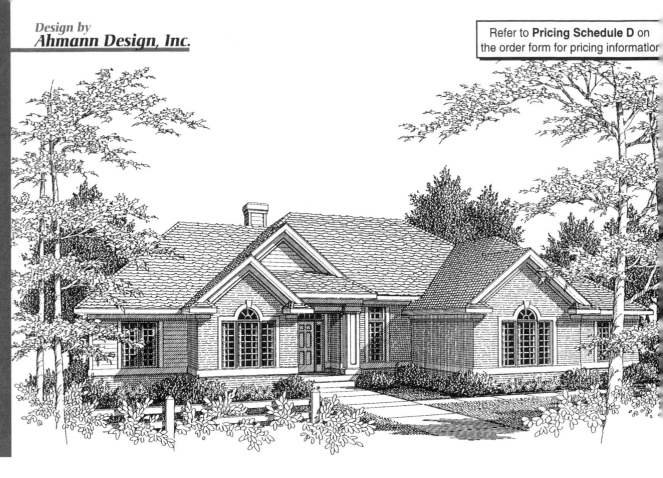

Perfect for Family Gatherings

■ This plan features:

— Three bedrooms

— Two full and one half baths

■ A screened Porch off the Nook creates a private area for relaxation

■ The Master Suite is your private retreat with a spa tub

■ Other amenities include a powder room, main floor Laundry Room and attached three-car Garage

■ No materials list is available for this plan

MAIN FLOOR — 2,469 SQ. FT.

TOTAL LIVING AREA:
2,469 SQ. FT

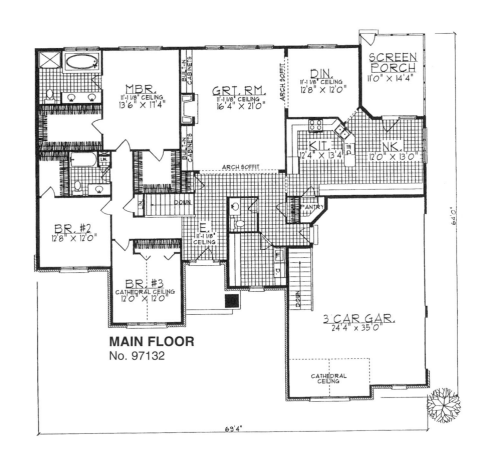

MAIN FLOOR
No. 97132

To order your Blueprints, call 1-800-235-5700

Refer to **Pricing Schedule C** on the order form for pricing information

SECOND FLOOR

BR.#3
11x12

rail

BR.#2
11x13

dn.

OPTIONAL BONUS
12x23

53'

52'

PORCH
5 x 16

16. Clg.

sloped ceiling

BREAKFAST
11x12

9' Clg.

FAMILY ROOM
18x15

MASTER
13x15
10' Clg.

KITCHEN
10x11

DINING
10x12

FOYER

up

dn.

D W

Workbench

GARAGE
20x23

Drive

FIRST FLOOR
No. 93410

Demonstrative Detail

■ This plan features:

— Three bedrooms

— Two full and one half baths

■ Keystone arched windows, stone and stucco combine with shutters and a flower box to create an eye-catching elevation

■ The Family Room has a sloped ceiling and is accented by a fire-place with windows to either side

■ The Kitchen/Breakfast Area has easy access to the rear Porch

■ Two roomy Bedrooms on the second floor share the full hall Bath

■ A bonus area over the Garage offers possibilities for expansion

FIRST FLOOR — 1,317 SQ. FT.
SECOND FLOOR — 537 SQ. FT.
BONUS — 312 SQ. FT.
BASEMENT — 1,317 SQ. FT.
GARAGE — 504 SQ. FT.

TOTAL LIVING AREA:
1,854 SQ. FT.

Design by
Studer Residential Design, Inc.

Refer to **Pricing Schedule C** on the order form for pricing information

Exciting Elevation

■ This plan features:

— Three bedrooms

— Two full and one half baths

■ A combination of materials, and varied rooflines make an exciting elevation

■ Dining Room defined by columns

■ The U-shaped Kitchen has access to the Dining Room and the Nook

■ A high ceiling and a fireplace highlight the Great Room

■ The first floor Master Suite has a decorative ceiling

■ Upstairs are two separate bonus rooms for future consideration

■ No materials list is available for this plan

FIRST FLOOR — 1,497 SQ. FT.
SECOND FLOOR — 473 SQ. FT.
BONUS ROOM — 401 SQ. FT.
BASEMENT — 1,420 SQ. FT.
GARAGE — 468 SQ. FT.

TOTAL LIVING AREA:
1,970 SQ. FT.

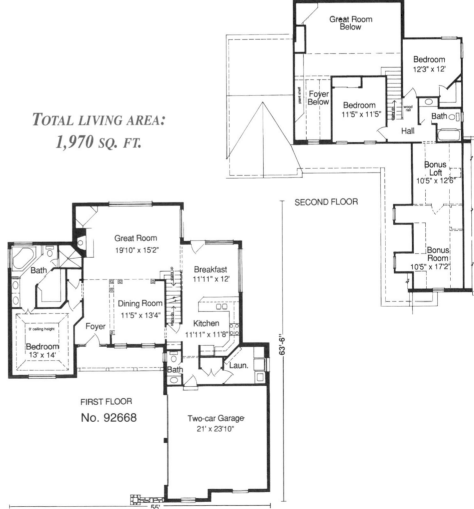

Design by
Frank Betz Associates, Inc.

Vaulted Ceilings

■ This plan features:

— Four bedrooms

— Two full and one half baths

■ The Family Room is topped by a vaulted ceiling and flows into the Dining Room

■ A vaulted ceiling also tops the efficient L-shaped Kitchen

■ The Master Suite has been designed with a tray ceiling in the Bedroom and a vaulted ceiling over the Master Bath

■ An optional basement or crawl space foundation — please specify when ordering

■ No materials list is available for this plan

MAIN FLOOR — 1,198 SQ. FT.
BASEMENT — 1,216 SQ. FT.
GARAGE — 410 SQ. FT.

TOTAL LIVING AREA:
1,198 SQ. FT.

47'- 4"

44'- 0"

© Frank Betz Associates

TRAPEZOID GLASS ABOVE

LINEN
SHWR
W.i.c.
Vaulted M. Bath
PLANT SHELF ABOVE

Bedroom 2
10⁰ x 10⁰

D.W.
RANGE
Vaulted Kitchen
PLANT SHELF ABOVE
PANTRY

FRENCH DOOR
Vaulted Dining Room
10' x 10⁰

REF.

RADIUS WINDOW

TRAY CLG.

Master Suite
12⁹ x 14²

LINEN
W.
D.
COATS
Bath

Vaulted Family Room
14⁵ x 15⁵

FPL

RADIUS WINDOW

W.H.

OPT. STAIRS TO BASEMENT

VAULT

Bedroom 3
10' x 10⁰

Covered Porch

Garage
19⁵ x 19⁸

MAIN FLOOR
No. 97256

Design by
Jannis Vann & Associates, Inc.

Refer to **Pricing Schedule C** on the order form for pricing information

Tall Window Brightens Center of Home

■ This plan features:

— Four bedrooms

— Two full and one half baths

■ Friendly Porch shelters entrance to open Foyer and graceful landing staircase

■ Open layout of formal Living and Dining rooms great for entertaining

■ Peninsula counter in Kitchen serves Breakfast Area, Family Room and Patio/Deck

■ Corner Master Bedroom with a decorative ceiling, large walk-in closet and double vanity Bath

■ Three Bedrooms share a double vanity Bath and convenient Laundry

■ An optional basement, slab or crawlspace foundation — please specify when ordering

FIRST FLOOR — 907 SQ. FT.
SECOND FLOOR — 1,129 SQ. FT.
BASEMENT — 907 SQ. FT.

TOTAL LIVING AREA:
2,036 SQ. FT.

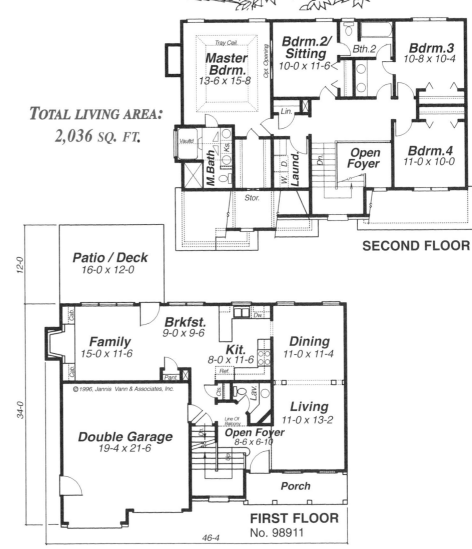

SECOND FLOOR

FIRST FLOOR
No. 98911

© 1996, Jannis Vann & Associates, Inc.

To order your Blueprints, call 1-800-235-5700

Design by
The Garlinghouse Company

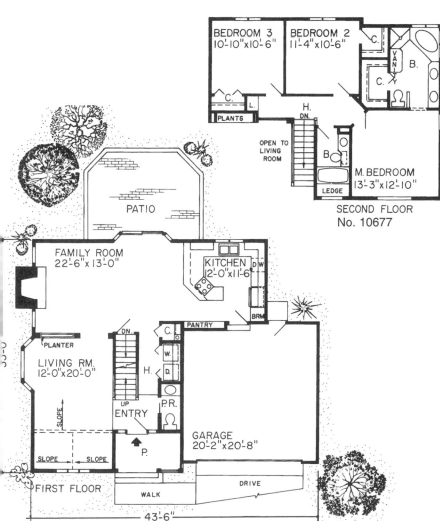

BEDROOM 3
10'-10"x10'-6"

BEDROOM 2
11'-4"x10'-6"

C.

VANITY

B.

C.

C.

L.

PLANTS

H.
DN.

OPEN TO
LIVING
ROOM

B

LEDGE

M. BEDROOM
13'-3"x12'-10"

SECOND FLOOR
No. 10677

PATIO

FAMILY ROOM
22'-6"x13'-0"

KITCHEN
12'-0"x11'-6"

DW

BRM

PANTRY

C.

PLANTER

DN.

W.

LIVING RM.
12'-0"x20'-0"

H.

D.

UP
ENTRY

P.R.

SLOPE

SLOPE   SLOPE

P.

GARAGE
20'-2"x20'-8"

FIRST FLOOR

WALK

DRIVE

43'-6"

Arches Grace Classic Facade

■ This plan features:

— Three bedrooms

— Two full and one half baths

■ Built-in planters and half walls to
define rooms

■ A balcony that connects three upstairs
Bedrooms

■ Double sinks and built-in vanity in the
Master Bath

■ Ample closet space

FIRST FLOOR — 932 SQ. FT.
SECOND FLOOR — 764 SQ. FT.
GARAGE — 430 SQ. FT.
BASEMENT — 920 SQ. FT.

TOTAL LIVING AREA:
1,696 SQ. FT.

Easy Family Living

■ This plan features:

— Three bedrooms

— Two full and one half baths

■ Sheltered entry leads into bright
Foyer with an angled staircase

■ Two-story Great Room with
hearth fireplace and atrium door

■ Convenient Kitchen has a serving
counter/snackbar

■ Quiet Master Suite has a walk-in
closet and double vanity bath

■ Two additional Bedrooms with
ample closets share a full Bath

FIRST FLOOR — 663 SQ. FT.
SECOND FLOOR — 740 SQ. FT.

TOTAL LIVING AREA:
1,403 SQ. FT.

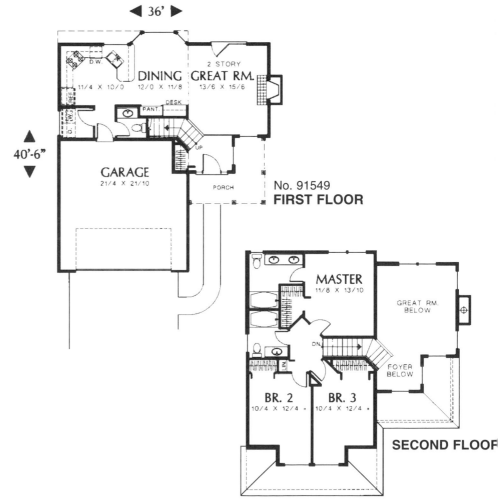

◄ 36' ►

40'-6"

DINING
11/4 X 10/0

2 STORY
GREAT RM.
13/6 X 15/6

DINING
12/0 X 11/8

DESK

PANT.

GARAGE
21/4 X 21/10

UP

PORCH

No. 91549
FIRST FLOOR

MASTER
11/8 X 13/10

GREAT RM.
BELOW

DN.

FOYER
BELOW

LIN

BR. 2
10/4 X 12/4

BR. 3
10/4 X 12/4

SECOND FLOOR

Refer to **Pricing Schedule F** on
the order form for pricing information

Design by
Patrick Morabito A.I.A.

SECOND FLOOR

ROOF

BR 4
14 x 12

ROOF

HALL

BR 3
14 x 12

B 2

FAMILY
(BELOW)

M/BATH

RAILING

FOYER
(BELOW)

BALCONY

MBR
14 X 20
STEPPED CLG

FIRST FLOOR
No. 93367

WIDTH-82'-0"
DEPTH-46'-0"

DECK

FAMILY
16 X 22
TRAY CLG

GARAGE
24 X 32

KITCHEN
13 X 16-6

DEN
12 X 14

HALL

BUILT-IN

STOR

E   LDY   DESK

DINING
14 X 14

FOYER

LIVING
14 x 18

PORCH

PORCH

Outstanding Family Home

■ This plan features:

— Four bedrooms

— Three full baths

■ Sheltered entrance into an open Foyer with a curved staircase and balcony

■ Formal Living and Dining Rooms off the Foyer for gracious entertaining

■ Pocket doors open to the Family Room with a hearth fireplace, tray ceiling and windows on three sides

■ Kitchen/Dinette has a cooktop/snackbar and built-in Pantry

■ Private Master Bedroom offers a step ceiling, huge walk-in closet and a plush Bath

■ Three additional Bedrooms share a Bath

■ No materials list is available for this plan

FIRST FLOOR — 1,895 SQ. FT.
SECOND FLOOR — 1,463 SQ. FT.
GARAGE — 768 SQ. FT.
BASEMENT — 1,895 SQ. FT.

TOTAL LIVING AREA:
3,358 SQ. FT.

Design by
Design Basics, Inc.

Refer to **Pricing Schedule D** on the order form for pricing information

Magnificent Elevation

■ This plan features:

— Four bedrooms

— Two full and one half baths

■ Impressive elevation masterfully combines brick and wood

■ The highlight of the sixteen-foot high Entry is an angled staircase

■ Formal Living and Dining rooms ideal for entertaining with tapered columns and decorative windows

■ Ideal Kitchen with a work island, adjoins the Breakfast bay and is open to the Family Room with a beamed ceiling and a fireplace

■ Double door entrance into the Master Bedroom suite that features a tiered ceiling, walk-in closet and a plush bath

FIRST FLOOR — 1,369 SQ. FT.
SECOND FLOOR — 1,111 SQ. FT.
BASEMENT — 1,369 SQ. FT.
GARAGE — 716 SQ. FT.

TOTAL LIVING AREA:
2,480 SQ. FT

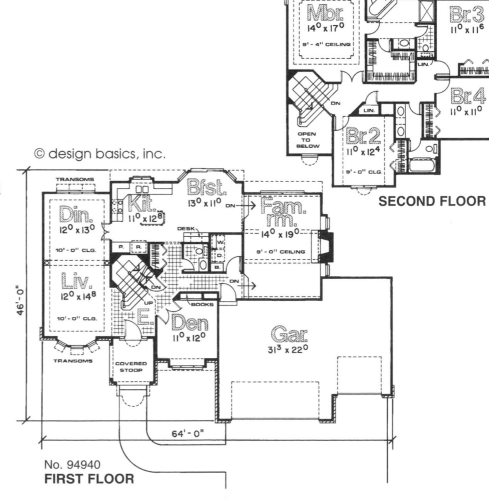

© design basics, inc.

SECOND FLOOR

No. 94940
FIRST FLOOR

To order your Blueprints, call 1-800-235-5700

Design by
Design Basics, Inc.

PLAN NO. 99400

© design basics, inc.

TOTAL LIVING AREA:
2,932 SQ. FT.

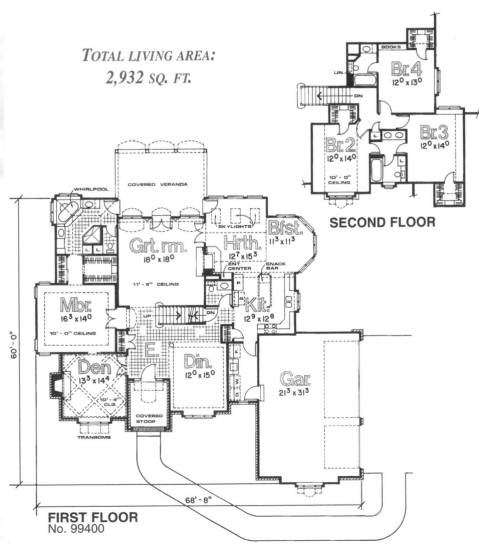

SECOND FLOOR

Br.4 12⁰ x 13⁰

Br.2 12⁰ x 14⁰ 10'-0" CEILING

Br.3 12⁰ x 14⁰

BOOKS

LIN.

WHIRLPOOL

COVERED VERANDA

Grt. rm. 18⁰ x 18⁰

11'-8" CEILING

SKYLIGHTS

Hrth. 12⁷ x 15³ ENT. CENTER

Bfst. 11³ x 11³ SNACK BAR

Mbr. 16³ x 14⁰ 10'-0" CEILING

Kit. 12⁹ x 12⁸

Den 13³ x 14⁴ 10'-4" CLG.

Din. 12⁰ x 15⁰

Gar. 21³ x 31³

COVERED STOOP

TRANSOMS

60'-0"

68'-8"

FIRST FLOOR
No. 99400

Stucco, Brick and Elegant Details

■ This plan features:

— Four bedrooms

—Three full and one half baths

■ Majestic Entry opens to Den and Dining Room

■ Expansive Great Room shares a see-thru fireplace with the Hearth Room

■ Lovely Hearth Room enhanced by three skylights and an entertainment center

■ Hub Kitchen with work island/snack bar, Pantry and bright Breakfast bay

■ Sumptuous Master Bedroom with corner windows, two closets and vanities

■ Second floor Bedrooms with walk-in closets and a private Bath

FIRST FLOOR — 2,084 SQ. FT.
SECOND FLOOR — 848 SQ. FT.
GARAGE — 682 SQ. FT.
BASEMENT— 2,084 SQ. FT.

PLAN NO. 91514

Large Front Window Provides Streaming Natural Light

■ This plan features:

— Three bedrooms

— Two full and one half baths

■ An outstanding, two-story Great Room with an unusual floor-to-ceiling, corner front window and cozy hearth fireplace

■ Kitchen with a work island and pantry opens to the Great Room, and a bright eating Nook

■ Master Suite has a vaulted ceiling and a spa tub

■ Two additional Bedrooms share a full hall Bath

FIRST FLOOR — 1,230 SQ. FT.
SECOND FLOOR — 477 SQ. FT.
BONUS ROOM — 195 SQ. FT.

TOTAL LIVING AREA:
1,707 SQ. FT.

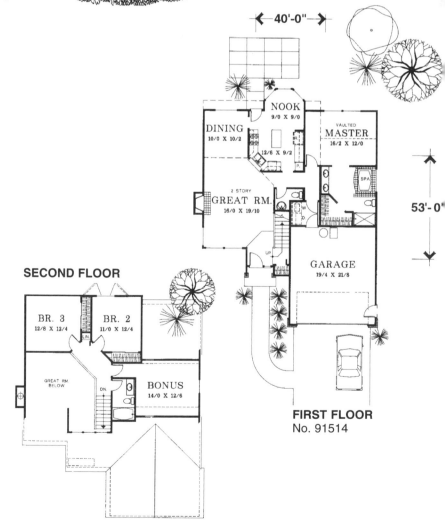

SECOND FLOOR

FIRST FLOOR
No. 91514

Design by
Design Basics, Inc.

SECOND FLOOR

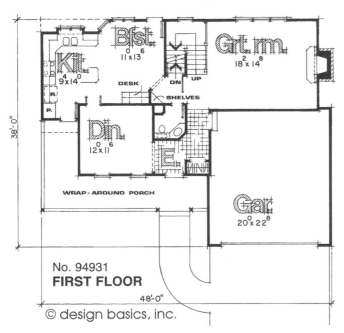

No. 94931
FIRST FLOOR

48'-0"

© design basics, inc.

Traditional Country Home

■ This plan features:

— Four bedrooms

— Two full and one half baths

■ Wraparound Porch accesses tiled Entry and Kitchen

■ Expansive Great Room has a triple window, inviting fireplace and a landing staircase

■ Large Kitchen has a built-in Pantry and desk, work island and a bright Breakfast Area

■ Private Master Bedroom has a decorative ceiling and a deluxe Bath

■ Three secondary Bedrooms share a double vanity Bath

FIRST FLOOR — 927 SQ. FT.
SECOND FLOOR — 1,163 SQ. FT.
BASEMENT — 927 SQ. FT.
GARAGE — 463 SQ. FT.

TOTAL LIVING AREA:
2,090 SQ. FT.

Design by
Studer Residential Design, Inc.

Refer to **Pricing Schedule D** on the order form for pricing information

Elegant Elevation

■ This plan features:

— Three bedrooms

— Two full and one half baths

■ Brick trim, sidelights and a transom window give a warm welcome to this home

■ High ceilings continue from Foyer into Great Room which counts among its amenities a fireplace and entertainment center

■ The Kitchen serves the formal and informal Dining Areas with ease

■ The Master Suite is positioned for privacy on the first floor

■ The second floor has loads of possibilities with a bonus space and a Study

■ Two Bedrooms each with walk-in closets share a full Bath

■ No materials list is available for this plan

FIRST FLOOR — 1,542 SQ. FT.
SECOND FLOOR — 667 SQ. FT.
BONUS — 236 SQ. FT.
BASEMENT — 1,367 SQ. FT.
GARAGE — 420 SQ. FT

TOTAL LIVING AREA:
2,209 SQ. FT.

FIRST FLOOR
No. 92662

SECOND FLOOR

To order your Blueprints, call 1-800-235-5700

Refer to **Pricing Schedule D** on the order form for pricing information

Design by
The Garlinghouse Company

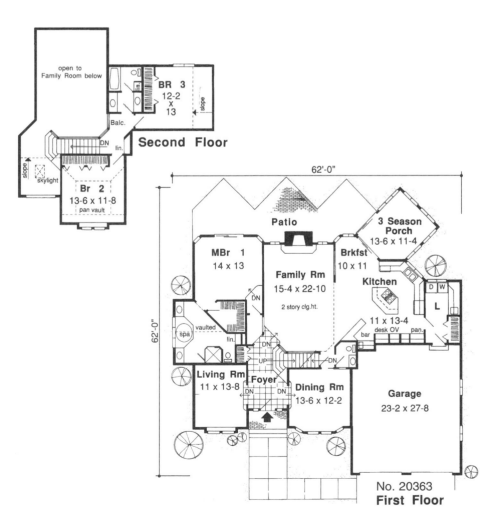

Second Floor

BR 3
12-2 x 13

open to Family Room below

Balc.

DN

Br 2
13-6 x 11-8
pan vault

slope

skylight

slope

No. 20363
First Floor

62'-0"

62'-0"

Patio

3 Season Porch
13-6 x 11-4

MBr 1
14 x 13

Brkfst
10 x 11

Family Rm
15-4 x 22-10
2 story clg. ht.

Kitchen
11 x 13-4

D W

L

vaulted

spa

lin.

DN

UP

DN

bar   desk OV   pan.

Living Rm
11 x 13-8

Foyer

DN   DN

Dining Rm
13-6 x 12-2

Garage
23-2 x 27-8

Comfort and Convenience

■ This plan features:

— Three bedrooms

— Two full and one half baths

■ Transom windows, skylights and an open plan combine to make this brick classic sun-filled

■ The Family Room includes a fireplace and open access to the Kitchen and Breakfast Area

■ The island Kitchen has a built-in bar to make mealtime preparation a breeze

■ The luxurious Master Suite has a vaulted Bath area including a garden spa

FIRST FLOOR — 1,859 SQ. FT.
SECOND FLOOR — 579 SQ. FT.
BASEMENT — 1,859 SQ. FT.
GARAGE — 622 SQ. FT.

TOTAL LIVING AREA:
2,438 SQ. FT.

Design by
Frank Betz Associates, Inc.

Refer to **Pricing Schedule C** on the order form for pricing informatio

Spectacular Front Window

■ This plan features:

— Three bedrooms

— Two full baths

■ A spectacular front window adorns the Dining Room

■ The Family Room is crowned in a vaulted ceiling and is accented by a fireplace

■ The Kitchen includes a walk-in Pantry

■ The Master Suite features a tray ceiling over the Bedroom and a vaulted ceiling over the Bath

■ An optional basement, crawl space or slab foundation — please specify when ordering

■ No materials list is available for this plan

MAIN FLOOR — 1,875 SQ. FT.
BASEMENT — 1,891 SQ. FT.
GARAGE — 475 SQ. FT.

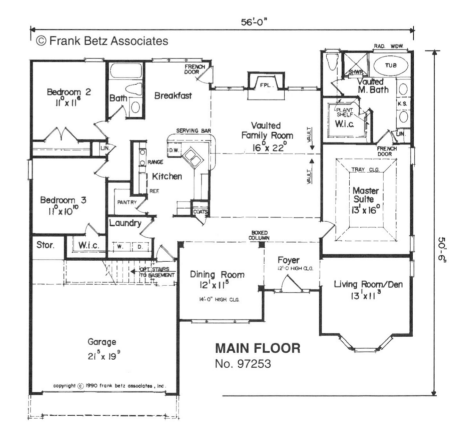

© Frank Betz Associates

MAIN FLOOR
No. 97253

copyright © 1990 frank betz associates, inc.

TOTAL LIVING AREA:
1,875 SQ. FT.

To order your Blueprints, call 1-800-235-5700

Design by
Building Science Associates

Sunroom with Vaulted Ceiling

■ This plan features:

— Four bedrooms

— Two full baths

■ In the rear find a Sunroom with a vaulted ceiling

■ A fireplace warms the Great Room

■ The Dining Room is located adjacent to the Kitchen with plenty of counter space

■ The Master Bedroom is well appointed and privately located

■ There is the option for a fourth Bedroom or a Study

■ No materials list is available for this plan

■ An optional slab or crawl space foundation — please specify when ordering

MAIN FLOOR — 2,201 SQ. FT.
GARAGE — 532 SQ. FT.

TOTAL LIVING AREA:
2,201 SQ. FT.

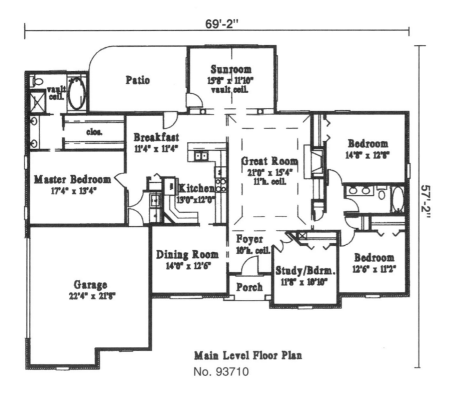

Main Level Floor Plan
No. 93710

Design by
Donald A. Gardner Architects, Inc.

Refer to **Pricing Schedule E** on the order form for pricing information

B. NATHAN

©1995 Donald A. Gardner Architects, Inc.

Dream Home for Contemporary Buyers

- This plan features:
- — Three bedrooms
- — Two full baths
- Gables, a center front dormer, and a touch of brick combine with desirable amenities and an efficient floor plan
- Dormer floods the Foyer with sunlight and intrigue, while a cathedral ceiling enlarges the Great Room
- The Kitchen and Breakfast Area, located next to the Great Room, is punctuated by interior columns
- Tray ceilings and arched picture windows are featured in the Dining Room and the Living Room
- Two family Bedrooms share a large full Bath with a double vanity in one wing, while the luxurious Master Suite enjoys privacy in the rear

MAIN FLOOR — 2,050 SQ. FT.
BONUS — 377 SQ. FT.
GARAGE — 503 SQ. FT.

TOTAL LIVING AREA
2,050 SQ. FT.

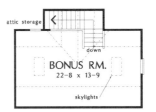

attic storage

down

BONUS RM.
22-8 x 13-9

skylights

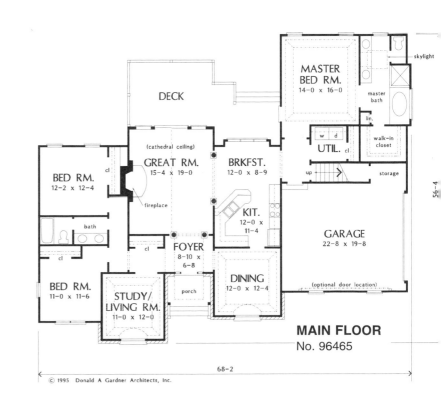

DECK

MASTER BED RM.
14-0 x 16-0

skylight

master bath

lin.

(cathedral ceiling)

GREAT RM.
15-4 x 19-0

BRKFST.
12-0 x 8-9

w   d

UTIL. cl

walk-in closet

BED RM.
12-2 x 12-4

cl

fireplace

KIT.
12-0 x 11-4

up

storage

56-4

bath

cl

FOYER
8-10 x 6-8

GARAGE
22-8 x 19-8

cl

BED RM.
11-0 x 11-6

STUDY/ LIVING RM.
11-0 x 12-0

porch

DINING
12-0 x 12-4

(optional door location)

MAIN FLOOR
No. 96465

68-2

© 1995 Donald A Gardner Architects, Inc.

To order your Blueprints, call 1-800-235-5700

Design by
Larry E. Belk

An Open Concept Floor Plan

■ This plan features:

— Four bedrooms

— Two full baths

■ The Kitchen, Breakfast Room and the Family Room are adjacent to one another, perfect for family gatherings

■ A well-appointed Kitchen has ample cabinet space, a peninsula counter, and is in close proximity to both the Dining Room and the Breakfast Room/Family Room

■ The private Master Suite has a large Master Bath

■ Two additional Bedrooms have walk-in closets

■ No materials list is available for this plan

MAIN FLOOR — 2,511 SQ. FT.
GARAGE — 469 SQ. FT.

TOTAL LIVING AREA:
2,511 SQ. FT.

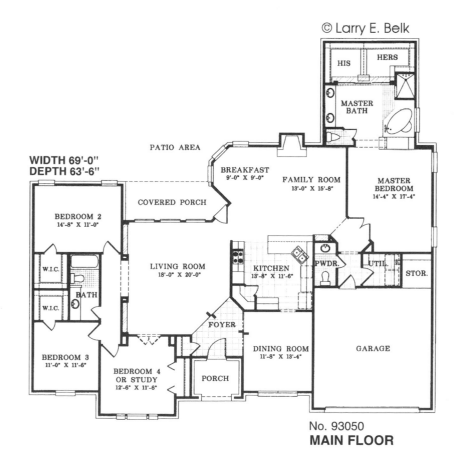

© Larry E. Belk

WIDTH 69'-0"
DEPTH 63'-6"

PATIO AREA

BREAKFAST
9'-0" X 9'-0"

FAMILY ROOM
13'-0" X 15'-8"

MASTER
BATH

HIS   HERS

MASTER
BEDROOM
14'-4" X 17'-4"

COVERED PORCH

BEDROOM 2
14'-8" X 11'-0"

W.I.C.

BATH

W.I.C.

LIVING ROOM
18'-0" X 20'-0"

KITCHEN
13'-8" X 11'-6"

PWDR.

UTIL.

STOR.

FOYER

BEDROOM 3
11'-0" X 11'-6"

BEDROOM 4
OR STUDY
12'-6" X 11'-6"

PORCH

DINING ROOM
11'-8" X 13'-4"

GARAGE

No. 93050
MAIN FLOOR

Design by
Studer Residental Design, Inc.

Refer to **Pricing Schedule C** on
the order form for pricing informatio

What a First Impression

■ This plan features:

— Three bedrooms

— Two full and one half baths

■ The Traditionally styled exterior makes a lasting first impression

■ Inside the Foyer, find a wood railed staircase that leads to the second floor

■ The sunken Great room with fireplace opens to both the Solarium and the Breakfast Nook

■ The Kitchen has a dual sided island with an eating bar and counter space

■ Upstairs the Master bedroom has a decorative high ceiling

■ If you need more space there is a Bonus Room provided over the Garage

■ No materials list is available for this plan

FIRST FLOOR —1,060 SQ. FT.
SECOND FLOOR — 927 SQ. FT.
BONUS — 267 SQ. FT.

TOTAL LIVING AREA:
1,987 SQ. FT.

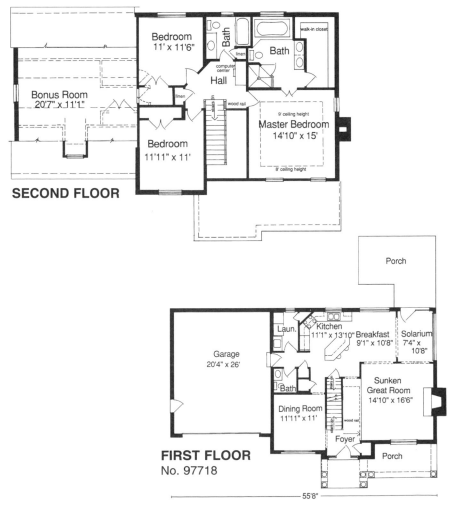

SECOND FLOOR

Bedroom 11' x 11'6"
Bath
Bath
walk-in closet
linen
computer center
Hall
Bonus Room 20'7" x 11'1"
linen
wood rail
9' ceiling height
Master Bedroom 14'10" x 15'
8' ceiling height
Bedroom 11'11" x 11'

Porch

Laun.
Kitchen 11'1" x 13'10"
Breakfast 9'1" x 10'8"
Solarium 7'4" x 10'8"
Garage 20'4" x 26'
Bath
Sunken Great Room 14'10" x 16'6"
Dining Room 11'11" x 11'
wood rail
Foyer
Porch

FIRST FLOOR
No. 97718

55'8"

To order your Blueprints, call 1-800-235-5700

Refer to **Pricing Schedule D** on the order form for pricing information

Cozy Yet Spacious

■ This plan features:

— Four bedrooms

— Three full baths

■ The Entry to the Gallery area has a brick floor and an 11-foot ceiling

■ The formal Dining Room and Living Room are located at an angle across the Gallery

■ The Family Room is crowned in a cathedral ceiling and features a fireplace

■ The Master Bedroom is topped by a vaulted ceiling and has a private covered Patio

■ The compartmental Master Bath features a whirlpool tub and a separate shower

■ No materials list is available for this plan

MAIN FLOOR — 2,526 SQ. FT.
GARAGE — 720 SQ. FT.

TOTAL LIVING AREA:
2,526 SQ. FT.

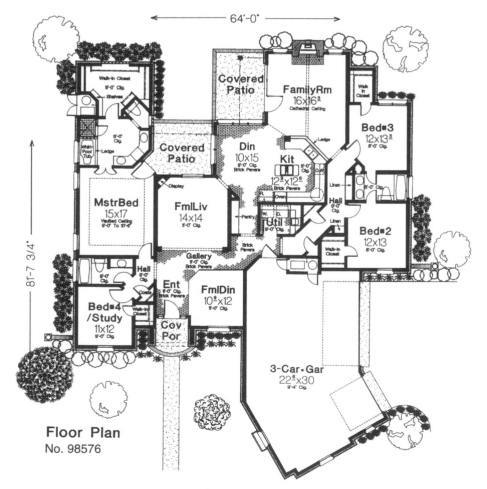

Floor Plan
No. 98576

Design by
Donald A. Gardner Architects, Inc.

Refer to **Pricing Schedule D** on the order form for pricing information

©1997 Donald A. Gardner Architects, Inc.

Arched Windows Make Wonderful Accents

■ This plan features:

— Three bedrooms

— Two full baths

■ Privacy and openness are balanced in this expandable home

■ The combined Great Room and Dining Area feature a cathedral ceiling, a fireplace and Deck access

■ A U-shaped Kitchen is convenient to Dining and Utility Areas

■ Crowned with a tray ceiling, the Master Bedroom includes a walk-in closet and private Bath

■ Two secondary Bedrooms, one an optional Study, share the second full Bath

MAIN FLOOR—1,542 SQ. FT.
BONUS —352 SQ. FT.
GARAGE —487 SQ. FT.

TOTAL LIVING AREA:
1,542 SQ. FT

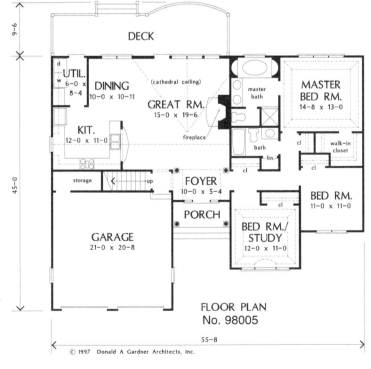

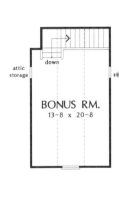

FLOOR PLAN
No. 98005

© 1997 Donald A Gardner Architects, Inc.

To order your Blueprints, call 1-800-235-5700

Design by
Donald A. Gardner Architects, Inc.

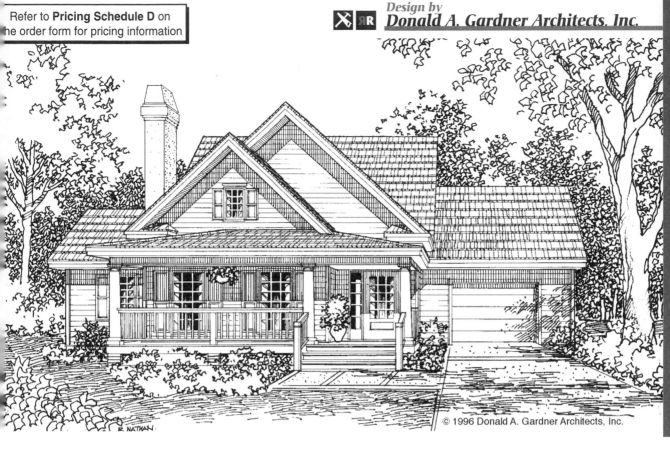

© 1996 Donald A. Gardner Architects, Inc.

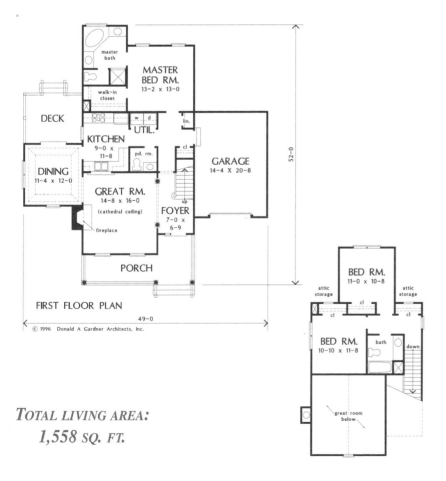

master bath

MASTER BED RM.
13-2 x 13-0

walk-in closet

DECK

KITCHEN
9-0 x 11-8

UTIL.

w d

pd. rm.

lin.

cl

GARAGE
14-4 X 20-8

DINING
11-4 x 12-0

GREAT RM.
14-8 x 16-0
(cathedral ceiling)

fireplace

FOYER
7-0 x 6-9

up

PORCH

FIRST FLOOR PLAN

52-0

49-0

© 1996 Donald A Gardner Architects, Inc.

BED RM.
11-0 x 10-8

attic storage

cl

attic storage

cl

cl

BED RM.
10-10 x 11-8

bath

down

great room below

SECOND FLOOR PLAN
No. 99883

TOTAL LIVING AREA:
1,558 SQ. FT.

Traditional Two-Story

■ This plan features:

— Three bedrooms

— Two full and one half baths

■ Great Room crowned in a cathedral ceiling and highlighted by a fireplace and colonnaded opening

■ A pass-through above the Kitchen sink making both serving and cleaning up a snap

■ Traffic flows easily into the Dining Room topped by a tray ceiling and spilling out onto the deck when needed

■ Secluded Master Suite highlighted by a generous walk-in closet and private Bath with separate shower, enclosed toilet, and corner garden tub

■ Two secondary Bedrooms upstairs share a full Bath

FIRST FLOOR — 1,116 SQ. FT.
SECOND FLOOR — 442 SQ. FT.
GARAGE & STORAGE — 313 SQ. FT.

Design by
Donald A. Gardner Architects, Inc.

Refer to **Pricing Schedule E** on the order form for pricing information

© 1997 Donald A. Gardner Architects, Inc.

B. NATHAN

Relaxed Country Living

■ This plan features:

— Three bedrooms

— Two full baths

■ Comfortable country home with deluxe Master Suite, two porches and dual-sided fireplace

■ Vaulted Great Room enjoys two clerestory dormers and a fireplace shared with the Breakfast bay

■ Dining Room and front Bedroom/ Study have tray ceilings

■ Master Bedroom features a vaulted ceiling, back Porch access, and a super Bath

■ Skylit Bonus Room over Garage provides extra space

MAIN FLOOR — 2,027 SQ. FT.
BONUS ROOM — 340 SQ. FT.
GARAGE & STORAGE — 532 SQ. FT.

TOTAL LIVING AREA:
2,027 SQ. FT.

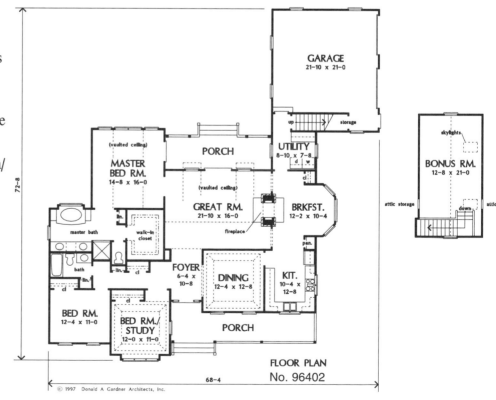

To order your Blueprints, call 1-800-235-5700

Design by
Ahmann Design, Inc.

SECOND FLOOR

MBR.
13'4" X 11'0"

B.R.#2
11'4" X 13'0"

LINEN

LIN.

DGN

BR.#3
12'0" X 13'0"

LINEN

OPEN TO
E.

PLANT LEDGE

BR.#4
12'0" X 12'8"

PLANT LEDGE

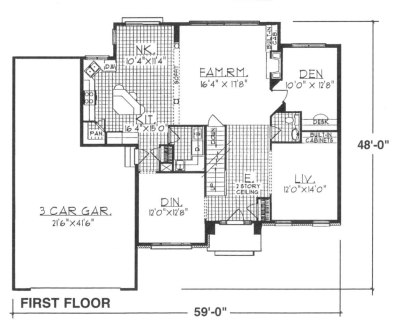

FIRST FLOOR

NK.
10'4"X11'4"

DW

FAM.RM.
16'4" X 17'8"

BUILT-IN CAB.

DEN
10'0" X 12'8"

KIT.
16'4"X15'0"

PAN.

DOWN

DESK

BUILT-IN CABINETS

E.
2 STORY CEILING

LIV.
12'0"X14'0"

3 CAR GAR.
21'6"X41'6"

DIN.
12'0"X12'8"

48'-0"

59'-0"

Adding Ease to Busy Lifestyles

■ This plan features:

— Three bedrooms

— Two full and one half baths

■ An elegant two-story Foyer leads to the Family Room

■ The Family Room has built-in cabinets surrounding the fireplace

■ A Den with a built-in desk is off the Family Room

■ An open Kitchen has ample counter space and a sunny Nook for family meals

■ The second floor Master Suite has a large walk-in closet and a private Bath with a garden spa tub

■ No materials list is available for this plan

FIRST FLOOR — 1,533 SQ. FT.
SECOND FLOOR — 1,255 SQ. FT.
BASEMENT — 1,533 SQ. FT.

TOTAL LIVING AREA:
2,788 SQ. FT.

Design by
The Garlinghouse Company

Refer to **Pricing Schedule C** on the order form for pricing information

Stone and Stucco Family Home

■ This plan features:

— Three bedrooms

— Two full and one half baths

■ The formal Living Room enjoys a large front window

■ A sloped ceiling and a stunning fireplace in the Hearth Room

■ The range-top island Kitchen has a corner double sink, built-in Pantry and ample counter space

■ The first-floor Master Suite is equipped with a luxurious Bath

FIRST FLOOR — 1,606 SQ. FT.
SECOND FLOOR — 543 SQ. FT.
BASEMENT — 1,606 SQ. FT.
GARAGE — 484 SQ. FT.

TOTAL LIVING AREA:
2,149 SQ. FT.

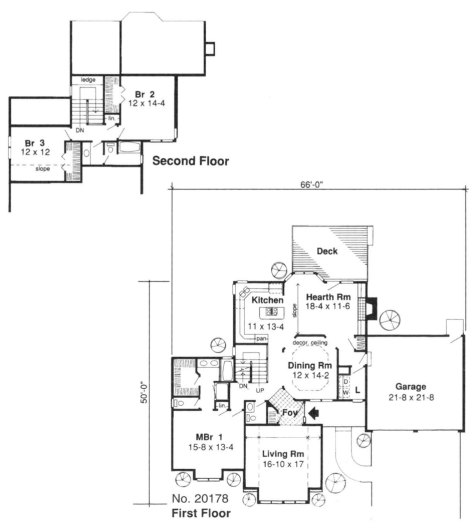

Second Floor

ledge

Br 2
12 x 14-4

lin.

DN

Br 3
12 x 12

slope

66'-0"

50'-0"

Deck

Kitchen
11 x 13-4

Hearth Rm
18-4 x 11-6

slope

pan.

decor. ceiling

Dining Rm
12 x 14-2

Garage
21-8 x 21-8

DN

UP

lin.

Foy

MBr 1
15-8 x 13-4

Living Rm
16-10 x 17

No. 20178
First Floor

To order your Blueprints, call 1-800-235-5700

Design by
Ahmann Design

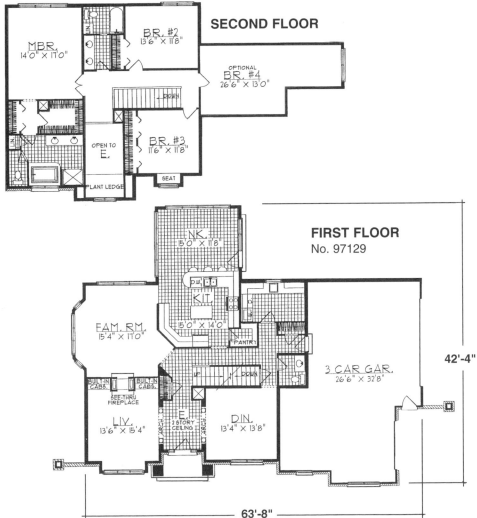

SECOND FLOOR

MBR.
14'0" × 17'0"

BR. #2
13'6" × 11'8"

OPTIONAL
BR. #4
26'6" × 13'0"

DOWN

OPEN TO
E.

BR. #3
11'6" × 11'8"

PLANT LEDGE

SEAT

NK.
15'0" × 11'8"

FIRST FLOOR
No. 97129

KIT.
15'0" × 14'0"

PANTRY

FAM. RM.
15'4" × 11'0"

BUILT-IN CABS.

BUILT-IN CABS.

SEE-THRU FIREPLACE

UP

DOWN

3 CAR GAR.
26'6" × 32'8"

42'-4"

LIV.
13'6" × 15'4"

E.
2 STORY CEILING

DIN.
13'4" × 13'8"

63'-8"

Perfect Look In Any Setting

■ This plan features:

— Three bedrooms

— Two full and one half baths

■ The Family Room has a see-through fireplace

■ The formal Living Room provides elegance while entertaining

■ The Kitchen has amenities such as wrap-around counters and a center island

■ An eating bar and a generous Breakfast Nook are perfect for family meals

■ Upstairs, the Master Bedroom is your private retreat

■ No materials list is available for this plan

FIRST FLOOR — 1,614 SQ. FT.
SECOND FLOOR — 1,103 SQ. FT.
BONUS — 318 SQ. FT.

TOTAL LIVING AREA:
2,717 SQ. FT.

Design by
Frank Betz Associates, Inc.

Refer to **Pricing Schedule D** on the order form for pricing information

Grand Styling

■ This plan features:

— Four bedrooms

— Two full and one half baths

■ The Family Room, Breakfast Room and Kitchen are laid out to create an open feeling

■ The Family Room has a serving bar between the Kitchen and the Breakfast Room

■ The Master Suite includes a walk-in closet and a cozy Sitting Room

■ An optional basement or crawl space foundation — please specify when ordering

■ No materials list is available for this plan

FIRST FLOOR — 1,205 SQ. FT.
SECOND FLOOR — 1,277 SQ. FT.
BASEMENT — 1,128 SQ. FT.
GARAGE — 528 SQ. FT.

TOTAL LIVING AREA:
2,482 SQ. FT.

No. 97255
FIRST FLOOR PLAN

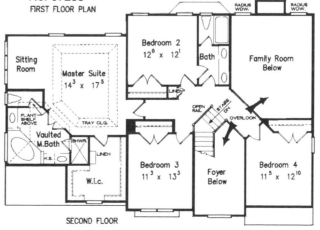

SECOND FLOOR

To order your Blueprints, call 1-800-235-5700

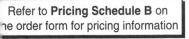

Design by
Fillmore Design Group

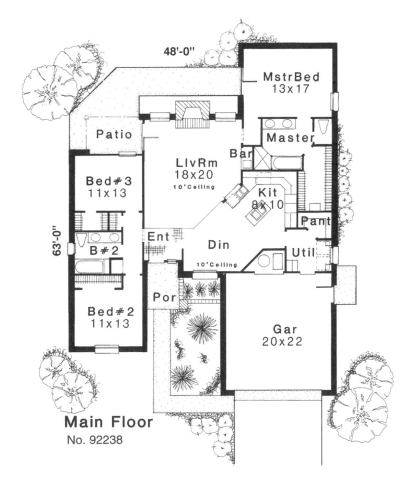

48'-0"

63'-0"

Patio

Bed#3
11x13

B # 2

Bed#2
11x13

Ent

Por

LivRm
18x20
10'Ceiling

Din
10'Ceiling

Bar

MstrBed
13x17

Master

Kit
8x10

Pant

Util

Gar
20x22

Main Floor
No. 92238

TOTAL LIVING AREA:
1,664 SQ. FT.

Easy Everyday Living

■ This plan features:

— Three bedrooms

— Two full baths

■ Front entrance accented by segmented arches, sidelight and transom windows

■ Open Living Room with focal point fireplace, wetbar and access to Patio

■ Dining Area open to both the Living Room and Kitchen

■ Efficient Kitchen with a cooktop island, walk-in Pantry and Utility Area with a Garage entry

■ Large walk-in closet, double vanity bath and access to Patio featured in the Master Bedroom

■ Two additional Bedrooms share a double vanity Bath

■ No materials list is available for this plan

MAIN FLOOR — 1,664 SQ. FT.
BASEMENT — 1,600 SQ. FT.
GARAGE — 440 SQ. FT

Design by
Greg Marquis & Associates

Refer to **Pricing Schedule B** on the order form for pricing information

Family Room with Skylights

■ This plan features:

— Three bedrooms

— Two full and one half baths

■ In the center of the home is the Family Room with skylights

■ The Dining Room is separated from the Foyer by columns

■ The Kitchen has a convenient working triangle

■ A wall of windows brightens the Breakfast Nook

■ The first floor Master Bedroom spans the width of the home

■ Upstairs, a balcony overlooks the Family Room below

■ No materials list is available for this plan

FIRST FLOOR — 1,299 SQ. FT.
SECOND FLOOR — 557 SQ. FT.
BONUS — 272 SQ. FT.
BASEMENT — 1,299 SQ. FT.
GARAGE — 494 SQ. FT.

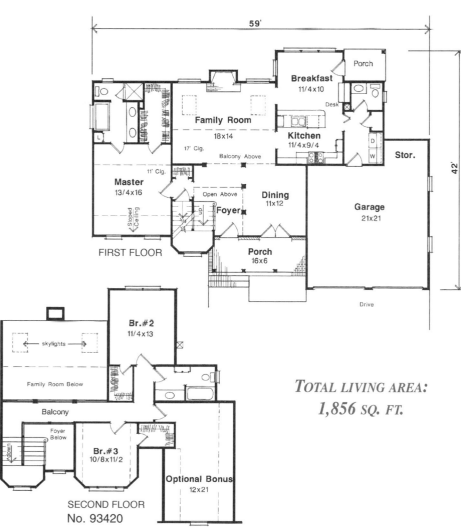

TOTAL LIVING AREA:
1,856 SQ. FT.

To order your Blueprints, call 1-800-235-5700

Design by
Frank Betz Associates, Inc.

Keystone and Arched Windows

■ This plan features:

— Three bedrooms

— Two full baths

■ An arched window in the Dining Room offers eye-catching appeal

■ A decorative column helps define the Dining Room and Great Room

■ A fireplace and French door to the rear yard are in the Great Room

■ An efficient Kitchen includes a serving bar, Pantry and pass through to the Great Room

■ A plush Master Suite includes a private bath and a walk-in closet

■ An optional basement, slab or crawl space foundation — please specify when ordering

MAIN FLOOR — 1,670 SQ. FT.
GARAGE — 240 SQ. FT.

TOTAL LIVING AREA:
1,670 SQ. FT.

54'-0"

OPT. BAY WINDOW

TRAY CLG.

Master Suite
13⁹ x 15⁶

Vaulted Breakfast

FRENCH DOOR

FPL.

Bedroom 2
11⁵ x 12⁸

SERVING BAR

D.W.

PASS-THRU

Great Room
16⁰ x 18⁴
(13'-2" HIGH CLG.)

RANGE

Kitchen

REF.

COATS

PANTRY

L.IN.

Bath

Vaulted M. Bath

SHWR.

W.

D.

Laun.

DECORATIVE COLUMN

LINEN

W.i.c.

PLANT SHELF ABOVE

W.H.

Dining Room
13⁰ x 11⁰
(14'-6" HIGH CLG.)

Foyer
(13'-2" HIGH CLG.)

Vaulted Bedroom 3
11⁵ x 12⁷

Covered Porch

52'-0"

Garage

MAIN FLOOR
No. 98432

© Frank Betz Associates

GARAGE LOCATION WITH BASEMENT

Design by
Studer Residental Design, Inc.

Refer to **Pricing Schedule B** on the order form for pricing information

Designed for a Narrow Lot

■ This plan features:

— Three bedrooms

— Two full and one half baths

■ Enter the home through the front door with transom and sidelights

■ The Great Room with its corner fireplace is just steps beyond the Foyer

■ The Dining Room accesses the rear Patio

■ The Kitchen is spacious enough for multiple chefs to stir the soup

■ The Bedrooms are all on the second floor and have ample closets

■ A Bonus Room is accessed from the second floor

■ No materials list is available for this plan

FIRST FLOOR — 798 SQ. FT.
SECOND FLOOR — 777 SQ. FT.
BONUS — 242 SQ. FT.
BASEMENT — 798 SQ. FT.

TOTAL LIVING AREA:
1,575 SQ. FT.

FIRST FLOOR
No. 97712

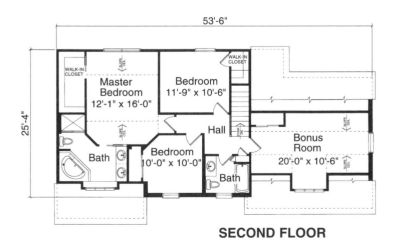

SECOND FLOOR

To order your Blueprints, call 1-800-235-5700

Design by
Fillmore Design Group

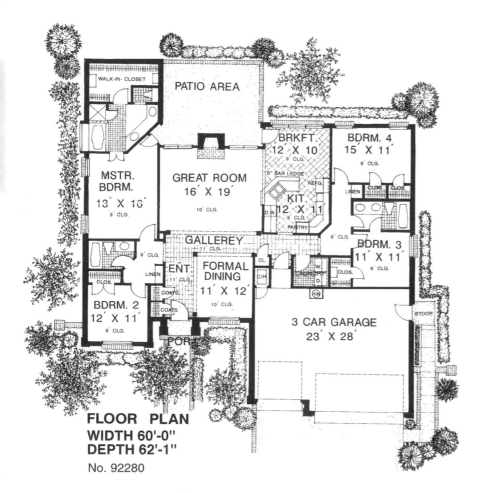

FLOOR PLAN
WIDTH 60'-0"
DEPTH 62'-1"

No. 92280

Lots of Living on One Level

■ This plan features:

— Four bedrooms

— Three full baths

■ Easy-care tiled Entry and Gallery opens to formal Dining Room and Great Room

■ Fireplace between double windows enhances the Great Room

■ Open Kitchen has an angled peninsula counter and a built-in Pantry

■ Private Master Bedroom offers Patio access, a walk-in closet and a lavish Bath

■ Three Bedrooms with ample closets have access to full Baths

■ No materials list is available for this plan

MAIN FLOOR — 2,132 SQ. FT.
GARAGE — 644 SQ. FT.

TOTAL LIVING AREA:
2,132 SQ. FT.

Design by
Design Basics, Inc.

Refer to **Pricing Schedule E** on the order form for pricing information

Luxury Found Within

■ This plan features:

— Four bedrooms

— Three full and one half baths

■ The covered stoop reveals the front door with sidelights and a transom

■ The Dining Room has a boxed bay window and a decorative ceiling

■ The Kitchen is equipped with a wetbar, a buffet and a center island

■ Upstairs find the Master Bedroom, which has a decorative ceiling

■ There are three additional Bedrooms and two full Baths on the second floor

FIRST FLOOR — 1,575 SQ. FT.
SECOND FLOOR — 1,295 SQ. FT.
GARAGE — 724 SQ. FT.

TOTAL LIVING AREA:
2,870 SQ. FT.

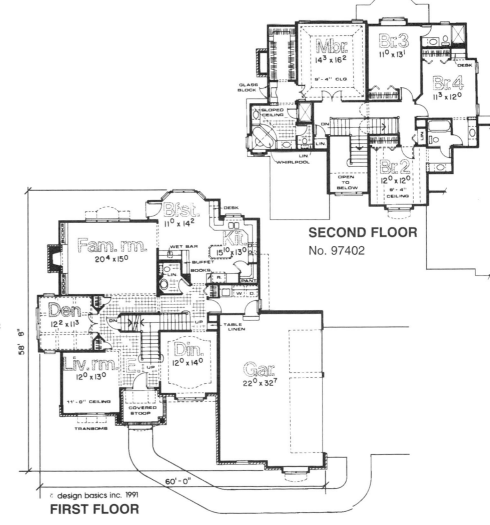

SECOND FLOOR
No. 97402

FIRST FLOOR
© design basics inc. 1991

To order your Blueprints, call 1-800-235-5700

Design by
Frank Betz Associates, Inc

PLAN NO. 98403

© Frank Betz Associates

64' - 6"

62' - 10"

FIRST FLOOR
No. 98403

SECOND FLOOR

Luxurious Yet Cozy

■ This plan features:

— Four bedrooms

— Three full and one half baths

■ Covered Porch offers a warm welcome

■ Decorative columns define Dining Room and Great Room

■ Inviting fireplace windows, and a vaulted ceiling in the Great Room

■ Kitchen with a work island, serving bar, Breakfast Area and walk-in Pantry

■ Corner Master Suite includes a cozy fireplace and a lavish Dressing Area

■ An optional basement, crawl space or slab foundation — please specify when ordering

FIRST FLOOR — 2,467 SQ. FT.
SECOND FLOOR — 928 SQ. FT.
BONUS — 296 SQ. FT.
BASEMENT — 2,467 SQ. FT.
GARAGE — 566 SQ. FT.

TOTAL LIVING AREA:
3,395 SQ. FT.

Design by
James Fahy, P.E., P.C.

Refer to **Pricing Schedule D** on the order form for pricing information

Appealing Gates

■ This plan features:

— Three or four bedrooms

— Two full and one half baths

■ The Foyer is highlighted by sidelights and a banister staircase

■ Formal Living Room is accented by a lovely bay window

■ Expansive Family Room has a cozy fireplace between windows

■ The efficient Kitchen has a work island and a Pantry

■ Master Bedroom offers a walk-in closet and private bath

■ No materials list is available for this plan

FIRST FLOOR — 1,009 SQ. FT.
SECOND FLOOR — 862 SQ. FT.
BASEMENT — 994 SQ. FT.
GARAGE — 506 SQ. FT.

TOTAL LIVING AREA:
1,871 SQ. FT.

WIDTH 60'-0"
DEPTH 33'-8"

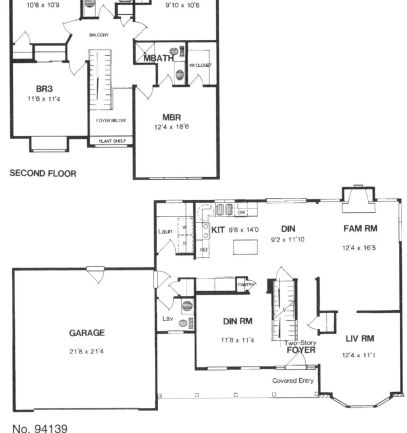

SECOND FLOOR

No. 94139
FIRST FLOOR

To order your Blueprints, call 1-800-235-5700

Design by
Frank Betz Associates, Inc.

© Frank Betz Associates

FIRST FLOOR
No. 97239

SECOND FLOOR

TOTAL LIVING AREA:
2,764 SQ. FT.

Impressive Presence

■ This plan features:

— Four bedrooms

— Three full and one half baths

■ The Living Room has a vaulted ceiling and a decorative window

■ The Dining Room features a boxed bay window

■ The Family Room has an arched entrance

■ The Kitchen is open to the Nook and has a center island

■ The Master Suite is secluded on the first floor

■ An optional basement or crawl space foundation — please specify when ordering

■ No materials list is available for this plan

FIRST FLOOR — 1,904 SQ. FT.
SECOND FLOOR — 860 SQ. FT.
BONUS — 388 SQ. FT.
BASEMENT — 1,904 SQ. FT.
GARAGE — 575 SQ. FT.

To order your Blueprints, call 1-800-235-5700

Design by
Design Basics, Inc.

Expansive Front Porch

■ This plan features:

— Four bedrooms

— Two full and one half baths

■ A wide front Porch and stylish windows highlight the facade

■ The Dining Room has a built-in hutch

■ A see-through fireplace in the Nook is shared with the Family Room

■ The L-shaped Kitchen has a center island with a cooktop

■ The Family Room is highlighted by a built-in entertainment center

■ Four large Bedrooms and two full Baths are on the second floor

FIRST FLOOR — 1,366 SQ. FT.
SECOND FLOOR — 1,278 SQ. FT.
BASEMENT — 1,366 SQ. FT.
GARAGE — 523 SQ. FT.

TOTAL LIVING AREA:
2,644 SQ. FT.

SECOND FLOOR

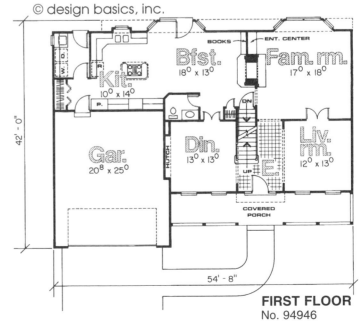

© design basics, inc.

FIRST FLOOR
No. 94946

To order your Blueprints, call 1-800-235-5700

Design by
Design Basics, Inc.

SECOND FLOOR

© design basics, inc.

"English Manor" House

■ This plan features:

— Four bedrooms

— Two full, one three quarter and one half baths

■ Stone facade enhances covered stoop and impressive entry

■ Formal Dining Room is accented by a decorative ceiling

■ Spectacular bow window and a raised, hearth fireplace highlight Living Room

■ The Kitchen has a walk-in Pantry, angled serving counter/snack bar and a bright Breakfast Alcove

■ Private Master Bedroom Suite has a Sitting Area and a luxurious Bath

FIRST FLOOR — 2,813 SQ. FT.
SECOND FLOOR — 1,091 SQ. FT.
BASEMENT — 2,813 SQ. FT.
GARAGE — 1,028 SQ. FT.

TOTAL LIVING AREA:
3,904 SQ. FT.

FIRST FLOOR
No. 99402

Design by
The Garlinghouse Company

Refer to **Pricing Schedule B** on the order form for pricing information

Family Room
With Fireplace

- This plan features:

— Four bedrooms

— One full, one half, and one three quarter baths

- A lovely Front Porch shades the entrance

- A spacious Living Room that opens into the Dining Area which flows into the efficient Kitchen

- The Family Room is equipped with a cozy fireplace and sliding glass doors to the Patio

- The Master Suite has a large walk-in closet and a private Bath with a step-in shower

- Three additional Bedrooms share a full hall Bath

FIRST FLOOR — 692 SQ. FT.
SECOND FLOOR — 813 SQ. FT.
BASEMENT — 699 SQ. FT.
GARAGE — 484 SQ. FT.

TOTAL LIVING AREA:
1,505 SQ. FT.

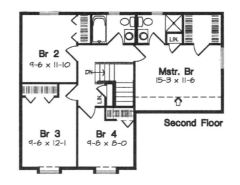

Second Floor

Br 2
9-6 x 11-10

Mstr. Br
15-3 x 11-6

Br 3
9-6 x 12-1

Br 4
9-8 x 8-0

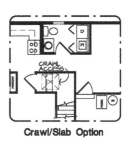

Crawl/Slab Option

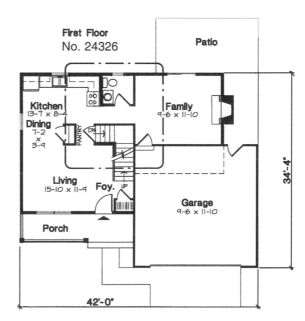

First Floor
No. 24326

Patio

Kitchen
13-7 x 8-4

Dining
7-2 x 3-9

Family
9-6 x 11-10

Living
15-10 x 11-9

Foy.

Garage
9-6 x 11-10

Porch

34'-4"

42'-0"

Design by
Design Basics, Inc.

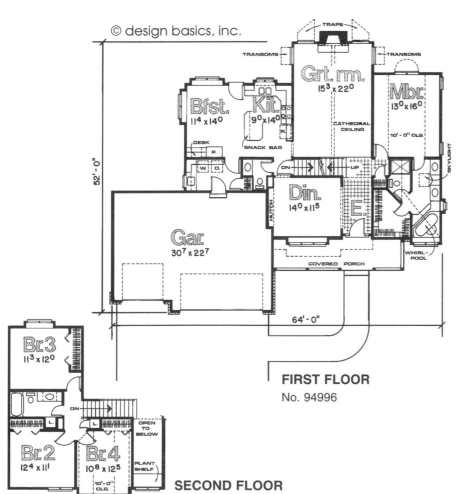

© design basics, inc.

FIRST FLOOR
No. 94996

SECOND FLOOR

Expansive Inside & Out

■ This plan features:
— Four bedrooms
— Two full and one half baths

■ Dramatic Entry opens to Dining Room with built-in hutch, and the Great Room with a fireplace set between decorative windows

■ Convenient Kitchen has an island snack bar, Breakfast Area, built-in desk and a Pantry

■ Master Bedroom wing with arched window, skylit Dressing Area, whirlpool tub and a walk-in closet

■ Three second floor Bedrooms, one with an arched window, share a full Bath

FIRST FLOOR — 1,505 SQ. FT.
SECOND FLOOR — 610 SQ. FT.
BASEMENT — 1,505 SQ. FT.
GARAGE — 693 SQ. FT.

TOTAL LIVING AREA:
2,115 SQ. FT.

Design by
Design Basics, Inc.

Refer to **Pricing Schedule C** on the order form for pricing information

Colonial Styling

■ This plan features:

— Four bedrooms

— Three full and one half baths

■ Colonial on the outside, thoroughly modern on the inside

■ The Dining Room has a built in hutch and a wetbar

■ The Great Room has a rear wall fireplace

■ The Kitchen is well designed and shares a snack bar with the Nook

■ The Master Bedroom is located on the first floor for privacy

FIRST FLOOR — 1,865 SQ. FT.
SECOND FLOOR — 774 SQ. FT.

TOTAL LIVING AREA:
2,639 SQ. FT.

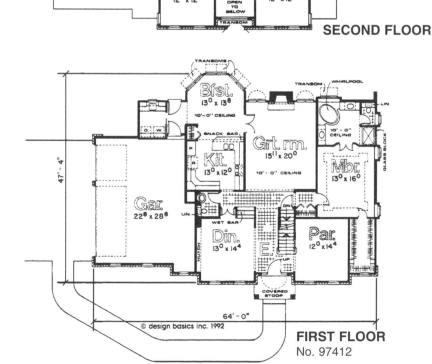

SECOND FLOOR

FIRST FLOOR
No. 97412

© design basics inc. 1992

Refer to **Pricing Schedule D** on the order form for pricing information

Design by
Studer Residential Design, Inc.

Breakfast 10'8" x 11'2"

Great Room 16' x 19'6"

Dressing

walk-in closet

Kitchen 13'5" x 14'

pantry

Laun.

Master Bedroom 14' x 14'1"

Foyer

Porch

Dining Room 12' x 13'10"

Two-car Garage 21' x 20'4"

Sitting Area 11'2" x 9'4"

48'

FIRST FLOOR
No. 92651

63'4"

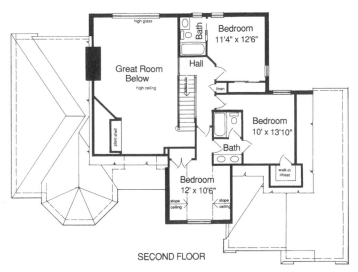

high glass

Bath

Bedroom 11'4" x 12'6"

Hall

Great Room Below
high ceiling

linen

plant shelf

Bath

Bedroom 10' x 13'10"

walk-in closet

Bedroom 12' x 10'6"

slope ceiling   slope ceiling

SECOND FLOOR

Eye-Catching Turret Adds to Master Suite

- This plan features:
  — Four bedrooms
  — Three full and one half baths
- Sheltered entry leads into open Foyer
- Great Room with high ceiling and hearth fireplace
- Columns frame entrance to Dining Room
- Efficient Kitchen with built-in Pantry and work island
- Master Bedroom wing with Sitting Area, walk-in closet and private Bath
- No materials list is available for this plan

FIRST FLOOR — 1,710 SQ. FT.
SECOND FLOOR — 693 SQ. FT.
BASEMENT — 1,620 SQ. FT.
GARAGE — 467 SQ. FT.

TOTAL LIVING AREA:
2,403 SQ. FT.

Design by
Jannis Vann & Associates, Inc.

Refer to **Pricing Schedule A** on
the order form for pricing information

Wonderful Open Spaces

■ This plan features:

— Three bedrooms

— Two full baths

■ A Family Room, Kitchen and
Breakfast Area that all connect to
form a great space

■ A central fireplace adds warmth
and atmosphere to the Family
Room, Kitchen and the Breakfast
Area

■ An efficient Kitchen that is highlighted by a peninsula counter
and doubles as a snack bar

■ The Master Suite includes a
walk-in closet, a double vanity,
separate shower and a tub

■ Two additional Bedrooms share a
full hall Bath

■ A wooden Deck that can be
accessed from the Breakfast Area

■ An optional crawl space or slab
foundation — please specify
when ordering

MAIN FLOOR — 1,388 SQ. FT.
GARAGE — 400 SQ. FT.

TOTAL LIVING AREA:
1,388 SQ. FT.

Patio
12-0 x 10-0

48-0

Dining
10-0 x 11-0

Brkfst. Bar

Dw.

**Living
Area**
13-8 x 17-6

Pass Thru
Fire Place

Vaulted Ceil.

**Master
Bdrm.**
13-6 x 12-2

Opt. Plant
Shelf Above

Kitchen
10-0 x 12-6

Ref. Pant.

Bth.2

W. D.

Cls.

Lnd.

Lin.

Stor.

Foyer

W/H

Fur.

M.Bath

Lin.

Bdrm.3
10-0 x 10-0

Bdrm.2
11-0 x 10-8

46-0

Double Garage
19-4 x 19-4

MAIN FLOOR
No. 93279

© 1988, Jannis Vann & Associates, Inc.

106

To order your Blueprints, call 1-800-235-5700

Design by
Patrick J. Morabito A.I.A.

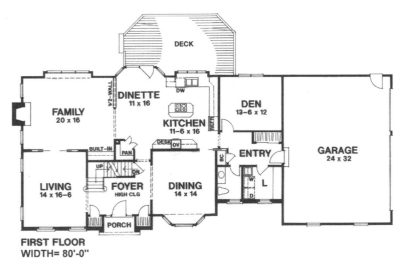

FIRST FLOOR
WIDTH= 80'-0"
DEPTH= 32'-6"

SECOND FLOOR
No. 93348

Luxury for the Family

■ This plan features:

— Four bedrooms

— Two full and one half baths

■ Central Foyer with a landing staircase, opens to the Living and Dining rooms

■ Informal Family Room has a cozy fireplace and decorative window

■ Hub Kitchen with a cooktop/serving island, walk-in Pantry and Dinette

■ Corner Master Bedroom offers a stepped ceiling, roomy walk-in closet and whirlpool Bath

■ Three additional Bedrooms with ample closets, share a full Bath

■ No materials list is available for this plan

FIRST FLOOR — 1,742 SQ. FT.
SECOND FLOOR — 1,331 SQ. FT.
BASEMENT — 1,742 SQ. FT.
GARAGE — 768 SQ. FT.

TOTAL LIVING AREA:
3,073 SQ. FT.

Design by
The Garlinghouse Company

Refer to **Pricing Schedule D** on the order form for pricing information

Arched Windows

■ This plan features:

— Three bedrooms

— Two full and one half baths

■ The vaulted Foyer is flanked by the soaring Living Room with a huge palladium window

■ The Family Room has a massive two-way fireplace

■ The Master Suite has a garden spa, private Deck access, and a walk-in closet

FIRST FLOOR — 1,752 SQ. FT.
SECOND FLOOR — 620 SQ. FT.
BASEMENT — 1,726 SQ. FT.
GARAGE — 714 SQ. FT.

TOTAL LIVING AREA:
2,372 SQ. FT.

Br 2
13-2 x 13-10
shelves

Loft

Br 3
12-6 x 10-8

Second Floor
No. 20368

First Floor

Deck

MBr 1
15 x 13-2
pan vault

Family Rm
15-6 x 19-2
vaulted

Dinette/Kitchen
22 x 13-8
bench

Balcony above

spa

UP DN
desk
pantry

Living Rm
13 x 13-8
vaulted

Foyer
vaulted

Dining Rm
11 x 13-8

Garage
21-4 x 31-4

64'-0"

52'-0"

Refer to **Pricing Schedule C** on the order form for pricing information

© design basics, inc.

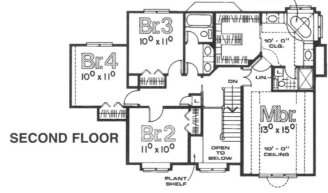

Sto. 10⁰ x 8⁴

Gar. 20⁸ x 21⁰

Bfst. 10⁰ x 11⁸

Kit. 10⁷ x 14⁰

Fam. rm. 13⁰ x 17⁰

Din. 11⁰ x 13⁰

Liv. rm. 13⁰ x 11⁸

SHELVES
CURIO
HUTCH
DESK
37' - 8"
55' - 4"
COVERED PORCH

FIRST FLOOR
No. 94941

Br. 3 10⁰ x 11⁰

Br. 4 10⁰ x 11⁰

Br. 2 11⁰ x 10⁰

Mbr. 13⁰ x 15⁰

WHIRLPOOL
10' - 0" CLG.
10' - 0" CEILING
OPEN TO BELOW
PLANT SHELF

SECOND FLOOR

Proportional Design

■ This plan features:

— Four bedrooms

— Two full and one half baths

■ The large covered Porch is framed by a wood railing

■ The Living Room is enhanced by a bay window and has a double French door to the Family Room

■ The Dining Room is crowned with a decorative ceiling and is accented by a built-in curio cabinet

■ The Family Room is enhanced by a cozy fireplace

■ Double doors open to the luxurious Master Bedroom with a distinctive vaulted ceiling

FIRST FLOOR — 1,093 SQ. FT.
SECOND FLOOR — 1,038 SQ. FT.
BASEMENT — 1,093 SQ. FT.
GARAGE — 527 SQ. FT.

TOTAL LIVING AREA:
2,131 SQ. FT.

Design by
Frank Betz Associates, Inc.

Refer to **Pricing Schedule F** on the order form for pricing information

Stately Stone and Stucco

■ This plan features:

— Four bedrooms

— Three full and one half baths

■ Two story Foyer with angled staircase

■ Expansive two story Great Room enhanced by a fireplace

■ Kitchen with a cooktop island with Pantry

■ Keeping Room accented by a wall of windows

■ Master Suite wing offers a plush Bath and roomy walk-in closet

■ An optional basement, crawl space, or slab foundation — please specify when ordering

FIRST FLOOR — 2,130 SQ. FT.
SECOND FLOOR — 897 SQ. FT.
BASEMENT — 2,130 SQ. FT.
GARAGE — 494 SQ. FT.

TOTAL LIVING AREA:
3,027 SQ. FT.

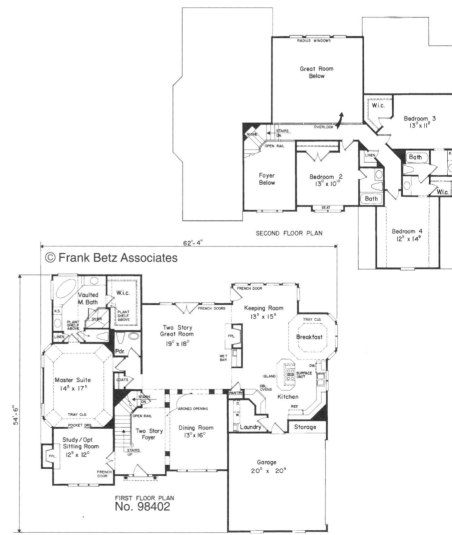

To order your Blueprints, call 1-800-235-5700

Design by
Greg Marquis & Associates

TOTAL LIVING AREA:
1,849 SQ. FT.

WIDTH 66'-4"
DEPTH 59'-10"

MAIN FLOOR
No. 93427

Attractive Styling

■ This plan features:

— Three bedrooms

— Two full baths

■ Tremendous style and presence created by windows, sidelights and transoms combined with a dramatic entrance

■ Formal Dining Room, off the Foyer, enjoying a view of the front yard and access to the Family Room

■ A grand fireplace, with windows to either side, serves as a focal point

■ Breakfast Room/Kitchen are open to the Family Room

■ Secluded Master Suite with walk-in closet, recessed ceiling and five-piece Bath

■ No materials list is available for this plan

MAIN FLOOR — 1,849 SQ. FT.
GARAGE — 555 SQ. FT.

Design by
Donald A. Gardner Architects, Inc.

Refer to **Pricing Schedule C** on the order form for pricing information

B. NATHAN

© 1996 Donald A. Gardner Architects,

For a Narrow Lot

■ This plan features:

— Three bedrooms

— Two full baths

■ The Great Room is topped by a cathedral ceiling and is accented by a fireplace

■ There is a convenient pass-through opening from the Kitchen

■ The Master Suite is loaded with luxuries, including a walk-in closet and a private Bath with a separate shower and garden tub

■ Two additional Bedrooms share a full Bath

MAIN FLOOR — 1,350 SQ. FT.
GARAGE & STORAGE — 309 SQ. FT.

TOTAL LIVING AREA:
1,350 SQ. FT.

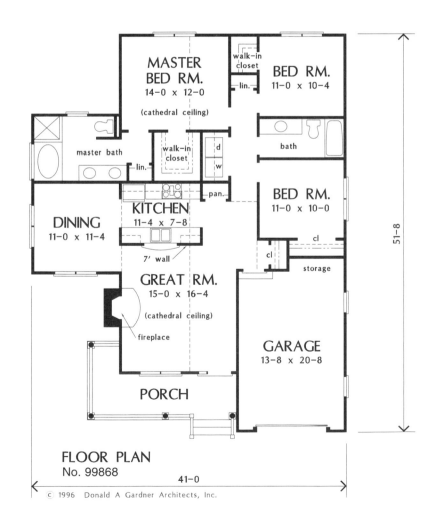

FLOOR PLAN
No. 99868

© 1996 Donald A Gardner Architects, Inc.

To order your Blueprints, call 1-800-235-5700

Refer to **Pricing Schedule D** on the order form for pricing information

Design by
The Garlinghouse Company

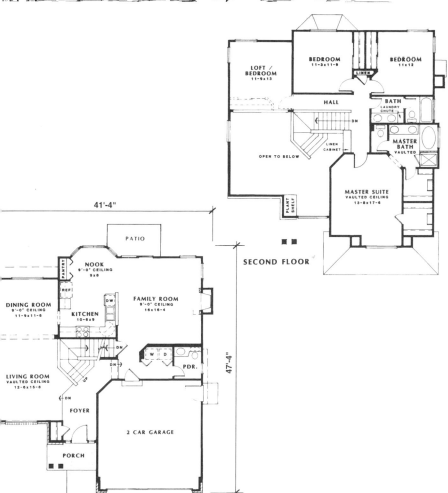

41'-4"

47'-4"

FIRST FLOOR
No. 24268

Stately Entrance Adds to Home's Exterior

■ This plan features:

— Three or four bedrooms

— Two full and one half baths

■ A vaulted ceiling in the Living Room adds to its spaciousness

■ A formal Dining Room

■ An efficient Kitchen has double sinks, and ample storage space

■ An informal Eating Nook with a built-in Pantry

■ Family Room with a fireplace

■ A plush Master Suite with a vaulted ceiling and luxurious Master Bath plus two walk-in closets

■ Two Bedrooms share a full Bath with a convenient laundry chute

FIRST FLOOR — 1,115 SQ. FT.
SECOND FLOOR — 1,129 SQ. FT.
BASEMENT — 1,096 SQ. FT.
GARAGE — 415 SQ. FT.

TOTAL LIVING AREA:
2,244 SQ. FT.

Design by
The Garlinghouse Company

Refer to **Pricing Schedule E** on
the order form for pricing informatio

Classic Front Porch

■ This plan features:

— Four bedrooms

— Two full and one half baths

■ Stone and columns accent the
wrap-around front Porch

■ The Living Room and Dining
Room adjoin with columns at
their entrances

■ The island Kitchen has a double
sink and a walk-in Pantry

■ The Breakfast Room flows into
the Family Room and the Kitchen

■ A corner fireplace and a built-in
entertainment center in the
Family Room

■ Lavish Master Suite with a decorative ceiling and an ultra Bath

FIRST FLOOR — 1,584 SQ. FT.
SECOND FLOOR — 1,277 SQ. FT.
GARAGE — 550 SQ. FT.
BASEMENT — 1,584 SQ. FT.

TOTAL LIVING AREA:
2,861 SQ. FT.

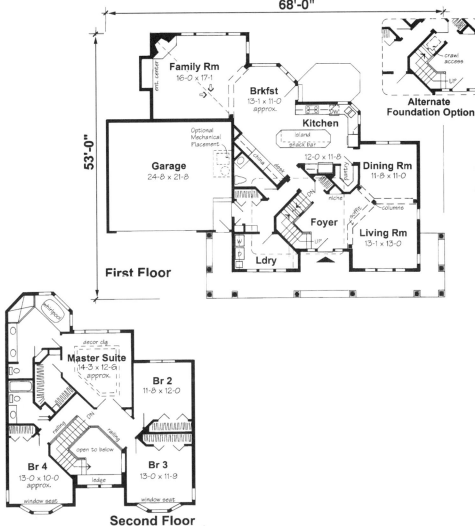

68'-0"

53'-0"

First Floor

Family Rm
16-0 x 17-1

Brkfst
13-1 x 11-0
approx.

Kitchen

Garage
24-8 x 21-8

12-0 x 11-8

Dining Rm
11-8 x 11-0

Foyer

Living Rm
13-1 x 13-0

Ldry

**Alternate
Foundation Option**

crawl
access

Second Floor

Master Suite
14-3 x 12-6
approx.

Br 2
11-8 x 12-0

Br 4
13-0 x 10-0
approx.

Br 3
13-0 x 11-9

open to below

To order your Blueprints, call 1-800-235-5700

Design by
Design Basics, Inc.

SECOND FLOOR
No. 99433

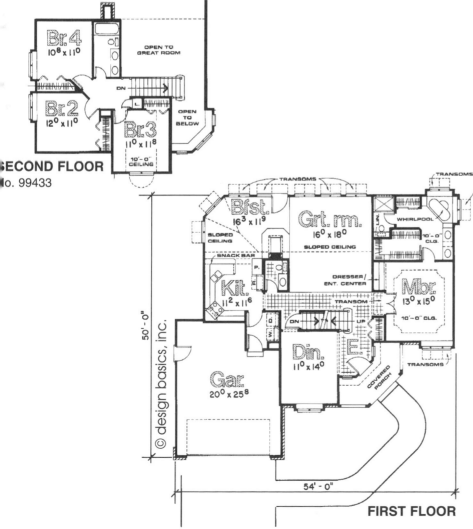

FIRST FLOOR

A Distinct Personality

■ This plan features:

— Four bedrooms

— Two full and one half baths

■ Unique angles give this home a distinct personality

■ From the tiled Entry enter the Dining Room with a boxed bay window on the front wall

■ A see-through fireplace warms both the Breakfast Nook and the Great Room

■ The Master Bedroom is located on the first floor for privacy and includes a boxed bay window

■ Upstairs find three Bedrooms that share a full Bath

FIRST FLOOR — 1,510 SQ. FT.
SECOND FLOOR — 579 SQ. FT.
BASEMENT — 1,510 SQ. FT.

TOTAL LIVING AREA:
2,089 SQ. FT.

Design by
Donald A. Gardner Architects, Inc.

Refer to **Pricing Schedule D** on the order form for pricing information

©1997 Donald A. Gardner Architects, Inc.

Pretty as a Picture

■ This plan features:

— Three bedrooms

— Two full baths

■ The wrapping front Porch is beautiful and functional

■ Inside the Great Room has a cathedral ceiling and a fireplace

■ The Dining Room has a tray ceiling and windows that overlook the front porch

■ The Kitchen has a convenient layout with a work triangle

■ The Master Bedroom is isolated and features a galley bath that leads into the walk-in closet

■ There is a bonus room over the Garage

MAIN FLOOR — 1,911 SQ. FT.
BONUS — 406 SQ. FT.
GARAGE — 551 SQ. FT.

TOTAL LIVING AREA:
1,911 SQ. FT.

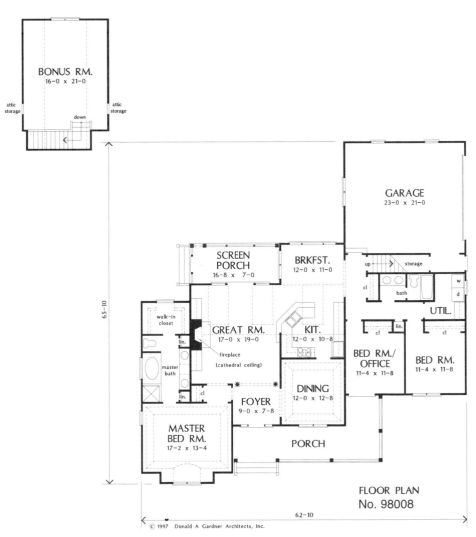

BONUS RM.
16-0 x 21-0

attic storage   attic storage

down

GARAGE
23-0 x 21-0

SCREEN PORCH
16-8 x 7-0

BRKFST.
12-0 x 11-0

up   storage

bath

UTIL.

walk-in closet

GREAT RM.
17-0 x 19-0

KIT.
12-0 x 10-8

fireplace
(cathedral ceiling)

master bath

BED RM./ OFFICE
11-4 x 11-8

BED RM.
11-4 x 11-8

DINING
12-0 x 12-8

FOYER
9-0 x 7-8

MASTER BED RM.
17-2 x 13-4

PORCH

65-10

62-10

FLOOR PLAN
No. 98008

© 1997 Donald A Gardner Architects, Inc.

To order your Blueprints, call 1-800-235-5700

Refer to **Pricing Schedule C** on the order form for pricing information

Design by
Design Basics, Inc.

Skylit Master Bath

■ This plan features:

— Two bedrooms

— Two full baths

■ A covered front stoop leads to the tiled formal Entry

■ The Great Room has a large rear wall fireplace

■ The Living Room has a 10-foot ceiling and a large front window

■ The Kitchen is laid out in a convenient manner

■ The bright Breakfast Nook has a rear wall bay and a 10-foot ceiling

■ The Master Bedroom has a decorative ceiling, two walk-in closets and a full Bath

■ Two-car Garage with a third bay in the rear

MAIN FLOOR — 1,996 SQ. FT.
GARAGE — 683 SQ. FT.

TOTAL LIVING AREA:
1,996 SQ. FT.

MAIN FLOOR
No. 94926

© design basics, inc.

Refer to **Pricing Schedule B** on the order form for pricing information

Traditional Ranch

■ This plan features:

— Three bedrooms

— Two full baths

■ A large front palladium window gives this home curb appeal, and allows a view of the front yard from the Living Room

■ A vaulted ceiling in the Living Room, adds to the architectural interest and the spacious feel of the room

■ Sliding glass doors in the Dining Room lead to a wood Deck

■ A built-in Pantry, double sink and breakfast bar in the efficient Kitchen

■ The Master Suite includes a walk-in closet and a private Bath with a double vanity

■ Two additional Bedrooms that share a full hall Bath

MAIN AREA —1,568 SQ. FT.
BASEMENT — 1,568 SQ. FT.
GARAGE — 509 SQ. FT.

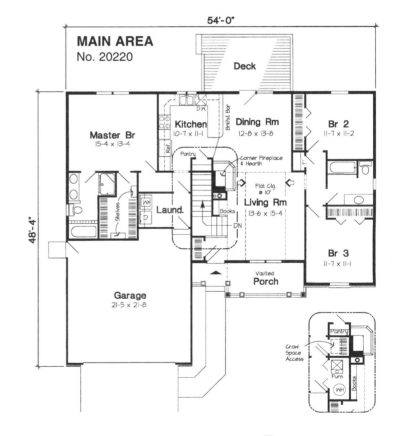

MAIN AREA
No. 20220

54'-0"

48'-4"

Deck

Kitchen
10-7 x 11-1

Master Br
15-4 x 13-4

Dining Rm
12-8 x 13-8

Br 2
11-7 x 11-2

Corner Fireplace & Hearth

Pantry

Laund.

Flat Clg. @ 10'

Living Rm
13-6 x 15-4

Shelves

Books

Garage
21-5 x 21-8

Vaulted Porch

Br 3
11-7 x 11-1

Crawl Space Access

Pantry

Furn

TOTAL LIVING AREA:
1,568 SQ. FT.

Design by
Larry E. Belk

© Larry E. Belk

SECOND FLOOR
No. 93099

BEDROOM 4
13-4 X 10-4

EXPANDABLE
17-4 X 18-0

LIN

BATH 3

+UP

BEDROOM 3
13-0 X 11-6

OPEN TO FOYER BELOW

PLANT LEDGE

WIDTH 64-10

MASTER BEDRM
13-4 X 16-4
10 FT TRAY CLG

BRKFST RM
11-4 X 13-0
10 FT TRAY CLG

PORCH

KITCHEN
16-6 X 13-4
9 FT CLG

MASTER BATH

GREAT ROOM
17-4 X 20-4
10 FT TRAY CLG

DESK

LIN

STORAGE

UTIL
11-4 X 6-0
9 FT CLG

PAN

BATH 2

LIN

GARAGE

DINING ROOM
12-6 X 15-4
10 FT CLG

FOYER
2 STORY CLG

ARCH

BEDROOM 2
12-6 X 13-6
9 FT CLG

PORCH

DEPTH 64-0

COPYRIGHT LARRY E. BELK

FIRST FLOOR

Out of the English Countryside

■ This plan features:

— Four bedrooms

— Three full baths

■ From the Foyer, arched entrances lead into the Dining Room and the Great Room

■ The Great Room is complimented by a 10-foot tray ceiling

■ The Master Suite is located in a secluded part of the first floor

■ The Breakfast Room shares a see-through fireplace with the Great Room

■ The Kitchen has a walk-in Pantry

■ No materials list is available for this plan

FIRST FLOOR — 2,050 SQ. FT.
SECOND FLOOR — 561 SQ. FT.
BONUS — 272 SQ. FT.
GARAGE — 599 SQ. FT.

TOTAL LIVING AREA:
2,611 SQ. FT.

Design by
Ahmann Design, Inc.

Refer to **Pricing Schedule C** on the order form for pricing information

Wonderful One-Level

■ This plan features:

— Three bedrooms

— Two full and one half baths

■ Charming front Porch accesses Entry

■ Central Great Room is enhanced by a cathedral ceiling

■ Large and convenient Kitchen has a work island/snackbar

■ Corner Master Bedroom features a walk-in closet and plush Bath with a double vanity and spa tub

■ Two additional Bedrooms with ample closets and double windows, share a full Bath

■ No materials list is available for this plan

MAIN FLOOR — 1,802 SQ. FT.
BASEMENT — 1,802 SQ. FT.

TOTAL LIVING AREA:
1,802 SQ. FT.

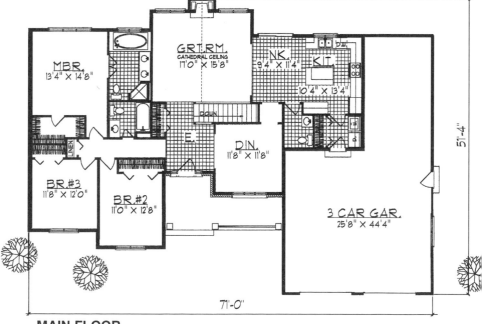

MAIN FLOOR
No. 93193

Refer to **Pricing Schedule D** on the order form for pricing information

Design by
Frank Betz Associates, Inc.

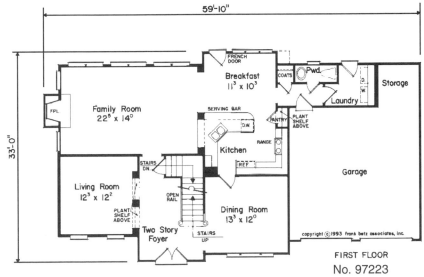

FIRST FLOOR
No. 97223

copyright ©1993 frank betz associates, inc.

© Frank Betz Associates

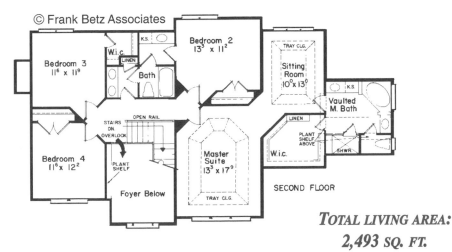

SECOND FLOOR

TOTAL LIVING AREA:
2,493 SQ. FT.

A Bold Statement

■ This plan features:

— Four bedrooms

— Two full and one half baths

■ The dramatic exterior creates a bold statement

■ Inside, the two-story Foyer has an open-rail staircase

■ The Living Room entry is separated by columns with a plant shelf above

■ The Dining Room has a bright front window

■ The Kitchen is separated from the Nook by a serving counter

■ The Master Suite is comprised of the Bedroom, a Sitting Area and a Bath

■ Three additional large Bedrooms are on the second floor

■ No materials list is available for this plan

FIRST FLOOR — 1,192 SQ. FT.
SECOND FLOOR — 1,301 SQ. FT.
BASEMENT — 1,192 SQ. FT.
GARAGE — 487 SQ. FT.

To order your Blueprints, call 1-800-235-5700

Design by
Frank Betz Associates, Inc.

Refer to **Pricing Schedule A** on
the order form for pricing information

Striking Style

■ This plan features:

— Three bedrooms

— Two full baths

■ Windows and exterior detailing create a striking elevation

■ The Foyer has a 12-foot ceiling

■ The Dining Room has a front window wall and arched openings

■ The secondary Bedrooms are in their own wing and share a Bath

■ The Breakfast Bay is open to the galley Kitchen

■ The Master Suite features a tray ceiling, a walk-in closet and a private Bath

■ An optional basement or crawl space foundation — please specify when ordering

MAIN FLOOR — 1,432 SQ. FT.
BASEMENT — 1,454 SQ. FT.
GARAGE — 440 SQ. FT.

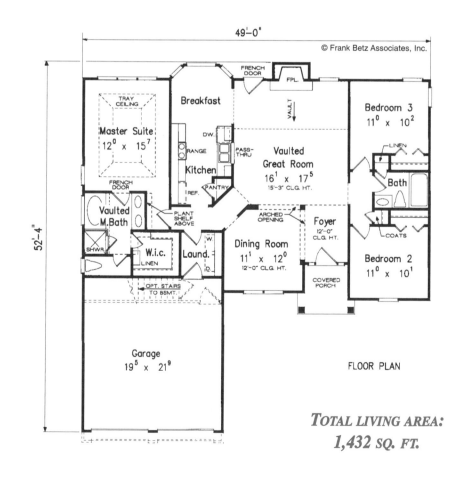

© Frank Betz Associates, Inc.

FLOOR PLAN

TOTAL LIVING AREA:
1,432 SQ. FT.

To order your Blueprints, call 1-800-235-5700

Refer to **Pricing Schedule A** on the order form for pricing information

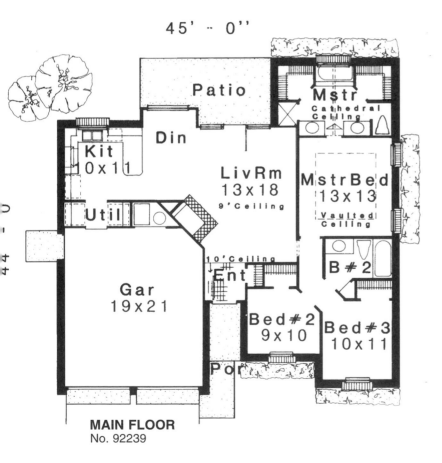

45' – 0''

44 – 0

Patio

Din

Kit
0 x 11

Mstr
Cathedral Ceiling

LivRm
13 x 18
9' Ceiling

Util

MstrBed
13 x 13
Vaulted Ceiling

10' Ceiling

Ent

B # 2

Gar
19 x 21

Bed #2
9 x 10

Bed #3
10 x 11

Po

MAIN FLOOR
No. 92239

Appealing Master Suite

■ This plan features:

— Three bedrooms

— Two full baths

■ Sheltered Entry leads into spacious Living Room with a corner fireplace and Patio access

■ Efficient Kitchen shares a serving counter with the Dining Area

■ Private Master Bedroom offers a vaulted ceiling and pampering bath with two vanities and walk-in closets and a garden window tub

■ Two additional Bedrooms with ample closets share a full Bath

■ No materials list is available for the plan

MAIN FLOOR — 1,198 SQ. FT.

TOTAL LIVING AREA:
1,198 SQ. FT.

Design by
Ahmann Design, Inc.

For a Growing Family

■ This plan features:

— Three bedrooms

— Two full and one half baths

■ Inside the Entry, find a two-story
ceiling and a lovely staircase

■ An arched opening leads into the
Dining Room

■ The Great Room has a fireplace
set between built-in cabinets

■ A three season Porch accesses a
covered Deck and Patio

■ The Kitchen is open to the Nook
and features a center island

■ There is a bonus room located
over the three-car Garage

■ No materials list is available for
this plan

FIRST FLOOR — 1,481 SQ. FT.
SECOND FLOOR — 1,319 SQ. FT.
BONUS — 487 SQ. FT.

TOTAL LIVING AREA:
2,800 SQ. FT

SECOND FLOOR

FIRST FLOOR
No. 97127

Refer to **Pricing Schedule B** on
he order form for pricing information

Design by
The Garlinghouse Company

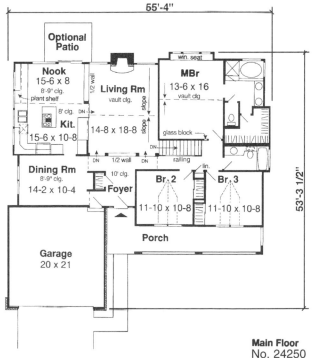

TOTAL LIVING AREA:
1,700 SQ. FT.

Optional Patio

Nook
15-6 x 8
8'-9" clg.
plant shelf

1/2 wall

Living Rm
vault clg.
14-8 x 18-8

MBr
13-6 x 16
vault clg.

win. seat

Kit.
15-6 x 10-8

8' clg.

glass block

Dining Rm
8'-9" clg.
14-2 x 10-4

10' clg.

1/2 wall

railing

lin.

Foyer

Br. 2
11-10 x 10-8

Br. 3
11-10 x 10-8

Porch

Garage
20 x 21

55'-4"

53'-3 1/2"

Main Floor
No. 24250

Clever Design Packs in Plenty of Living Space

- This plan features:
— Three bedrooms
— Two full baths
- Custom, volume ceilings
- A sunken Living Room that includes a vaulted ceiling and a fireplace with oversized windows framing it
- A center island and an eating nook in the Kitchen that has more than ample counter space
- A formal Dining Room adjoins the Kitchen, allowing for easy entertaining
- The spacious Master Suite includes a vaulted ceiling and a lavish Bath
- Secondary bedrooms with custom ceiling treatments have use of a full hall Bath

MAIN FLOOR — 1,700 SQ. FT.
BASEMENT — 1,700 SQ. FT.
GARAGE — 462 SQ. FT.

Design by
Kent & Kent, Inc.

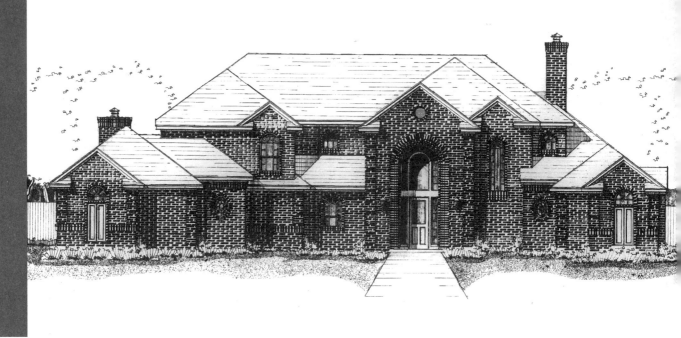

Room to Roam

- This plan features:
— Four bedrooms
— Three full and one half baths

- Gables and bumpouts add distinction to the brick facade

- The two-story Foyer is adorned by a curved staircase

- Straight ahead is the Dining Room with a curved window wall

- The informal areas include the Kitchen, Nook and angled Family Room

- The Master Suite shares a see-through fireplace with the Study

- Upstairs find three Bedrooms, two Baths, a Game Room and plenty of storage space

- No materials list is available for this plan

FIRST FLOOR — 2,974 SQ. FT.
SECOND FLOOR — 1,518 SQ. FT.
GARAGE — 599 SQ. FT.

TOTAL LIVING AREA:
4,492 SQ. FT.

WIDTH 96'-4"
DEPTH 67'-6"

To order your Blueprints, call 1-800-235-5700

Refer to **Pricing Schedule D** on the order form for pricing information

Design by
Frank Betz Associates, Inc.

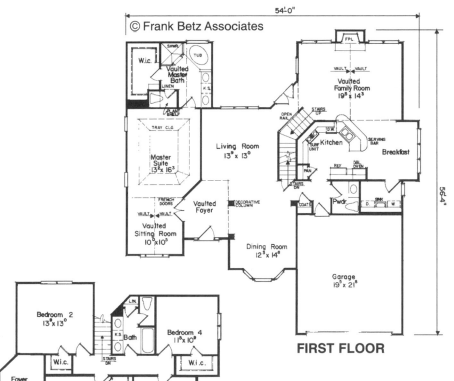

© Frank Betz Associates

54'-0"

FIRST FLOOR

W.i.c.
SHWR.
TUB
Vaulted Master Bath
LINEN
K.S.
PLANT SHELF
TRAY CLG.
Master Suite 13⁵ x 16³
Living Room 13⁹ x 13⁰
FRENCH DOORS
VAULT VAULT
Vaulted Sitting Room 10⁵ x 10⁵
Vaulted Foyer
DECORATIVE COLUMN
Dining Room 12³ x 14⁸

FPL
VAULT VAULT
Vaulted Family Room 19⁵ x 14³
OPEN RAIL
STAIRS UP
D.W.
SURF. UNIT
Kitchen
SERVING BAR
Breakfast
PAN
REF.
DBL. OVEN
STAIRS DN.
COATS
Pwdr.
SINK
D. W.
Garage 19³ x 21⁸

56'-4"

SECOND FLOOR

Bedroom 2 13⁹ x 13⁰
LIN.
K.S.
Bath
Bedroom 4 11⁹ x 10⁹
W.i.c.
STAIRS DN.
W.i.c.
Foyer Below
W.i.c.
Bedroom 3 12³ x 12³
Opt. Bonus Room 11⁶ x 24³

Attention to Details

■ This plan features:

— Four bedrooms

— Two full baths

■ The Family Room has a rear wall fireplace set between windows

■ The Kitchen shares a serving bar with the Nook

■ The Master Suite has a tray ceiling

■ Upstairs, find three Bedrooms all with walk-in closets

■ An optional basement, slab or crawl space foundation — please specify when ordering

■ No materials list is available for this plan

FIRST FLOOR — 1,750 SQ. FT.
SECOND FLOOR — 718 SQ. FT.
BONUS — 294 SQ. FT.
BASEMENT — 1,750 SQ. FT.
GARAGE — 440 SQ. FT.

TOTAL LIVING AREA:
2,468 SQ. FT.

Design by
Design Basics, Inc.

Refer to **Pricing Schedule C** on the order form for pricing information

Distinctive Design

■ This plan features:

— Three bedrooms

— Two full and one half baths

■ Living Room is distinguished by warmth of bay window and French doors leading to Family Room

■ Built-in curio cabinet adds interest to formal Dining Room

■ Well-appointed Kitchen with island cooktop and Breakfast area designed to save you steps

■ Family Room with fireplace for informal gatherings

■ Spacious Master Bedroom with vaulted ceiling, decorative window and plush dressing area with double walk-in closet, dual vanity and a corner whirlpool tub

■ Secondary Bedrooms share a double vanity Bath

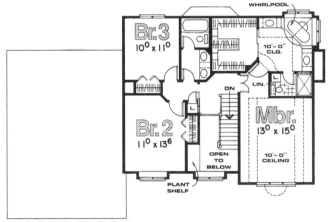

SECOND FLOOR

FIRST FLOOR — 1,093 SQ. FT.
SECOND FLOOR — 905 SQ. FT.
BASEMENT — 1,093 SQ. FT.
GARAGE — 527 SQ. FT.

TOTAL LIVING AREA:
1,998 SQ. FT.

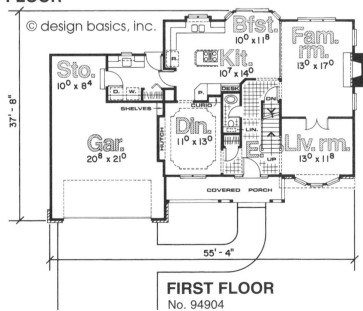

FIRST FLOOR
No. 94904

To order your Blueprints, call 1-800-235-5700

Refer to **Pricing Schedule C** on the order form for pricing information

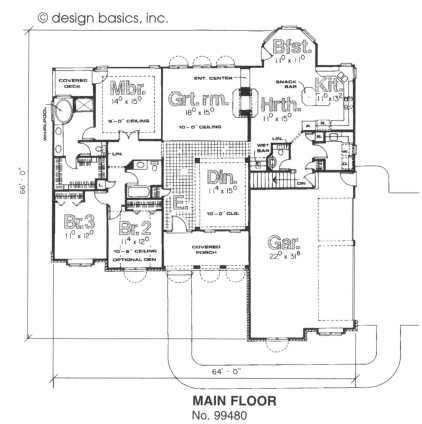

© design basics, inc.

MAIN FLOOR
No. 99480

Arched Interest

■ This plan features:

— Three bedrooms

— Two full and one half baths

■ The covered Porch has triple arches and columns

■ A tiled entry opens into the Dining Room

■ The Great Room features a see-through fireplace and rear window wall

■ The Hearth Room is warmed by a fireplace and opens into the breakfast bay and kitchen

■ The Master Bedroom features a 9-foot ceiling, whirlpool Bath and a private covered Deck

■ Bedroom two, or an optional den, has a high ceiling and a magnificent front window

MAIN FLOOR — 2,187 SQ. FT.

TOTAL LIVING AREA:
2,187 SQ. FT.

Design by
Urban Design Group

Refer to **Pricing Schedule F** on the order form for pricing information

Unusual and Dramatic

■ This plan features:

— Four bedrooms

— Three full and one half baths

■ Elegant Entry with decorative windows, arched openings and a double curved staircase

■ Cathedral ceilings crown arched windows in the Den and Living Room

■ Spacious Family Room with a vaulted ceiling and a fireplace

■ Hub Kitchen with a work island/serving counter

■ Secluded Master Suite with a lovely bay window, two walk-in closets and a plush Bath

■ Three second floor Bedrooms, one with a private Bath, offer ample closets

FIRST FLOOR — 2,646 SQ. FT.
SECOND FLOOR — 854 SQ. FT.
BASEMENT — 2,656 SQ. FT.

TOTAL LIVING AREA:
3,500 SQ. FT.

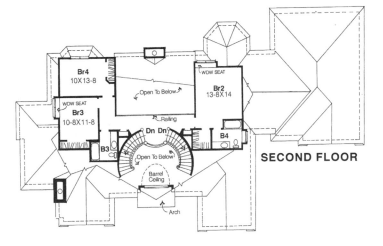

SECOND FLOOR

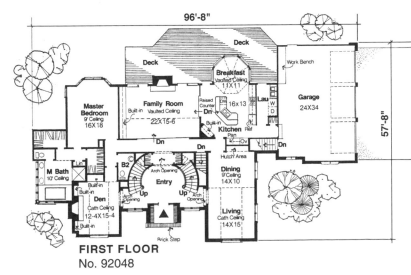

FIRST FLOOR
No. 92048

To order your Blueprints, call 1-800-235-5700

Design by
Jannis Vann & Associates, Inc.

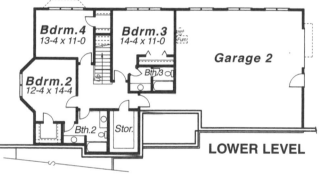

Bdrm. 4
13-4 x 11-0

Bdrm. 3
14-4 x 11-0

Garage 2

Bdrm. 2
12-4 x 14-4

Bth. 3

Bth. 2

Stor.

LOWER LEVEL

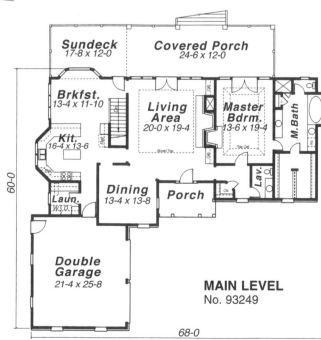

Sundeck
17-8 x 12-0

Covered Porch
24-6 x 12-0

Brkfst.
13-4 x 11-10

Living Area
20-0 x 19-4

Master Bdrm.
13-6 x 19-4

M. Bath

Kit.
16-4 x 13-6

Lav.

Laun.

Dining
13-4 x 13-8

Porch

60-0

Double Garage
21-4 x 25-8

MAIN LEVEL
No. 93249

68-0

With Room for All

■ This plan features:

— Four bedrooms

— Three full and one half baths

■ An extensive Living Area with a fireplace, built-in shelves, double doors to the rear Porch and an embellished ceiling

■ The U-shaped Kitchen has a peninsula counter and an island

■ A sunny bayed Breakfast Room and a the Dining Room are on separate sides of the Kitchen

■ The Master Suite has a decorative ceiling and a private Bath

■ No materials list is available for this plan

MAIN LEVEL — 1,871 SQ. FT.
LOWER LEVEL — 1,015 SQ. FT.
BASEMENT — 826 SQ. FT.
GARAGE — 558 SQ. FT.

TOTAL LIVING AREA:
2,886 SQ. FT.

Design by
Design Basics, Inc.

Refer to **Pricing Schedule B** on the order form for pricing information

Simplicity at it's Finest

■ This plan features:

— Three bedrooms

— Two full and one half baths

■ A covered Porch gives the home a nostalgic feel

■ The volume Great Room offers a fireplace with transom windows on both sides

■ A built-in planning desk and Pantry in the Breakfast Area

■ A snack bar for informal meals highlights the Kitchen

■ The formal Dining Room over-looks the Porch, which has easy access to the Kitchen

■ An isolated Master Suite has a five-piece Bath and a walk-in closet

FIRST FLOOR — 1,298 SQ. FT.
SECOND FLOOR — 396 SQ. FT.
BASEMENT — 1,298 SQ. FT.
GARAGE — 513 SQ. FT.

TOTAL LIVING AREA:
1,694 SQ. FT.

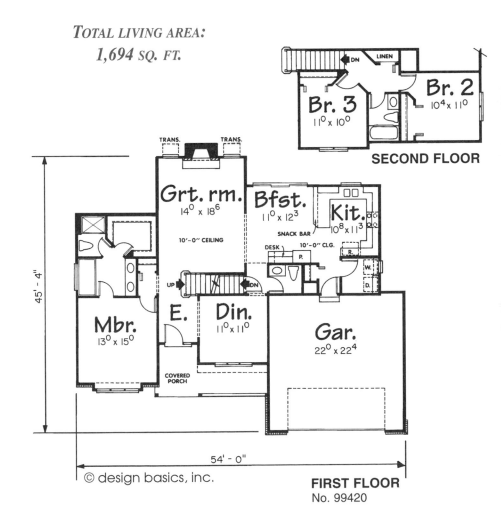

© design basics, inc.

SECOND FLOOR

FIRST FLOOR
No. 99420

To order your Blueprints, call 1-800-235-5700

Design by
Design Basics, Inc.

P L A N   N O .   9 4 9 0 0

SECOND FLOOR

Br. 2
11⁰ x 11⁴

Br. 4
11⁰ x 10⁰

OPEN TO BELOW

DESK

L.

DN

UNFINISHED STORAGE
14⁶ x 12⁶

Br. 3
11³ x 11³
10'-0" CEILING

© design basics, inc.

TRANSOMS

TRANS.

TRANS.

LIN.

WHIRLPOOL

Grt. rm.
15³ x 19⁹
12'-10" CEILING

Bfst.
12⁶ x 13⁷
SNACK BAR

Kit.
10⁰ x 11³

SHELVES

DESK

R.

P.

UP

DN

D.   W.

Mbr.
13⁰ x 16³
11'-6" CLG.

E.

Din.
12³ x 12⁸

HUTCH

Gar.
20⁸ x 23⁰

COVERED PORCH

TRANSOMS

BENCH

52' - 0"

FIRST FLOOR
No. 94900

Quaint Front Porch and Lovely Details

■ This plan features:
— Four bedrooms
— Two full and one half baths

■ A Covered Porch and Victorian touches create unique elevation

■ A one and a half story entry hall leads into formal Dining Room

■ A volume ceiling, abundant windows and a see-through fireplace highlight the Great Room

■ Kitchen/Breakfast Area share a fireplace and a snack bar

■ Laundry Area provides access to Garage and side yard

■ Secluded Master Suite crowned by a vaulted ceiling

■ Three additional Bedrooms on the second floor share a full Bath

TOTAL LIVING AREA : 1,999 SQ. FT.

FIRST FLOOR — 1,421 SQ. FT.
SECOND FLOOR — 578 SQ. FT.
BASEMENT — 1,421 SQ. FT.
GARAGE — 480 SQ. FT.

Design by
Design Basics, Inc.

Refer to **Pricing Schedule B** on the order form for pricing information

Keystone Arches and Decorative Windows

■ This plan features:

— Three bedrooms

— One full and one three quarter baths

■ Brick and stucco enhance the dramatic front elevation

■ Inviting Entry leads into expansive Great Room with hearth fireplace framed by transom windows

■ The Dining Room is topped by decorative ceiling and is convenient to the Great Room and the Kitchen/Breakfast Area

■ Corner Master Suite enjoys a tray ceiling, roomy walk-in closet and a plush bath with a double vanity and whirlpool window tub

■ Two additional Bedrooms with large closets, share a full Bath

MAIN FLOOR — 1,666 SQ. FT.
BASEMENT — 1,666 SQ. FT.
GARAGE — 496 SQ. FT.

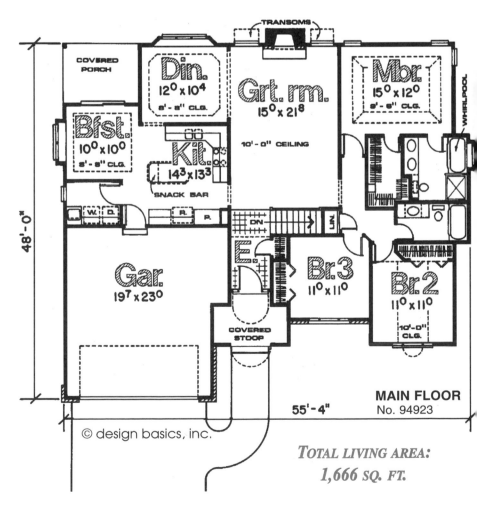

MAIN FLOOR
No. 94923

© design basics, inc.

TOTAL LIVING AREA:
1,666 SQ. FT.

Design by
The Garlinghouse Company

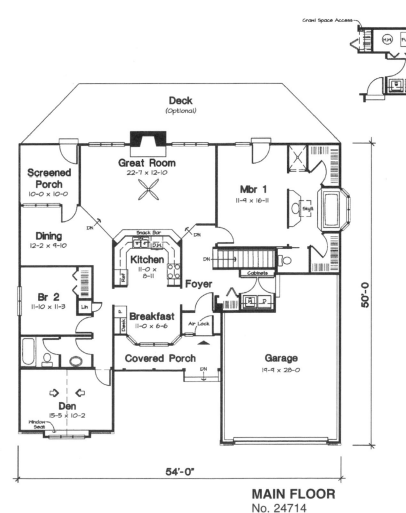

Deck
(Optional)

Screened Porch
10-0 x 10-0

Great Room
22-7 x 12-10

Mbr 1
11-9 x 16-11

Dining
12-2 x 9-10

Snack Bar

Kitchen
11-0 x 8-11

Foyer

Cabinets

Br 2
11-10 x 11-3

Breakfast
11-0 x 6-6

Air Lock

Covered Porch

Garage
19-9 x 28-0

Den
15-5 x 10-2

Window Seat

50'-0"

54'-0"

Crawl Space Access
H.W. Furn.

MAIN FLOOR
No. 24714

Energy Efficient Air-Lock Entry

■ This plan features:

— Two bedrooms

— Two full baths

■ The attractive covered Porch highlights the curb appeal of this charming home

■ A window seat and a vaulted ceiling enhance the private Den

■ The sunken Great Room is accented by a fireplace that is nestled between windows

■ A screened Porch, accessed from the Dining Room, extends the living space to the outdoors

■ The Master Bath features a garden tub, separate shower, his-n-her walk-in closets and a skylight

■ No materials list is available for this plan

MAIN FLOOR — 1,771 SQ. FT.
BASEMENT — 1,194 SQ. FT.
GARAGE — 517 SQ. FT.

TOTAL LIVING AREA:
1,771 SQ. FT.

Design by
Design Basics, Inc.

Refer to **Pricing Schedule C** on the order form for pricing information

Easy Traffic Flow

■ This plan features:

— Four bedrooms

— Two full and one half baths

■ Covered Porch welcomes all and shelters entry

■ Formal Dining Room highlighted by a boxed window

■ Fireplace and a wall of windows accent the Family Room

■ Bayed Breakfast Area with access to back yard part of the efficient Kitchen

■ Kitchen adjoins Dining Room, half-Bath, Laundry and Garage entry

■ Master Bedroom offers two walk-in closets and a double vanity Bath

■ Three additional Bedrooms share a full hall Bath

FIRST FLOOR — 925 SQ. FT.
SECOND FLOOR — 960 SQ. FT.
BONUS — 258 SQ. FT.
BASEMENT — 925 SQ. FT.
GARAGE — 455 SQ. FT.

TOTAL LIVING AREA:
1,885 SQ. FT.

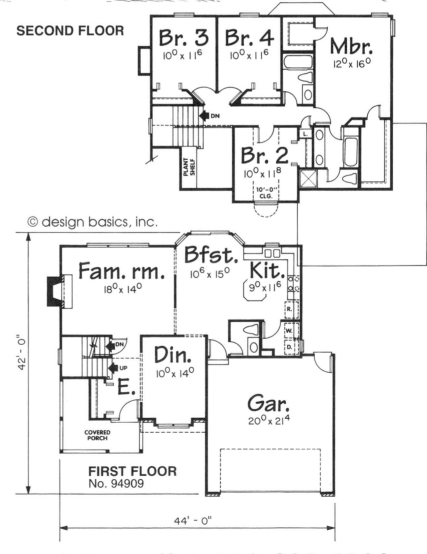

SECOND FLOOR

Br. 3
10⁰ x 11⁶

Br. 4
10⁰ x 11⁶

Mbr.
12⁰ x 16⁰

DN

PLANT SHELF

Br. 2
10⁰ x 11⁸
10'-0" CLG.

© design basics, inc.

Fam. rm.
18⁰ x 14⁰

Bfst.
10⁶ x 15⁰

Kit.
9⁰ x 11⁶

42' - 0"

DN

UP

E.

Din.
10⁰ x 14⁰

Gar.
20⁰ x 21⁴

COVERED PORCH

FIRST FLOOR
No. 94909

44' - 0"

To order your Blueprints, call 1-800-235-5700

Refer to **Pricing Schedule D** on the order form for pricing information

MAIN AREA — 1,959 SQ. FT.
GARAGE — 512 SQ. FT.

TOTAL LIVING AREA:
1,959 SQ. FT.

MAIN AREA
No. 92515

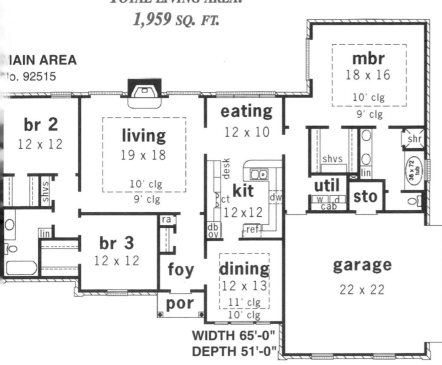

WIDTH 65'-0"
DEPTH 51'-0"

Elegant and Efficient

■ This plan features:

— Three bedrooms

— Two full baths

■ Covered entrance into the Foyer leads to the Living Room with a decorative ceiling, and hearth fireplace

■ A decorative window and ceiling highlight the formal Dining Room

■ A large, Country Kitchen has double ovens, a cooktop and a peninsula snackbar

■ The Master Bedroom has a decorative ceiling, a walk-in closet and a plush Bath

■ Two additional Bedrooms have walk-in closets and share a full Bath

■ An optional slab or crawl space foundation — please specify when ordering

Design by
Ahmann Design, Inc. ℞R

Refer to **Pricing Schedule C** on
the order form for pricing information

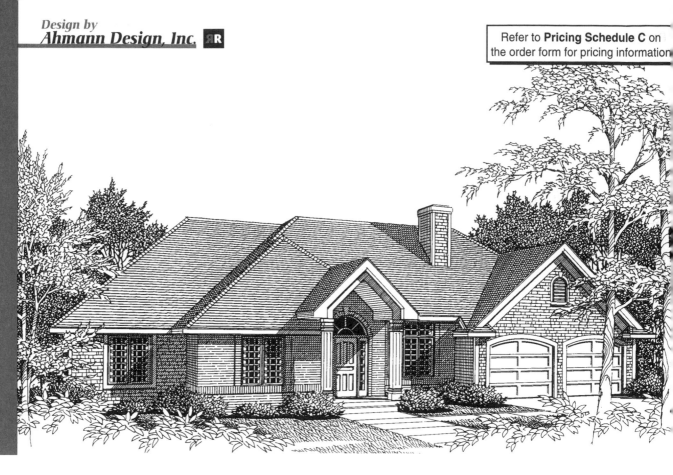

Charming Brick Home

■ This plan features:

— Three bedrooms

— Two full baths

■ Covered entrance leads to the
Living Room with a fireplace

■ Island Kitchen, open to the
Dining Room, offers ample space
for entertaining

■ The Master Bedroom has a walk-
in closet, access to the Patio, and
a plush Bath

■ Two additional Bedrooms, with
decorative windows, share a full
hall Bath

■ No materials list is available for
this plan

MAIN FLOOR — 1,868 SQ. FT
BASEMENT — 1,868 SQ. FT.
GARAGE — 782 SQ. FT.

TOTAL LIVING AREA:
1,868 SQ. FT.

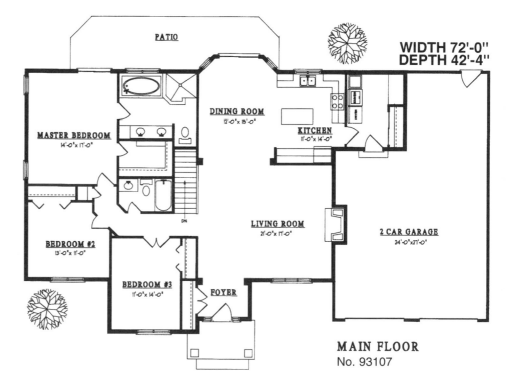

WIDTH 72'-0"
DEPTH 42'-4"

PATIO

MASTER BEDROOM
14'-0" x 17'-0"

DINING ROOM
12'-0" x 15'-0"

KITCHEN
11'-0" x 14'-0"

BEDROOM #2
13'-0" x 11'-0"

BEDROOM #3
11'-0" x 14'-0"

FOYER

LIVING ROOM
21'-0" x 17'-0"

2 CAR GARAGE
24'-0" x 27'-0"

DN

MAIN FLOOR
No. 93107

To order your Blueprints, call 1-800-235-5700

Refer to **Pricing Schedule D** on
the order form for pricing information

Design by
Donald A. Gardner Architects, Inc.

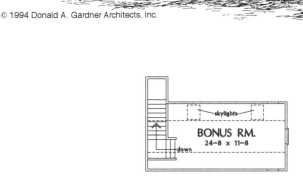

© 1994 Donald A. Gardner Architects, Inc.   B. NATHAN

Didn't Waste An Inch of Space

■ This plan features:

— Three bedrooms

— Two full baths

■ Great Room with fireplace and built-in cabinets share a cathedral ceiling with angled Kitchen

■ Separate Dining Room allows for more formal entertaining

■ Master bedroom topped by a cathedral ceiling, walk-in closet, and well appointed Bath

■ Front and rear Covered Porches encourage relaxation

■ Skylit Bonus Room makes a great Recreation Room or Office in the future

MAIN FLOOR — 1,575 SQ. FT.
BONUS ROOM — 276 SQ. FT.
GARAGE — 536 SQ. FT.

TOTAL LIVING AREA:
1,575 SQ. FT.

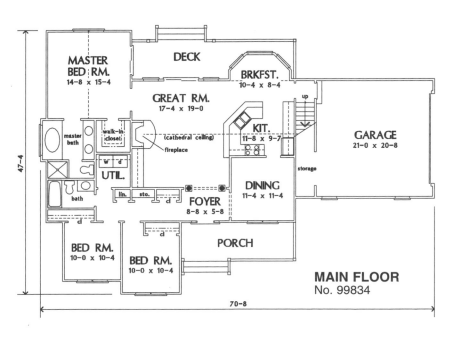

BONUS RM.
24-8 x 11-8
skylights

MASTER BED RM.
14-8 x 15-4

DECK

BRKFST.
10-4 x 8-4

GREAT RM.
17-4 x 19-0

KIT.
11-8 x 9-7

GARAGE
21-0 x 20-8

master bath
walk-in closet
(cathedral ceiling)
fireplace
w d

UTIL.

storage

lin. sto.

DINING
11-4 x 11-4

bath

FOYER
8-8 x 5-8

BED RM.
10-0 x 10-4

BED RM.
10-0 x 10-4

PORCH

MAIN FLOOR
No. 99834

47-4

70-8

Design by
Frank Betz Associates, Inc.

Refer to **Pricing Schedule E** on the order form for pricing information

Stucco & Stone

■ This plan features:

— Three bedrooms

— Two full and one half baths

■ Decorative columns define the Dining Room

■ A built-in Pantry and a radius window in the Kitchen

■ A tray ceiling over the Master Bedroom and a vaulted ceiling in the Bath

■ An optional basement, crawl space or slab foundation — please specify when ordering

■ No material list is available for this plan

FIRST FLOOR — 1,796 SQ. FT.
SECOND FLOOR — 629 SQ. FT.
BONUS ROOM — 208 SQ. FT.
BASEMENT — 1,796 SQ. FT.
GARAGE — 588 SQ. FT.

TOTAL LIVING AREA:
2,425 SQ. FT.

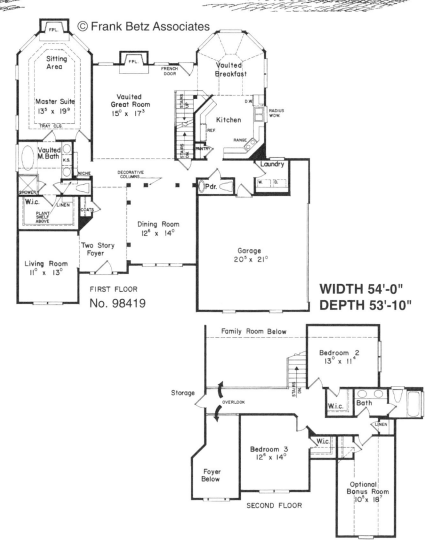

© Frank Betz Associates

FIRST FLOOR
No. 98419

Sitting Area

Master Suite
13⁵ x 19⁹
TRAY CLG.

Vaulted
M. Bath

Vaulted Great Room
15⁰ x 17³

Vaulted Breakfast

FRENCH DOOR

Kitchen

Living Room
11⁰ x 13⁰

Two Story Foyer

Dining Room
12⁶ x 14⁰

DECORATIVE COLUMNS

Pdr.

Laundry

Garage
20⁵ x 21⁰

WIDTH 54'-0"
DEPTH 53'-10"

SECOND FLOOR

Family Room Below

Bedroom 2
13⁰ x 11⁴

Storage

Bedroom 3
12⁶ x 14⁰

Foyer Below

Bath

Optional Bonus Room
10⁵ x 18⁷

To order your Blueprints, call 1-800-235-5700

Refer to **Pricing Schedule F** on
the order form for pricing information

Design by
Jannis Vann & Associates, Inc.

SECOND FLOOR

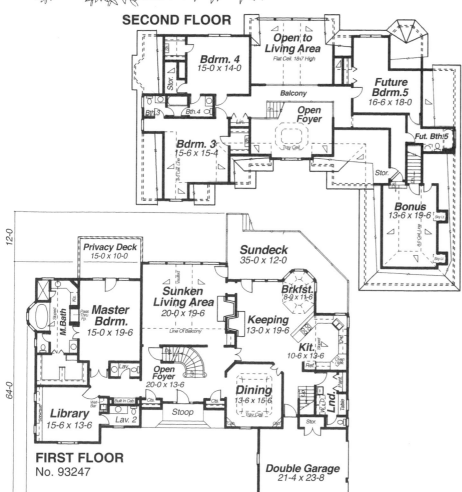

Bdrm. 4
15-0 x 14-0

Open to Living Area
Flat Ceil. 18x7 High

Stor.

Balcony

Bth.3   Bth.4

Lin.

Open Foyer
Tray Ceil.

Bdrm. 3
15-6 x 15-4

18-0 Ceil. Line

Future Bdrm.5
16-6 x 18-0

Fut. Bth.5

Stor.

Bonus
13+6 x 19-6

Sky Lt

8-0 Ceil Line

Sky Lt

12-0

Privacy Deck
15-0 x 10-0

Sundeck
35-0 x 12-0

M. Bath

Pass Thru Fp

Master Bdrm.
15-0 x 19-6

Line Of Balcony

Sunken Living Area
20-0 x 19-6

Brkfst.
8-0 x 11-6

Keeping
13-0 x 19-6

Kit.
10-6 x 13-6

Ref.

64-0

Lav.

Open Foyer
20-0 x 13-6

Stoop

Dining
13-6 x 15-6
Tray Ceil.

Wet Bar   Built In Cab

Library
15-6 x 13-6

Lav. 2

Lnd.

Stor.

FIRST FLOOR
No. 93247

Double Garage
21-4 x 23-8

© 1988, Jannis Vann & Associatres, Inc.

78-0

Quoins and Keystones Accent Stucco

■ This plan features:

— Three bedrooms

— Two full and four half baths

■ Impressive entrance with two-story Foyer

■ Spacious Living Room with a vaulted ceiling above a wall of windows

■ Elegant Dining Room with decorative ceiling and corner built-ins

■ Ideal Kitchen with extended cooktop serving counter

■ Palatial Master Bedroom with a fireplace and private Deck

■ No materials list is available for this plan

FIRST FLOOR — 2,656 SQ. FT.
SECOND FLOOR — 1,184 SQ. FT.
GARAGE — 528 SQ. FT.
BONUS — 508 SQ. FT.
BASEMENT — 2,642 SQ. FT.

TOTAL LIVING AREA:
3,840 SQ. FT.

Design by
Donald A. Gardner Architects, Inc.

Refer to **Pricing Schedule E** on the order form for pricing information

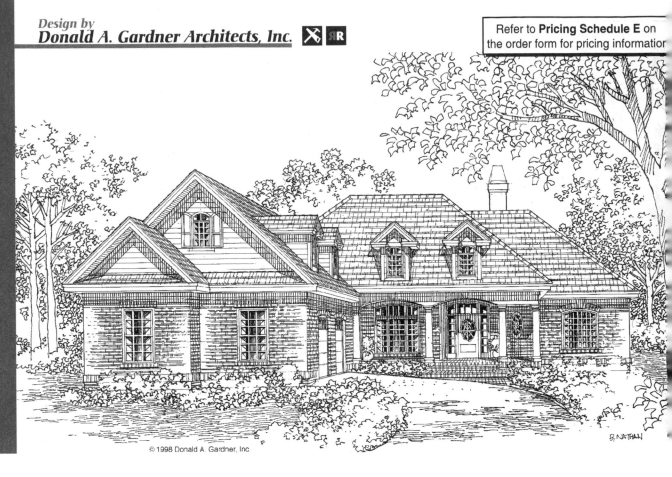

© 1998 Donald A. Gardner, Inc.

B. NATHAN

Stately Arched Entry

■ This plan features:

— Three bedrooms

— Two full and one half baths

■ The stately arched entry Porch is supported by columns

■ The Dining Room has a tray ceiling and is defined by columns

■ The Great Room has a fireplace and accesses the rear Porch/Deck

■ The Kitchen is full of cabinet and counter space

■ The Master Bedroom has a bay window and a tray ceiling

■ The Master Bath features dual vanities and walk in closets

MAIN FLOOR — 2,024 SQ. FT.
BONUS — 423 SQ. FT.
GARAGE — 623 SQ. FT.

TOTAL LIVING AREA:
2,024 SQ. FT.

FLOOR PLAN
No. 98011

© 1998 Donald A Gardner, Inc.

To order your Blueprints, call 1-800-235-5700

Refer to **Pricing Schedule C** on the order form for pricing information

WIDTH 65-0

DEPTH 46-2

MASTER BATH

MASTER BEDROOM
14-6 X 15-6

GREAT ROOM
16-10 X 15-6

BRKFST RM
11-4 X 11-6

UTIL

STORAGE

KITCHEN
11-4 X 13-6

PAN

GARAGE

BATH 2

ENTRY

BEDROOM 2
12-4 X 13-2

BEDROOM 3
11-4 X 12-0

PORCH

DINING ROOM
11-6 X 12-0

NOTE: ALL CEILINGS 10 FT

MAIN AREA
No. 93000

Cozy Traditional

■ This plan features:

— Three bedrooms

— Two full baths

■ An angled eating bar separates the Kitchen, Breakfast Room and Great Room, while leaving these areas open for easy entertaining

■ An efficient, well-appointed Kitchen is convenient to both the formal Dining Room and the sunny Breakfast Room

■ The spacious Master Suite has an oval tub, step-in shower, double vanity and walk-in closet

■ Two additional Bedrooms with ample closet space share a full hall Bath

■ No materials list is available for this plan

MAIN AREA — 1,862 SQ. FT.
GARAGE — 520 SQ. FT.

TOTAL LIVING AREA:
1,862 SQ. FT.

Refer to **Pricing Schedule C** on the order form for pricing information

Appealing Roofline

■ This plan features:

— Three bedrooms

— Two full baths

■ Perfectly symmetrical, this home has an appealing look thanks to the roofline

■ A covered Porch provides space and shelter from the elements

■ The tiled Entry is illuminated by the front doors sidelights

■ The Great Room has a fireplace set between windows

■ The Master Bedroom has a large walk-in closet and a Bath with a skylight

■ Two secondary Bedrooms each have a distinctive front wall window

MAIN FLOOR — 1,850 sq. ft.
GARAGE — 487 sq. ft.

TOTAL LIVING AREA:
1,850 sq. ft.

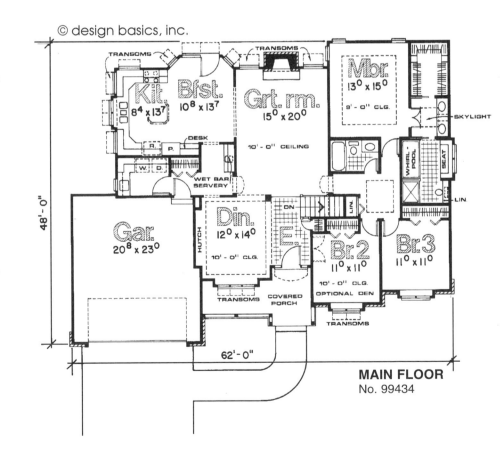

© design basics, inc.

MAIN FLOOR
No. 99434

Refer to **Pricing Schedule D** on the order form for pricing information

Design by
The Garlinghouse Company

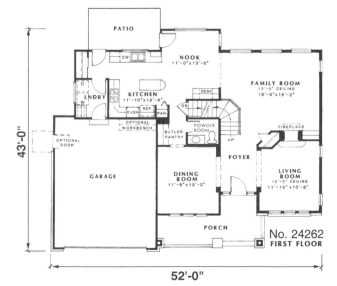

SECOND FLOOR

Attractive Hip and Valley Style Roof

■ This plan features:

— Four bedrooms

— Two full and one half baths

■ A see-through fireplace between the Living Room and the Family Room

■ A gourmet Kitchen with an island, built-in Pantry and double sink

■ A Master Bedroom with a vaulted ceiling

■ A Master Bath with large double vanity, linen closet, corner tub, separate shower, compartmented toilet and huge walk-in closet

■ Three additional Bedrooms, one with a walk-in closet, share full hall Bath

FIRST FLOOR — 1,241 SQ. FT.
SECOND FLOOR — 1,170 SQ. FT.
GARAGE — 500 SQ. FT.

TOTAL LIVING AREA:
2,411 SQ. FT.

No. 24262
FIRST FLOOR

ALTERNATE KITCHEN

OPTIONAL RETREAT

Design by
Rick Garner

Refer to **Pricing Schedule D** on the order form for pricing information

European Styling with a Georgian Flair

■ This plan features:

— Four bedrooms

— Two full baths

■ Elegant European styling spiced up with Georgian Styling

■ Arched windows, quoins and shutters on the exterior, a columned covered front and a rear Porch

■ Formal Foyer gives access to the Dining Room to the left and spacious Den straight ahead

■ Kitchen flows into the informal Eating Area and is separated from the Den by an angled extended counter eating bar

■ Split Bedroom plan, Master Suite privately place to the rear

■ Three additional Bedrooms share a full Bath in the hall

■ An optional crawl space or slab foundation — please specify when ordering

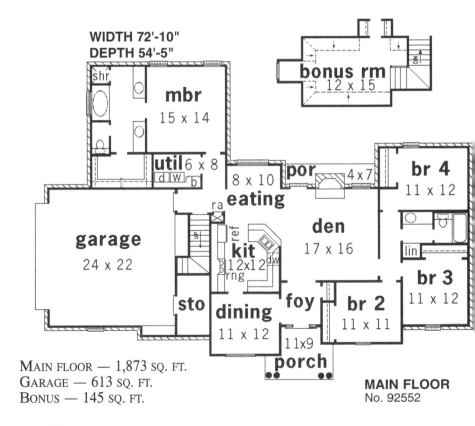

WIDTH 72'-10"
DEPTH 54'-5"

MAIN FLOOR — 1,873 SQ. FT.
GARAGE — 613 SQ. FT.
BONUS — 145 SQ. FT.

MAIN FLOOR
No. 92552

TOTAL LIVING AREA:
1,873 SQ. FT.

To order your Blueprints, call 1-800-235-5700

Design by
Donald A. Gardner Architects, Inc.

© 1994 Donald A. Gardner Architects, Inc.   B. NATHAN

Dynamic Open Floor Plan

■ This plan features:

— Four bedrooms

— Two full and one half baths

■ Elegant columns separate the Great room from the angled Kitchen

■ The Great room accesses the covered rear Porch and the Deck

■ The Master Suite features a well-appointed bath with a corner whirlpool tub

■ The front Bedroom may be used as a Study

■ The bonus room over the Garage adds flexibility

MAIN FLOOR — 2,625 SQ. FT.
BONUS ROOM — 447 SQ. FT.
GARAGE — 753 SQ. FT.

TOTAL LIVING AREA:
2,625 SQ. FT.

MAIN FLOOR
No. 99839

DECK
spa
skylights
covered porch
BED RM.
14-10 x 12-0
cl
cl
bath
BRKFST.
12-0 x 9-10
MASTER BED RM.
15-8 x 16-8
GREAT RM.
18-0 x 19-2
(cathedral ceiling)
fireplace
KITCHEN
12-0 x 15-4
walk-in closet
BED RM.
11-0 x 12-0
lin.
lin. pd. rm.
walk-in closet
master bath
cl
FOYER
15-2 x 5-10
cl
skylight
90-2
BED RM./ STUDY
12-0 x 12-0
PORCH
DINING
12-0 x 13-8
up
UTIL.
7-8 x 9-0
d w
storage
GARAGE
23-0 x 25-6
63-1

down
BONUS RM.
15-0 x 22-0

© Donald A. Gardner Architects, Inc.

Design by
Frank Betz Associates, Inc.

Refer to **Pricing Schedule D** on the order form for pricing information

Elegant in Stature

- This plan features:

— Three bedrooms

— Two full and one half baths

- Elegant in stature and classic in style

- A covered entry leads into a two-story Foyer

- A vaulted ceiling and a boxed bay window highlight the Living Room

- The Family Room features a fireplace and a vaulted ceiling

- The Master Suite has a tray ceiling, a Sitting Room and a private Bath

- An optional basement or crawl space foundation — please specify when ordering

FIRST FLOOR — 1,135 SQ. FT.
SECOND FLOOR — 1,077 SQ. FT.
BASEMENT — 1,135 SQ. FT.
GARAGE — 452 SQ. FT.

TOTAL LIVING AREA:
2,212 SQ. FT

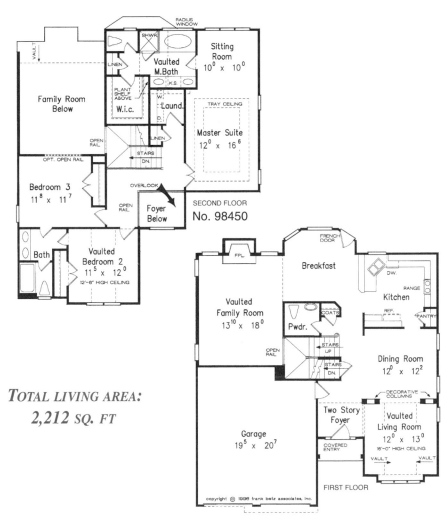

To order your Blueprints, call 1-800-235-5700

Refer to **Pricing Schedule B** on the order form for pricing information

Design by
Ahmann Design, Inc.

TOTAL LIVING AREA:
1,761 SQ. FT.

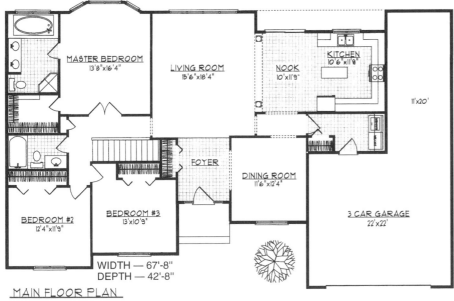

MASTER BEDROOM
13'8"x16'4"

LIVING ROOM
15'6"x18'4"

NOOK
10'x11'9"

KITCHEN
10'6"x11'9"

11'x20'

FOYER

DINING ROOM
11'6"x12'4"

3 CAR GARAGE
22'x22'

BEDROOM #2
12'4"x11'9"

BEDROOM #3
13'x10'9"

WIDTH — 67'-8"
DEPTH — 42'-8"

MAIN FLOOR PLAN
No. 93133

Triple Tandem Garage

■ This plan features:

— Three bedrooms

— Two full baths

■ A large Foyer leads to the bright and spacious Living Room

■ The open Kitchen has a central work island

■ The handy Laundry Room has a pantry and garage access

■ The Master Suite has a bay windowed Sitting Area and French doors, as well as a private Master Bath

■ Two additional front Bedrooms share a full Bath

■ A triple tandem garage with space for a third car, boat or just extra space

■ No materials list is available for this plan

MAIN FLOOR — 1,761 SQ. FT.
BASEMENT — 1,761 SQ. FT.
GARAGE — 658 SQ. FT.

Design by
The Garlinghouse Company

Refer to **Pricing Schedule B** on the order form for pricing information

Secluded Master Suite

■ This plan features:

— Three bedrooms

— Two full and one half baths

■ Great Room with a vaulted ceiling, sunburst window and hearth fireplace

■ Columns frame entrance to formal Dining Room with decorative ceiling

■ Kitchen with breakfast bar, and Breakfast Area

■ Master Bedroom offers an angled ceiling, private Deck, a large walk-in closet and plush Bath

■ Two additional Bedrooms with ample closets, share a full Bath

FIRST FLOOR — 900 SQ. FT.
SECOND FLOOR — 841 SQ. FT.
GARAGE — 609 SQ. FT.
BASEMENT — 891 SQ. FT.

TOTAL LIVING AREA:
1,741 SQ. FT.

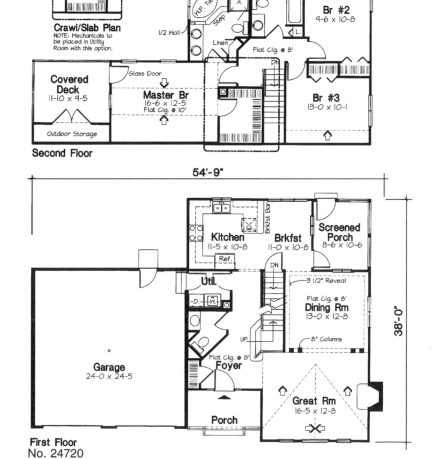

Crawl/Slab Plan
NOTE: Mechanicals to be placed in Utility Room with this option.

Second Floor

Br #2
9-6 x 10-8

Br #3
13-0 x 10-1

Covered Deck
11-10 x 9-5

Master Br
16-6 x 12-5
Flat Clg. @ 10'

Outdoor Storage

54'-9"

38'-0"

Kitchen
11-5 x 10-8

Brkfst
11-0 x 10-8

Screened Porch
8-6 x 10-6

Util.

Dining Rm
13-0 x 12-8

Garage
24-0 x 24-5

Foyer

Great Rm
16-5 x 12-8

Porch

First Floor
No. 24720

To order your Blueprints, call 1-800-235-5700

Design by
Design Basics, Inc.

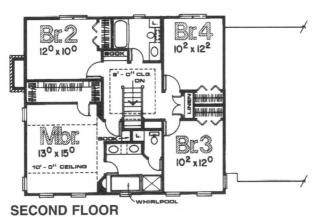

SECOND FLOOR

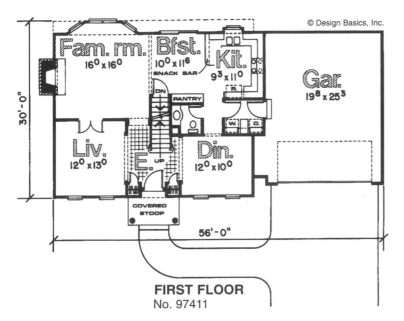

© Design Basics, Inc.

FIRST FLOOR
No. 97411

Classic Colonial

■ This plan features:

— Four bedrooms

— Two full and one half baths

■ This Colonial style home is a classic example

■ Columns punctuate the entrance to both the Living and Dining Rooms

■ The Family Room has a fireplace and a large bay window arrangement

■ The Master Bedroom has a huge walk-in closet and a private Bath

■ On the second floor, three additional Bedrooms share a full Bath

FIRST FLOOR — 1,000 SQ. FT.
SECOND FLOOR — 993 SQ. FT.
GARAGE — 534 SQ. FT.

TOTAL LIVING AREA:
1,993 SQ. FT.

Design by
Design Basics, Inc.

Delightful Decorative Windows

This plan features:

— Four bedrooms

— Two full, one three-quarter and one half baths

■ Arched transom window highlights two-story Entry

■ Dining Room enhanced by hutch space and a bow window

■ Living Room features a volume ceiling and see-through fireplace

■ Spacious Family Room has a dual entertainment center

■ Octagonal Breakfast Bay, a walk-in Pantry, work island and planning desk compliment the Kitchen

■ Secluded Master Bedroom offers a decorative ceiling, double walk-in closet and a lavish Bath

FIRST FLOOR — 1,860 SQ. FT.
SECOND FLOOR — 848 SQ. FT.
BASEMENT — 1,860 SQ. FT.
GARAGE — 629 SQ. FT.

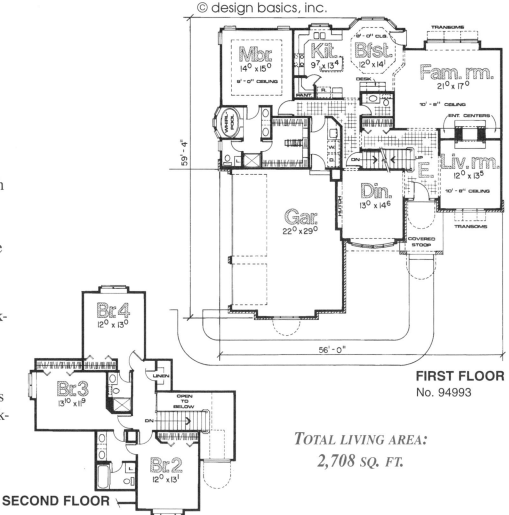

© design basics, inc.

FIRST FLOOR
No. 94993

SECOND FLOOR

TOTAL LIVING AREA:
2,708 SQ. FT.

© design basics inc.

© design basics, inc.

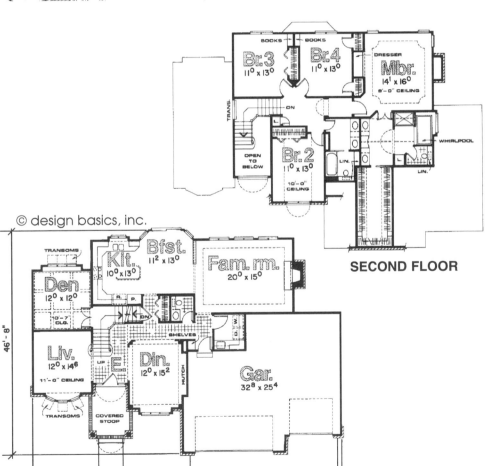

SECOND FLOOR

Br. 3
11⁰ x 13⁰

Br. 4
11⁰ x 13⁰

DRESSER

Mbr.
14¹ x 16⁰
8'-0" CEILING

WHIRLPOOL

Br. 2
11⁰ x 13⁰
10'-0" CEILING

OPEN TO BELOW

BOOKS   BOOKS

TRANS.

LIN.   LIN.

Kit.
10⁰ x 13⁰

Bfst.
11² x 13⁰

Fam. rm.
20⁰ x 15⁰

Den
12⁰ x 12⁰
10'-7" CLO.

Liv.
12⁰ x 14⁶
11'-0" CEILING

Din.
12⁰ x 15²

Gar.
32⁸ x 25⁴

TRANSOMS

SHELVES

COVERED STOOP

TRANSOMS

46' - 8"

64' - 8"

FIRST FLOOR
No. 99446

Classical Details

■ This plan features:

— four bedrooms

— two full and one half baths baths

■ Decorative windows and digni-
fied brick exterior combine with
classical details to create a
sophisticated facade

■ The volume Living Room and
formal Dining Room reflect
elegance with a large bayed
window

■ The sensible Kitchen provides a
large Pantry, two Lazy Susans
and a large center work island

■ The distinctive Master Suite is
highlighted by a built-in dresser,
extra-large walk-in closet and
luxurious bath with an arched
opening to the whirlpool and
shower area

FIRST FLOOR — 1,469 SQ. FT.
SECOND FLOOR — 1,306 SQ. FT.
BASEMENT — 1,469 SQ. FT.

TOTAL LIVING AREA:
2,775 SQ. FT.

Design by
Iannis Vann & Associates, Inc.

Refer to **Pricing Schedule C** on the order form for pricing information

Varied Roof Lines Add Interest

TOTAL LIVING AREA: 2,192 SQ. FT.

■ This plan features:

— Three bedrooms

— Two full and one half baths

■ A modern, convenient floor plan

■ Formal areas located at the front of the home

■ A decorative ceiling in the Dining Room

■ Columns accent the Living Room

■ A large Family Room with a cozy fireplace and direct access to the Deck

■ An efficient Kitchen located between the formal Dining Room and the informal Breakfast Room

■ A private Master Suite with a Master Bath and walk-in closet

■ Two additional bedrooms share a full hall bath

MAIN FLOOR — 2,192 SQ. FT.
BASEMENT — 2,192 SQ. FT.
GARAGE — 564 SQ. FT.

Sundeck
16-4 x 12-0

Brkfst.
11-8 x 10-0

Bdrm.3
13-4 x 11-0

Master Bdrm.
17-6 x 13-10

Family
15-8 x 19-6
Vaulted

Kit.
13-10 x 11-6

M. Bath

Lav.

Bth.2

Dining
11-6 x 13-6
Boxed Tray

Foyer

Living
11-8 x 13-2

Bdrm.2
13-4 x 11-6

Double Garage
21-4 x 25-8

MAIN FLOOR
No. 93255

64-0

70-0

To order your Blueprints, call 1-800-235-5700

Design by
Design Basics, Inc.

FIRST FLOOR — 1,405 SQ. FT.
SECOND FLOOR — 453 SQ. FT.
BONUS ROOM — 300 SQ. FT.
BASEMENT — 1,405 SQ. FT.
GARAGE — 490 SQ. FT.

TOTAL LIVING AREA:
1,858 SQ. FT.

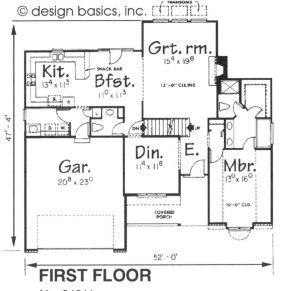

FIRST FLOOR

No. 94911

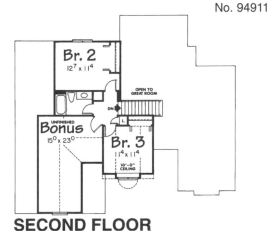

SECOND FLOOR

Fieldstone Facade and Arched Windows

■ This plan features:

— Three bedrooms

— Two full and one half baths

■ Inviting Covered Porch shelters entrance

■ Expansive Great Room enhanced by warm fireplace and three transom windows

■ Breakfast area adjoins Great Room giving a feeling of more space

■ An efficient Kitchen with counter snack bar and nearby Laundry and Garage entry

■ A first floor Master Bedroom with an arched window below a sloped ceiling and a double vanity Bath

■ Two additional Bedrooms share a Bonus area and a full Bath on the second floor

Design by
Design Basics, Inc.

Refer to **Pricing Schedule B** on the order form for pricing information

Quaint, Cozy Exterior

■ This plan features:

— Four bedrooms

— Two full and one half baths

■ Covered Porch leads into tiled Entry with banister staircase

■ Formal Dining Room doubles as a Parlor

■ The Kitchen has a serving counter/snackbar, Pantry and Breakfast Area

■ Spacious Family Room has an inviting fireplace

■ Corner Master Bedroom offers a roomy walk-in closet and a pampering Bath

FIRST FLOOR — 866 SQ. FT.
SECOND FLOOR — 905 SQ. FT.
BASEMENT — 866 SQ. FT.
GARAGE — 541 SQ. FT.

TOTAL LIVING AREA:
1,771 SQ. FT.

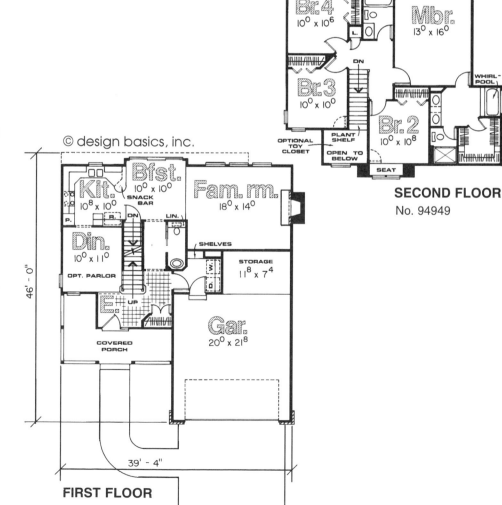

© design basics, inc.

SECOND FLOOR
No. 94949

FIRST FLOOR

To order your Blueprints, call 1-800-235-5700

Design by
The Meredith Corporation

Photography by The Meredith Corporation

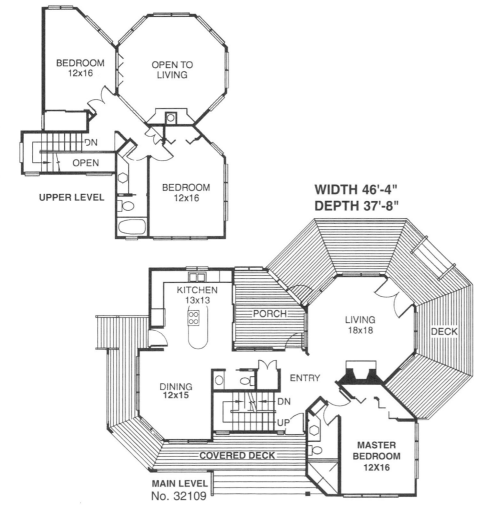

BEDROOM
12x16

OPEN TO
LIVING

DN

OPEN

BEDROOM
12x16

UPPER LEVEL

WIDTH 46'-4"
DEPTH 37'-8"

KITCHEN
13x13

PORCH

LIVING
18x18

DECK

DINING
12x15

ENTRY

DN

UP

COVERED DECK

MASTER
BEDROOM
12X16

MAIN LEVEL
No. 32109

Prairie Style Retreat

■ This plan features:

— Three bedrooms

— Two full and one half baths

■ Shingle siding, tall expanses of glass and wrapping decks accent the exterior

■ The octagonal shaped Living Room has a two-story ceiling and French doors

■ The Kitchen is enhanced by a cooktop island

■ The main level Master Suite offers a private Bath

■ Two additional, second floor bedrooms share the full bath in the hall

MAIN LEVEL — 1,213 SQ. FT.
UPPER LEVEL — 825 SQ. FT.
BASEMENT — 1,213 SQ. FT.

TOTAL LIVING AREA:
2,038 SQ. FT.

Design by
Frank Betz Associates, Inc.

Refer to **Pricing Schedule B** on the order form for pricing information

Bathed in Natural Light

■ This plan features:

— Three bedrooms

— Two full and one half baths

■ A high arched window illuminates the Foyer

■ Vaulted ceilings in the formal Dining Room, Breakfast Room and Great Room create volume

■ The Master Suite is crowned with a decorative tray ceiling

■ The Master Bath has a double vanity, oval tub, separate shower and a walk-in closet

■ Two additional Bedrooms, a full Bath and a loft highlight the second floor

■ The Loft has the option of becoming a fourth bedroom

■ An optional basement or crawl space foundation available — please specify when ordering

FIRST FLOOR — 1,133 SQ. FT.
SECOND FLOOR — 486 SQ. FT.
BASEMENT — 1,133 SQ. FT.
BONUS — 134 SQ. FT.
GARAGE — 406 SQ. FT.

TOTAL LIVING AREA:
1,619 SQ. FT.

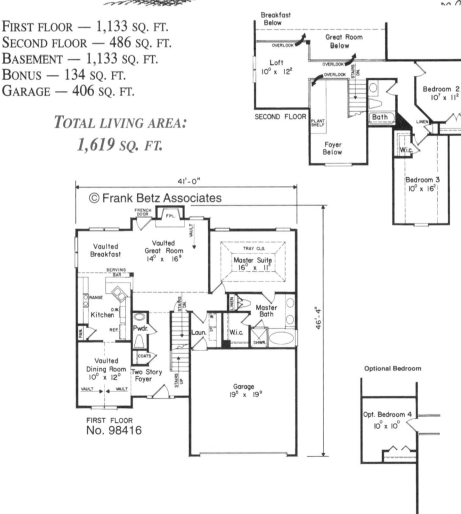

To order your Blueprints, call 1-800-235-5700

Design by
Frank Betz Associates, Inc.

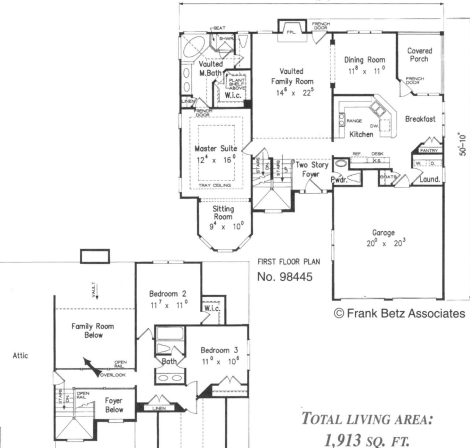

FIRST FLOOR PLAN
No. 98445

© Frank Betz Associates

48'-0"

50'-10"

Seat
SHWR.
Vaulted M.Bath
Plant Shelf Above
W.i.c.
Linen
French Door
Master Suite 12⁴ x 16⁰
TRAY CEILING
Sitting Room 9⁴ x 10⁰

FPL
French Door
Vaulted Family Room 14⁶ x 22⁵
Stairs UP Stairs DN
Two Story Foyer

Dining Room 11⁸ x 11⁰
Covered Porch
French Door
Breakfast
Kitchen
RANGE DW.
Pantry
REF. DESK K.S.
Pwdr. Coats W. D. Laund.
Garage 20⁰ x 20³

SECOND FLOOR PLAN

VAULT
Bedroom 2 11⁷ x 11⁰
W.i.c.
Family Room Below
Attic
Open Rail
Overlook
Bath
Bedroom 3 11⁰ x 10⁶
Stairs DN
Open Rail
Foyer Below
Linen
Opt. Bonus Room 12⁰ x 23⁷

TOTAL LIVING AREA:
1,913 SQ. FT.

Beautiful Stucco & Stone

■ This plan features:

— Three bedrooms

— Two full and one half baths

■ This home features keystone arches and a turret styled roof

■ The vaulted Family Room is highlighted by a fireplace

■ The Dining Room adjoins the Family Room

■ The Master Bedroom is crowned by a tray ceiling, while the Master Bath has a vaulted ceiling

■ A Balcony overlooks the Family Room and Foyer below

■ An optional basement, slab or crawl space foundation — please specify when ordering

■ No materials list is available for this plan

FIRST FLOOR — 1,398 SQ. FT.
SECOND FLOOR — 515 SQ. FT.
BASEMENT — 1,398 SQ. FT.
BONUS — 282 SQ. FT.
GARAGE — 421 SQ. FT.

Design by
Wesplan Building Design

Refer to **Pricing Schedule D** on
the order form for pricing information

Stately Manor

- This plan features:
— Three bedrooms
— Two full and one half baths
- A Porch serves as a grand entrance
- A very spacious Foyer with an open staircase and lots of angles
- A beautiful Kitchen equipped with a cook top island and a full bay window wall that includes a roomy Breakfast Nook
- The Living Room has a vaulted ceiling
- The grand Master Suite is equipped with a walk-in closet and five-piece private Bath

FIRST FLOOR — 1,383 SQ. FT.
SECOND FLOOR — 997 SQ. FT.
BASEMENT — 1,374 SQ. FT.
GARAGE — 420 SQ. FT.

TOTAL LIVING AREA:
2,380 SQ. FT.

MAIN FLOOR
No. 90966

WIDTH 54'-0"
DEPTH 47'-0"

SECOND FLOOR

To order your Blueprints, call 1-800-235-5700

Design by
Larry E. Belk

French Influenced Design

- This plan features:
- — Three bedrooms
- — Two full baths
- The formal Dining Room has a ten-foot coffered, decorative ceiling
- The over-sized Living Room includes built-in bookcases
- An angled bar separates the Kitchen and Breakfast Room
- The Master Bedroom includes a luxurious Master Bath with a walk-in closet, his-n-hers vanities and a whirlpool tub
- No materials list is available for this plan

MAIN FLOOR — 1,890 SQ. FT.
GARAGE — 565 SQ. FT.

TOTAL LIVING AREA:
1,890 SQ. FT.

WIDTH 65'-10"
DEPTH 53'-5"

MASTER BATH
SEAT

PORCH

BRKFST RM
10-8 X 11-8
10 FT CLG

UTIL
8-0 X 5-8

STORAGE

STORAGE

MASTER BEDRM
14-4 X 15-6
10 FT CLG

FP

BUILT INS

BUILT INS

LIVING ROOM
17-4 X 15-8
10 FT CLG

45° LEDGE

KITCHEN
10-8 X 13-6
10 FT CLG

PAN

COPYRIGHT LARRY E. BELK

GARAGE

BATH 2

LIN

SLOPE

PORCH

FOYER
10 FT CLG

DINING ROOM
11-0 X 13-0
10 FT COFFERED CLG

MAIN FLOOR
No. 96601

BEDROOM 2
12-6 X 11-6

BEDROOM 3
12-0 X 13-4
10 FT CLG

PORCH

Design by
Donald A. Gardner Architects, Inc.

Refer to **Pricing Schedule D** on the order form for pricing information

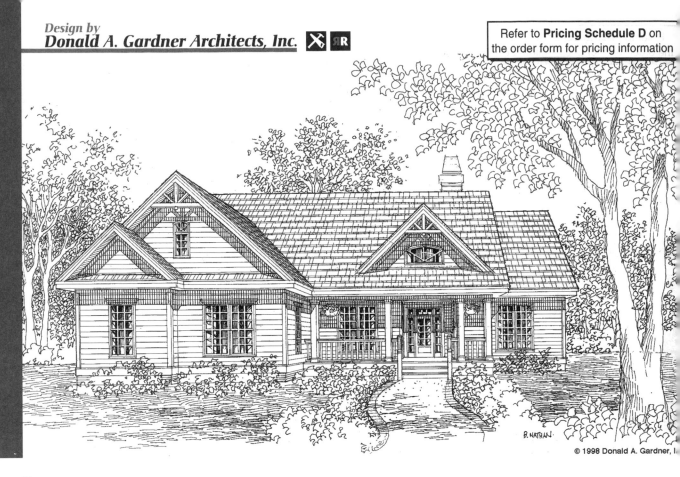

© 1998 Donald A. Gardner, I

Open Spaces

■ This plan features:

— Three bedrooms

— Two full baths

■ Covered Porches front and rear add to your living space

■ The Dining Room has a decorative ceiling and is punctuated by columns

■ The Great Room has a fireplace set between built-in shelves

■ The Master Bedroom has a decorative ceiling and dual walk in closets

■ Two secondary Bedrooms and a full Bath are located on the opposite side of the home

MAIN FLOOR — 1,762 SQ. FT.
BONUS ROOM — 316 SQ. FT.
GARAGE — 520 SQ. FT.

TOTAL LIVING AREA:
1,762 SQ. FT.

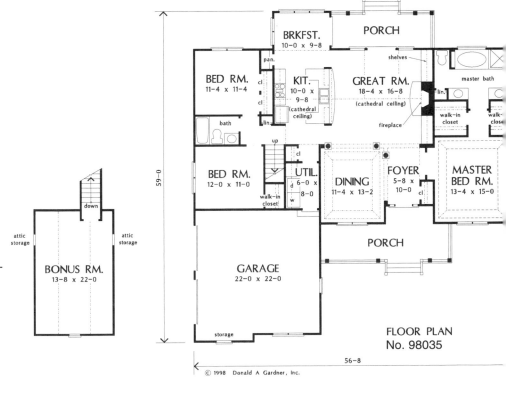

To order your Blueprints, call 1-800-235-5700

Refer to **Pricing Schedule D** on the order form for pricing information

Design by
Fillmore Design Group

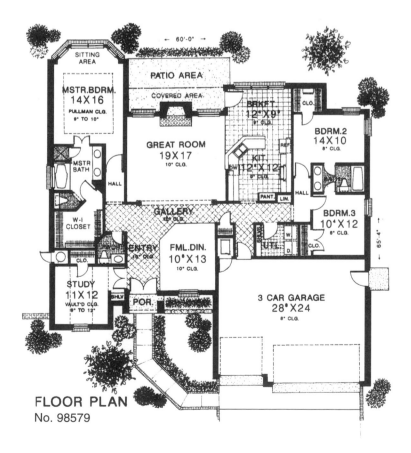

FLOOR PLAN
No. 98579

Expansive Master Suite

■ This plan features:

— Three bedrooms

— Two full and one half baths

■ There is a large Master Bedroom with a bayed Sitting Area, a five-piece Master Bath, and a walk-in closet

■ The Study is topped by a vaulted ceiling and has French doors

■ The Kitchen is open to the Breakfast Room which is open to the Great Room

■ The peninsula counter adds to the work space in the Kitchen

■ The fireplace in the Great Room is flanked by windows

■ No materials list is available for this plan

MAIN FLOOR — 2,214 SQ. FT.
GARAGE — 687 SQ. FT.

TOTAL LIVING AREA:
2,214 SQ. FT.

Design by
Donald A. Gardner Architects, Inc.

Refer to **Pricing Schedule E** on the order form for pricing information

© 1997 Donald A Gardner Architects, Inc.

Dressed to Impress

■ This plan features:

— Three bedrooms

— Two full and one half baths

■ The Great Room has a cathedral ceiling and adjoins the Breakfast Area

■ The Kitchen is enhanced by an angled counter with stove top, a Pantry, and easy access to the formal Dining Room

■ A separate Utility Room with built-in cabinets and a counter top with laundry sink add efficiency

■ Double doors lead into the Master Suite with a box bay window, two walk-in closets, and a lavish Bath

■ Two more Bedrooms are located upstairs along with a full Bath, linen closet and skylit bonus room

FIRST FLOOR — 1,572 SQ. FT.
SECOND FLOOR — 549 SQ. FT.
BONUS ROOM — 384 SQ. FT.
GARAGE & STORAGE — 540 SQ. FT.

TOTAL LIVING AREA:
2,121 SQ. FT.

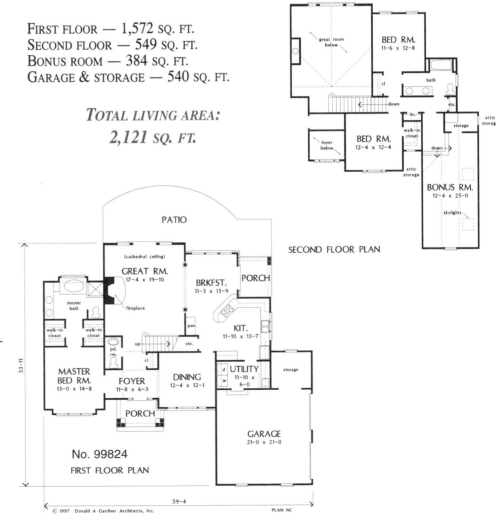

SECOND FLOOR PLAN

No. 99824
FIRST FLOOR PLAN

© 1997 Donald A Gardner Architects, Inc.   PLAN NC

164

Design by
Garrell Associates, Inc.

SECOND FLOOR

TOTAL LIVING AREA:
3,029 SQ. FT.

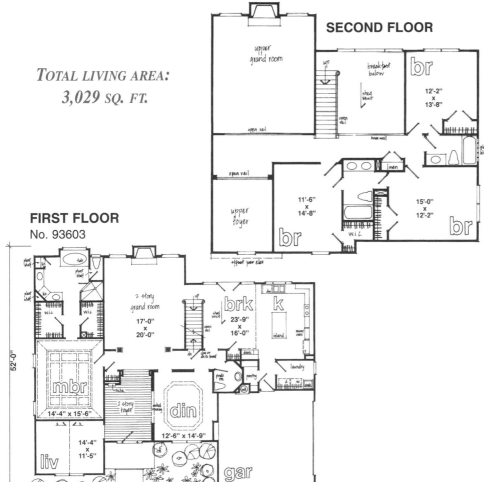

FIRST FLOOR
No. 93603

Stately Columns and Keystones

■ This plan features:

— Four bedrooms

— Three full and one half baths

■ Gracious two-story Foyer opens to vaulted Living Room and arched Dining Room

■ Expansive, two-story Grand Room with impressive fireplace

■ Spacious and efficient Kitchen with a work island, Breakfast area with back yard access, and nearby Laundry/Garage entry

■ Private Master Bedroom offers a decorative ceiling, two walk-in closets and vanities, and a garden window tub

■ No materials list is available for this plan

FIRST FLOOR — 2,115 SQ. FT.
SECOND FLOOR — 914 SQ. FT.
BASEMENT — 2,115 SQ. FT.
GARAGE — 448 SQ. FT.

Design by
Design Basics, Inc.

Refer to **Pricing Schedule E** on the order form for pricing information

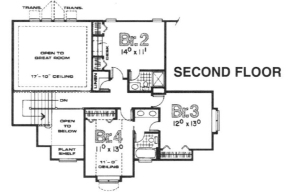

© design basics inc.

Traditional Home

■ This plan features:

— Four bedrooms

— Two full, one three-quarter and one half baths

■ Dining Room has a built-in hutch and a bay window

■ Cozy Den and Great Room have high ceilings and transom windows

■ Conveniently arranged Kitchen adjoins the Breakfast Nook

■ The Gathering Room features a fireplace and a cathedral ceiling

■ The secluded Master Bedroom is a world away from the busy areas

■ Upstairs are three Bedrooms and two full Baths

FIRST FLOOR — 2,158 SQ. FT.
SECOND FLOOR — 821 SQ. FT.
BASEMENT — 2,158 SQ. FT.
GARAGE — 692 SQ. FT.

TOTAL LIVING AREA:
2,979 SQ. FT.

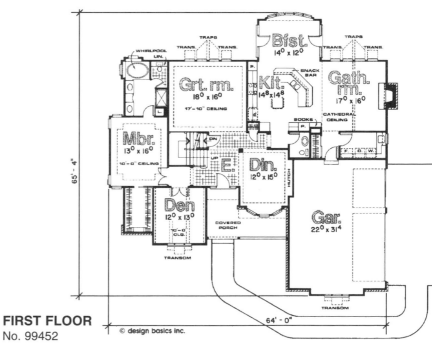

SECOND FLOOR

FIRST FLOOR
No. 99452
© design basics inc.

Design by
Frank Betz Associates, Inc.

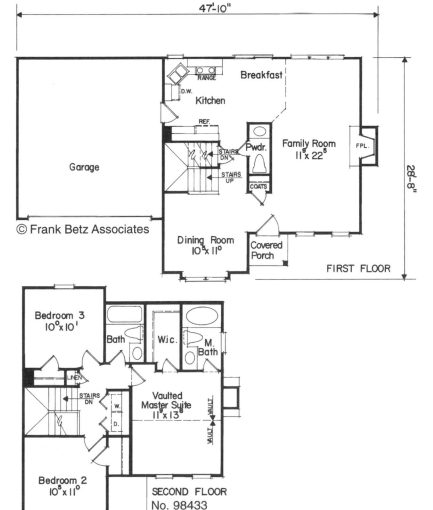

© Frank Betz Associates

Garage

Breakfast

RANGE

D.W.

Kitchen

REF.

STAIRS DN

STAIRS UP

Pwdr.

COATS

Family Room
11⁹ x 22⁵

FPL.

Dining Room
10⁵ x 11⁰

Covered Porch

FIRST FLOOR

47'-10"

28'-8"

Bedroom 3
10⁰ x 10¹

Bath

Wic.

M. Bath

LINEN

STAIRS DN

W.

D.

Vaulted Master Suite
11⁹ x 13⁸

VAULT

Bedroom 2
10⁵ x 11⁰

SECOND FLOOR
No. 98433

A Good Traffic Pattern

■ This plan features:

— Three bedrooms

— Two full and one half baths

■ The open layout of this home creates a good traffic pattern for daily activities

■ A covered front Porch shelters you in inclement weather

■ The Dining Room has a boxed bay window

■ The Master Suite includes a vaulted ceiling, a walk-in closet, and a private Bath

■ An optional basement, slab or crawl space foundation — please specify when ordering

FIRST FLOOR — 670 SQ. FT.
SECOND FLOOR — 651 SQ. FT.
BASEMENT — 670 SQ. FT.
GARAGE — 404 SQ. FT.

TOTAL LIVING AREA:
1,321 SQ. FT.

Design by
Frank Betz Associates, Inc.

Refer to **Pricing Schedule C** on the order form for pricing information

Outstanding Four Bedroom

■ This plan features:

— Four bedrooms

— Two full baths

■ Radius window highlights exterior and formal Dining Room

■ Vaulted ceiling enhances the Great Room accented by a fireplace framed by windows

■ Arched opening to the Kitchen from the Great Room

■ Breakfast Room topped by a vaulted ceiling and enhanced by a French door

■ Tray ceiling and a five-piece compartmental Bath provides luxury in the Master Suite

■ An optional basement or crawl space foundation — please specify when ordering

MAIN FLOOR — 1,945 SQ. FT.

TOTAL LIVING AREA:
1,945 SQ. FT.

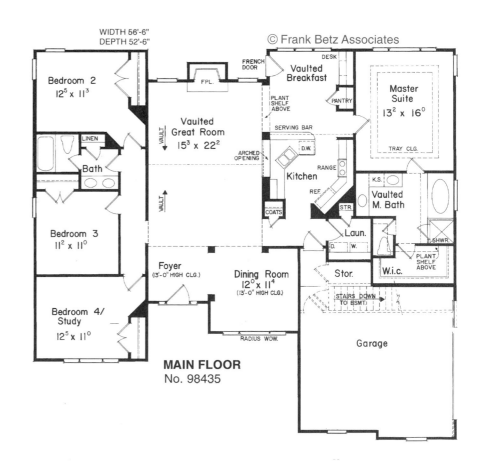

WIDTH 56'-6"
DEPTH 52'-6"

© Frank Betz Associates

Bedroom 2
12⁵ x 11³

Vaulted Breakfast

FRENCH DOOR

DESK

Master Suite
13² x 16⁰

FPL.

PLANT SHELF ABOVE

PANTRY

TRAY CLG.

LINEN

Vaulted Great Room
15³ x 22²

SERVING BAR

Bath

VAULT

ARCHED OPENING

D.W.

RANGE

K.S.

Bedroom 3
11² x 11⁰

VAULT

Kitchen

REF.

Vaulted M. Bath

COATS

STR.

Laun.
D. W.

SHWR.

PLANT SHELF ABOVE

Foyer
(13'-0" HIGH CLG.)

Dining Room
12⁰ x 11⁴
(13'-0" HIGH CLG.)

Stor.

W.i.c.

Bedroom 4/ Study
12⁵ x 11⁰

STAIRS DOWN TO BSMT.

RADIUS WDW.

Garage

MAIN FLOOR
No. 98435

To order your Blueprints, call 1-800-235-5700

Design by
Design Basics, Inc.

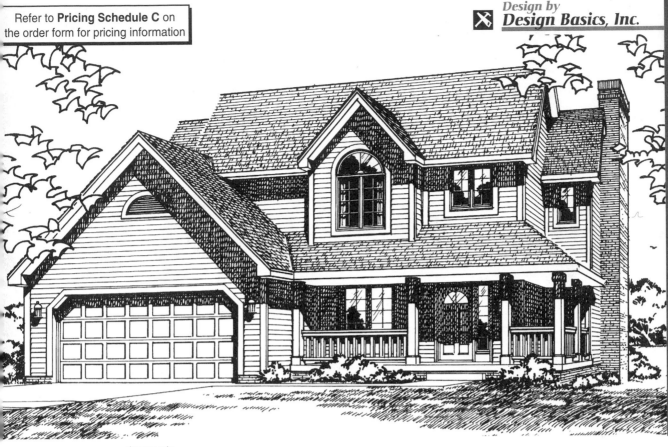

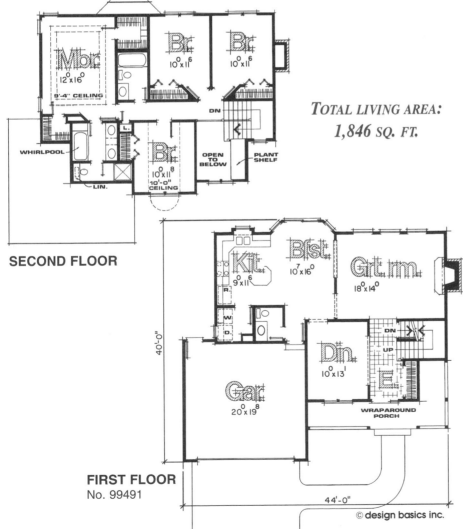

SECOND FLOOR

TOTAL LIVING AREA:
1,846 SQ. FT.

FIRST FLOOR
No. 99491

© design basics inc.

Wrap-Around Porch Adds Style

■ This plan features:

— Four bedrooms

— Two full and one half baths

■ The two-story Entry includes a large coat closet and a plant shelf

■ Many windows and a fireplace highlight the Great Room

■ The island Kitchen with a boxed window over the sink flows freely into the Breakfast Area

■ There is a volume ceiling and an arched window in the front Bedroom

■ The large Master Suite has his-n-her walk-in closets and a private Bath

■ An optional basement or slab foundation — please specify when ordering

FIRST FLOOR — 919 SQ. FT.
SECOND FLOOR — 927 SQ. FT.
GARAGE — 414 SQ. FT.

Design by
Design Basics, Inc.

Refer to **Pricing Schedule C** on the order form for pricing information

Notable Windows

■ This plan features:

— Four bedrooms

— Two full and one half baths

■ Gables and accenting arches enhance this home

■ Open Entry between formal Living and Dining rooms

■ Comfortable Family Room offers a fireplace, wetbar, and a wall of windows

■ Kitchen includes an island counter and adjoins the Breakfast Bay

■ Luxurious Master Bedroom has a Bath with a skylight

FIRST FLOOR — 1,179 SQ. FT.
SECOND FLOOR — 1,019 SQ. FT.
BASEMENT — 1,179 SQ. FT.
GARAGE — 466 SQ. FT.

TOTAL LIVING AREA:
2,198 SQ. FT.

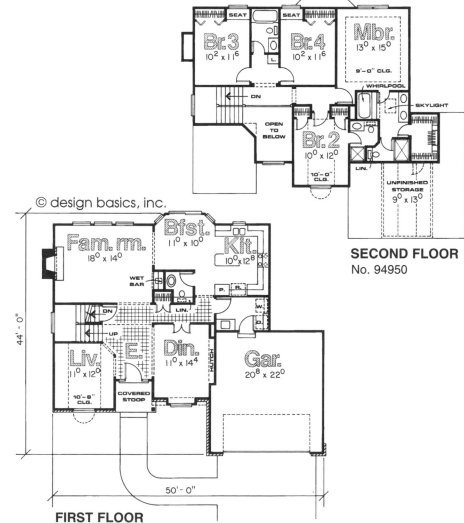

SECOND FLOOR
No. 94950

© design basics, inc.

FIRST FLOOR

To order your Blueprints, call 1-800-235-5700

Refer to **Pricing Schedule C** on
he order form for pricing information

Design by
Design Basics, Inc.

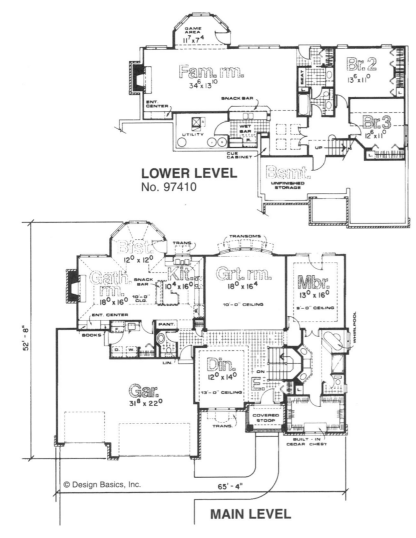

LOWER LEVEL
No. 97410

MAIN LEVEL

© Design Basics, Inc.

65' - 4"

52' - 8"

Expand Your Options

■ This plan features:

— One Bedroom

— One full and one half baths

■ This plan has an optional lower level that includes two more Bedrooms

■ Also on the lower level, find a Family Room with a fireplace and a bar

■ On the main level, the Dining Room has a towering front wall window

■ The Great Room has a rear bow window

■ The Master Bedroom has a French door to the rear yard

MAIN LEVEL — 1,887 SQ. FT.
LOWER LEVEL — 1,388 SQ. FT.
GARAGE — 738 SQ. FT.

TOTAL LIVING AREA:
1,887 SQ. FT.

Design by
Studer Residential Design, Inc.

Refer to **Pricing Schedule D** on the order form for pricing information

Exciting Arched Accents Give Impact

■ This plan features:

— Three bedrooms

— Two full and one half baths

■ Keystone arch accents entrance into open Foyer

■ Great Room enhanced by an entertainment center

■ Efficient, angled Kitchen offers work island/snackbar

■ Master Bedroom wing with a lavish Bath; two vanities, and corner window tub

■ Two bedrooms with walk-in closets share a skylit Study and a double vanity bath

■ No materials list is available for this plan

FIRST FLOOR — 1,542 SQ. FT.
SECOND FLOOR — 667 SQ. FT.
BONUS ROOM — 236 SQ. FT.
BASEMENT — 1,470 SQ. FT.
GARAGE — 420 SQ. FT.

TOTAL LIVING AREA:
2,209 SQ. FT.

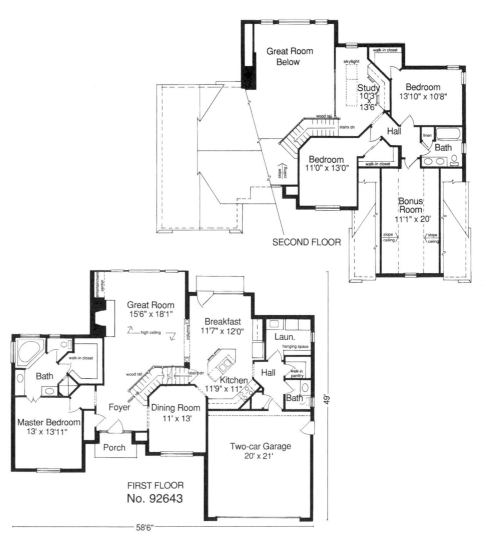

SECOND FLOOR

FIRST FLOOR
No. 92643

To order your Blueprints, call 1-800-235-5700

Design by
Fillmore Design Group

Elegant Palladian Window

■ This plan features:

— Four bedrooms

— Two full baths

■ Entry with columns framing Living and Breakfast rooms

■ Living Room enhanced by a cathedral ceiling, palladian window and hearth fireplace

■ Efficient Kitchen with corner Pantry, and peninsula counter serving Breakfast Area and Patio

■ Corner Master Bedroom offers a cozy Sitting Area, Patio access, walk-in closet and lavish Bath

■ Three additional Bedrooms with over-sized closets, share a double vanity Bath

■ No materials list is available for this plan

MAIN FLOOR — 1,696 SQ. FT.
GARAGE — 389 SQ. FT.

TOTAL LIVING AREA:
1,696 SQ. FT.

No. 92290
Floor Plan

Design by
Larry E. Belk

Refer to **Pricing Schedule E** on the order form for pricing information

Vintage America

■ This plan features:

— Four bedrooms

— Two full and one half baths

■ Wide front Porch framing the front of the home

■ Huge Great Room opening through classic arches to the Kitchen and Breakfast Room

■ Kitchen with all the amenities, a large work island complete with cooktop and raised eating bar

■ Luxurious Master Suite with his-n-her vanity and closets

■ A second large covered Porch at the rear of the home

■ All bedrooms feature picturesque dormer windows, perfect for a built-in window seat or toy box

■ No material list is available for this plan

FIRST FLOOR — 1,785 SQ. FT.
SECOND FLOOR — 830 SQ. FT.
BONUS ROOM — 280 SQ. FT.
GARAGE — 583 SQ. FT.

TOTAL LIVING AREA:
2,615 SQ. FT.

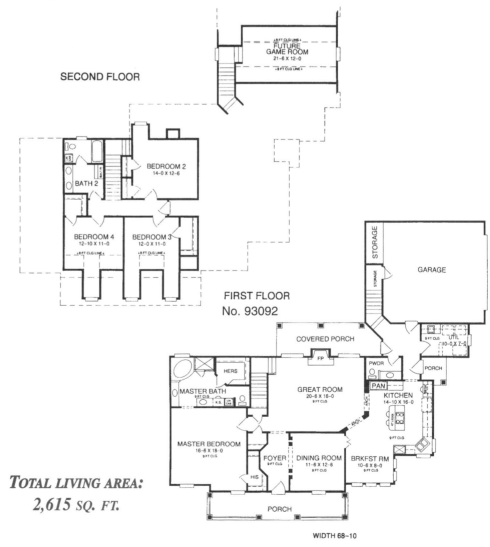

To order your Blueprints, call 1-800-235-5700

Design by
Studer Residential Design, Inc.

SECOND FLOOR

Bedroom
11-4 x 11-4

Bath

Great Room
Below
12' ceiling

Hall

Master
Bedroom
12 x 16

Foyer
Below
12' ceiling

stairs dn

Bath

tray ceiling

Bedroom
11-4 x 9-6

walk-in closet

Porch

Breakfast
10 x 13-4

Kitchen
8-6 x 11

Bath

Laundry

Sunken
Great Room
13 x 17-4

stairs up

stairs dn

walk-in
closet

Foyer

Dining Room
11-4 x 12

WIDTH 55'-4"
DEPTH 40'-4"

Porch

furniture
alcove

Two-car Garage
20-4 x 20

FIRST FLOOR
No. 92609

A Little Drama

■ This plan features:

— Three bedrooms

— Two full and one half baths

■ A 12-foot high Entry with a transom and sidelights

■ The sunken Great Room has a fireplace and access to a rear Porch

■ The Breakfast Bay and Kitchen flow into each other and access a rear Porch

■ The Master Bedroom has a tray ceiling, walk-in closet and a private Master Bath

■ No materials list is available for this plan

FIRST FLOOR — 960 SQ. FT.
SECOND FLOOR — 808 SQ. FT.
BASEMENT — 922 SQ. FT.
GARAGE — 413 SQ. FT.

TOTAL LIVING AREA:
1,768 SQ. FT.

Design by
Frank Betz Associates, Inc.

Refer to **Pricing Schedule C** on the order form for pricing information

Family Size Accommodations

■ This plan features:

— Four bedrooms

— Two full and one half baths

■ The two-story Foyer with a vaulted ceiling sets the tone

■ A vaulted ceiling tops the Family Room that also boasts a fireplace

■ The family size Kitchen features an island, a Pantry and ample counter space

■ The first floor Master Suite is crowned with a tray ceiling

■ On the second floor three additional Bedrooms share the full hallway Bath

■ An optional basement or a crawl space foundation available — please specify when ordering.

MAIN FLOOR — 1,320 SQ. FT.
UPPER FLOOR — 554 SQ. FT.
BONUS ROOM — 155 SQ. FT.
BASEMENT — 1,320 SQ. FT.
GARAGE — 406 SQ. FT.

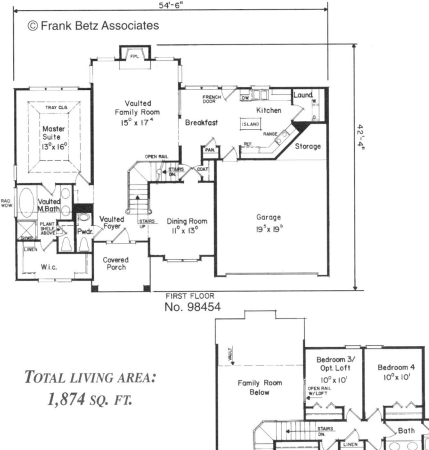

© Frank Betz Associates

54'-6"

42'-4"

Master Suite 13⁰ x 16⁰ — TRAY CLG.

Vaulted M.Bath

RAD. WDW.

PLANT SHELF ABOVE

SHWR.

LINEN

W.i.c.

Pwdr.

Vaulted Foyer

Covered Porch

Vaulted Family Room 15⁰ x 17⁴

OPEN RAIL

STAIRS DN.

STAIRS UP

COAT

PAN.

Dining Room 11⁰ x 13⁰

Breakfast

FRENCH DOOR

Kitchen

ISLAND

RANGE

REF

DW

Laund.

W

D

Storage

Garage 19⁵ x 19⁹

FPL

FIRST FLOOR
No. 98454

TOTAL LIVING AREA:
1,874 SQ. FT.

VAULT

Family Room Below

OPEN RAIL W/LOFT

STAIRS DN.

LINEN

VAULT

Foyer Below

Bedroom 3/ Opt. Loft 10⁰ x 10'

Bedroom 4 10⁰ x 10'

Bath

Bedroom 2 11⁰ x 10⁰

Opt. Bonus Room 10⁹ x 13⁶

SECOND FLOOR

To order your Blueprints, call 1-800-235-5700

Design by
Donald A. Gardner Architects, Inc.

© 1994 Donald A. Gardner Architects, Inc.

No. 99841
SECOND FLOOR PLAN

FIRST FLOOR PLAN

© 1994 Donald A Gardner Architects, Inc.

Four Dramatic Gables

■ This plan features:

— Three bedrooms

— Two full and one half baths

■ Four dramatic gables lend curb appeal to this home

■ Two fireplaces add warmth, one in the Family Room, the other in the Study/Living Room

■ Vaulted and nine-foot ceilings create maximum volume

■ First floor Master Suite, with an angled hall entrance for privacy, features a sitting bay, whirlpool tub, and a shower

■ Extra room is added on the upper level by a skylit bonus room and attic storage

FIRST FLOOR — 2,162 SQ. FT.
SECOND FLOOR — 671 SQ. FT.
BONUS — 345 SQ. FT.
GARAGE — 587 SQ. FT.

TOTAL LIVING AREA:
2,833 SQ. FT.

Design by
Design Basics, Inc.

Refer to **Pricing Schedule E** on the order form for pricing information

See-Through Fireplace

◼ This plan features:

— Four bedrooms

— Two full and one half baths

◼ The formal rooms have beautiful bayed windows

◼ The Family Room has a wetbar and shares a see-through fireplace with the Kitchen

◼ The large Kitchen with a Pantry and snack bar adjoins the bayed Breakfast Area

◼ Upstairs, double doors open into the Master Bedroom

FIRST FLOOR — 1,392 SQ. FT.
SECOND FLOOR — 1,335 SQ. FT.
BASEMENT — 1,392 SQ. FT.
GARAGE — 545 SQ. FT.

TOTAL LIVING AREA:
2,727 SQ. FT.

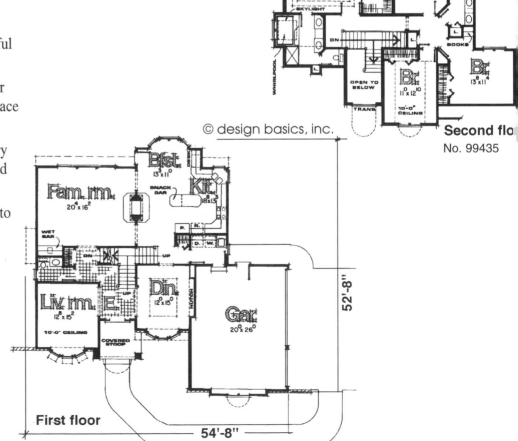

© design basics, inc.

Second flo
No. 99435

First floor

54'-8"

52'-8"

To order your Blueprints, call 1-800-235-5700

Refer to **Pricing Schedule D** on the order form for pricing information

Design by
Corley Plan Service

SECOND FLOOR PLAN

TOTAL LIVING AREA:
2,398 SQ. FT.

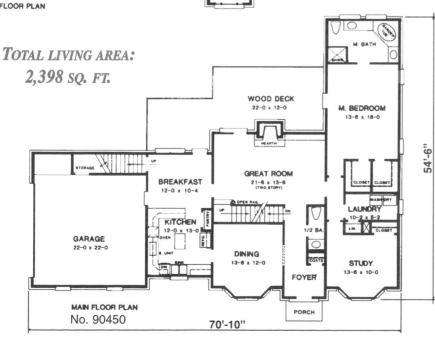

MAIN FLOOR PLAN
No. 90450

70'-10"

54'-6"

Elegant Brick Two-Story

■ This plan features:

— Four bedrooms

— Two full and one half baths

■ A large two-story Great Room with a fireplace and access to a wood Deck

■ A secluded Master Suite with two walk-in closets and a private, lavish, Master Bath

■ A large island Kitchen serving the formal Dining Room and the sunny Breakfast Nook with ease

■ Three additional Bedrooms, two with walk-in closets, share a full hall Bath

■ An optional Bonus Room with a private entrance from below

■ An optional basement or crawl space foundation — please specify when ordering

FIRST FLOOR — 1,637 SQ. FT.
SECOND FLOOR — 761 SQ. FT.
BONUS AREA — 453 SQ. FT.

Design by
Donald A. Gardner Architects, Inc.

Refer to **Pricing Schedule D** on the order form for pricing information

© 1996 Donald A Gardner Architects, Inc.

Great As A Mountain Retreat

■ This plan features:

— Three bedrooms

— Two full baths

■ Board and batten siding, stone, and stucco combine to give this popular plan a casual feel

■ User friendly Kitchen with huge Pantry for ample Storage and island counter

■ Casual family meals in sunny Breakfast bay; formal gatherings in the columned Dining Area

■ Master Suite is topped by a deep tray ceiling, has a large walk-in closet, an extravagant private Bath and direct access to back Porch

MAIN FLOOR — 1,912 SQ. FT.
GARAGE — 580 SQ. FT.
BONUS — 398 SQ. FT.

TOTAL LIVING AREA:
1,912 SQ. FT.

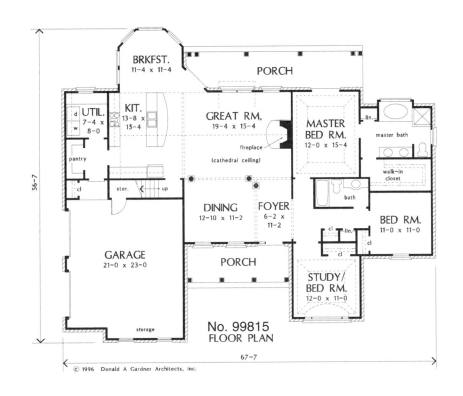

No. 99815
FLOOR PLAN

© 1996 Donald A Gardner Architects, Inc.

To order your Blueprints, call 1-800-235-5700

Design by
Design Basics, Inc.

© 1987 design basics inc.

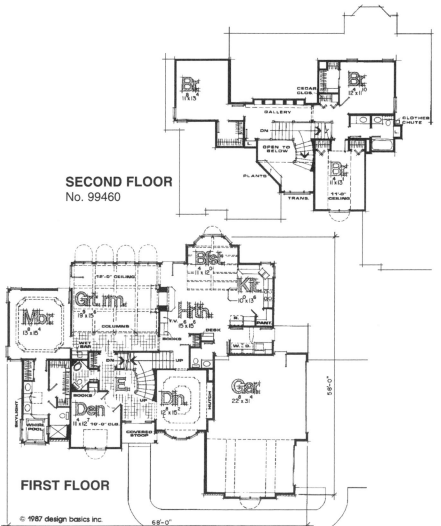

SECOND FLOOR
No. 99460

FIRST FLOOR

© 1987 design basics inc.

Stately Lines Allude to Elegance

■ This plan features:

— Four bedrooms

— Two full and one half baths

■ The dynamic entry views the Den, formal Dining Room and curved stairway

■ French doors access the Den topped by a volume ceiling

■ A unique ceiling detail and outdoor access highlight the bayed Dinette

■ The Kitchen features an island, a walk-in Pantry and an abundance of counter space with built-ins

■ The Master Bedroom has well placed bright windows and a decorative ceiling treatment

FIRST FLOOR — 2,040 SQ. FT.
SECOND FLOOR — 927 SQ. FT.

TOTAL LIVING AREA:
2,967 SQ. FT.

Design by
Fillmore Design Group

Refer to **Pricing Schedule E** on the order form for pricing information

Room for All

■ This plan features:

— Four bedrooms

— Three full and one half baths

■ The Master Bath includes a whirlpool tub and a divided walk-in closet

■ French door open into the Study/Living room, which includes a hard wood floor

■ A vaulted ceiling and a decorative window highlight the Dining Room

■ The Great Room overlooks the rear Patio and is warmed by a fireplace

■ No materials list is available for this plan

MAIN FLOOR — 2,039 SQ. FT.
UPPER FLOOR — 978 SQ. FT.
BONUS — 234 SQ. FT.
GARAGE — 738 SQ. FT.

TOTAL LIVING AREA:
3,017 SQ. FT.

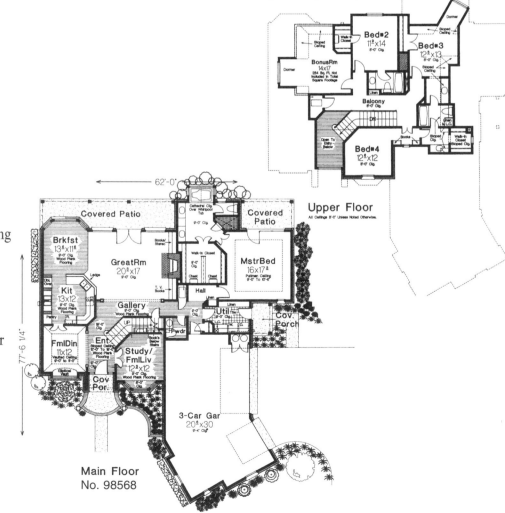

Upper Floor

Main Floor
No. 98568

To order your Blueprints, call 1-800-235-5700

Refer to **Pricing Schedule D** on the order form for pricing information

Design by
Studer Residential Design, Inc.

TOTAL LIVING AREA:
2,205 SQ. FT.

Bedroom
11' x 13'2"

Master Bedroom
12'6" x 16'

Bath

walk-in closet

Hall

Bath

stairs dn

Bedroom
12'8" x 11'1"

SECOND FLOOR
No. 92675

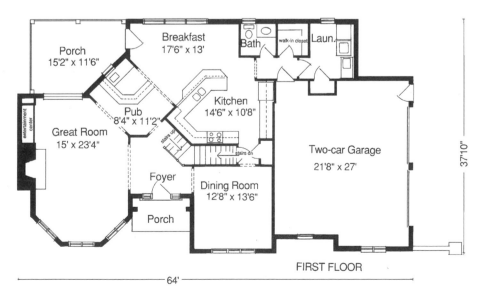

Porch
15'2" x 11'6"

Breakfast
17'6" x 13'

Bath

walk-in closet

Laun.

entertainment center

Great Room
15' x 23'4"

Pub
8'4" x 11'2"

Kitchen
14'6" x 10'8"

stairs up

stairs dn

Two-car Garage
21'8" x 27'

Foyer

Dining Room
12'8" x 13'6"

Porch

37'10"

64'

FIRST FLOOR

Detailed Brick and Fieldstone Facade

■ This plan features:

— Three bedrooms

— Two full and one half baths

■ Open Foyer enhanced by a graceful, banister staircase

■ Great Room highlighted by a twelve foot ceiling, an alcove of windows, fireplace, built-in entertainment center and Porch access

■ Spacious Kitchen and Breakfast Area with extended counter/snackbar and nearby Pub

■ Comfortable Master Bedroom with a large walk-in closet and double vanity Bath

■ Two additional Bedrooms share a double vanity Bath

■ No materials list is available for this plan

FIRST FLOOR — 1,192 SQ. FT.
SECOND FLOOR — 1,013 SQ. FT.
BASEMENT — 1,157 SQ. FT.

Design by
Fillmore Design Group

Refer to **Pricing Schedule F** on
the order form for pricing information

Luxurious One Floor Living

TOTAL LIVING AREA:
3,254 SQ. FT.

■ This plan features:

— Four bedrooms

— Three full baths

■ Decorative windows enhance front entrance of elegant home

■ Formal Living Room accented by fireplace between windows overlooking rear yard

■ Formal Dining Room highlighted by decorative window

■ Breakfast bar, work island, and an abundance of storage and counter space featured in Kitchen

■ Bright alcove for informal Dining and Family Room with access to covered Patio adjoin Kitchen

■ Spacious Master Bedroom with access to covered Patio, a lavish bath and huge walk-in closet

■ No materials list is available for this plan

MAIN FLOOR — 3,254 SQ. FT.
GARAGE — 588 SQ. FT.

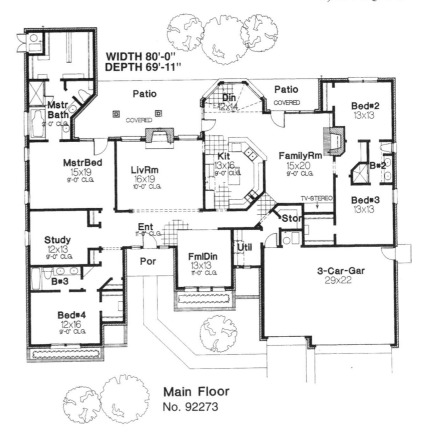

WIDTH 80'-0"
DEPTH 69'-11"

Mstr Bath

Patio COVERED

Din 12x14

Patio COVERED

Bed#2 13x13

MstrBed 15x19 9'-0" CLG.

LivRm 16x19 10'-0" CLG.

Kit 13x16 9'-0" CLG.

FamilyRm 15x20 9'-0" CLG.

B#2

TV-STEREO

Bed#3 13x13

Study 12x13 9'-0" CLG.

Ent 11'-0" CLG.

Stor

Por

FmlDin 13x13 11'-0" CLG.

Util

3-Car-Gar 29x22

B#3

Bed#4 12x16 9'-0" CLG.

Main Floor
No. 92273

Design by
Donald A. Gardner Architects, Inc.

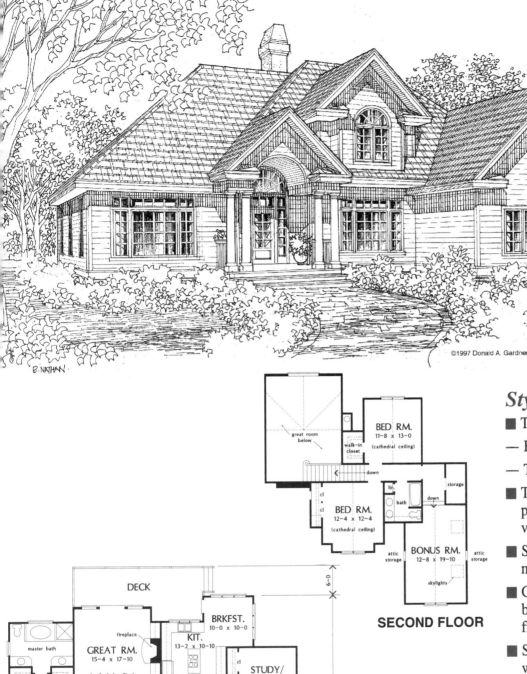

©1997 Donald A. Gardner Architects, Inc.

B. NATHAN

SECOND FLOOR

great room below

BED RM.
11-8 x 13-0
(cathedral ceiling)

walk-in closet

down

BED RM.
12-4 x 12-4
(cathedral ceiling)

lin.

bath

storage

down

attic storage

BONUS RM.
12-8 x 19-10

attic storage

skylights

FIRST FLOOR
No. 96494

© 1997 Donald A Gardner Architects, Inc.

DECK

master bath

walk-in closet

walk-in closet

GREAT RM.
15-4 x 17-10
(cathedral ceiling)

fireplace

BRKFST.
10-0 x 10-0

KIT.
13-2 x 10-10

STUDY/
BED RM.
11-8 x 12-0

MASTER
BED RM.
13-0 x 16-0

up

UTIL.

w
d

bath

storage

FOYER
6-6 x
8-1

DINING
12-4 x 12-4

PORCH

GARAGE
21-0 x 20-8

6-0

49-4

59-2

Style and Versatility

■ This plan features:

— Four Bedrooms

— Three full baths

■ Traditional hip roof arched and picture windows, and a barrel vaulted entrance

■ Stunning Great Room with magnificent cathedral ceiling

■ Cozy fireplace with space saving built-ins shields the Great Room from Kitchen noise

■ Secluded Master Suite with twin walk-in closets and a stately tray ceiling in the Bedroom

■ Cathedral ceiling enhances both Bedrooms on the second floor

■ First floor Study/Bedroom providing ample flexibility

FIRST FLOOR — 1,687 SQ. FT.
SECOND FLOOR — 514 SQ. FT.
BONUS — 336 SQ. FT.
GARAGE — 489 SQ. FT.

TOTAL LIVING AREA:
2,201 SQ. FT.

Design by
Fillmore Design Group

Refer to **Pricing Schedule D** on
the order form for pricing information

Easy Street

■ This plan features:

— Four bedrooms

— Two full and one half baths

■ This home offers privacy by
using a split-bedroom floor plan

■ The Master Suite features a
whirlpool Bath and a vaulted
ceiling over the Bedroom

■ The Entry, Gallery, Kitchen,
Dining Room, Powder Room,
Utility Room and secondary Bath
have tiled floors

■ The formal Dining and Living
Rooms adjoin and are enhanced
by the bay window featured at
the front of the house

■ The fireplaced Family Room and
Dining Room are adjoined

■ No materials list is available for
this plan

MAIN FLOOR — 2,370 SQ. FT.
GARAGE — 638 SQ. FT.

TOTAL LIVING AREA:
2,370 SQ. FT.

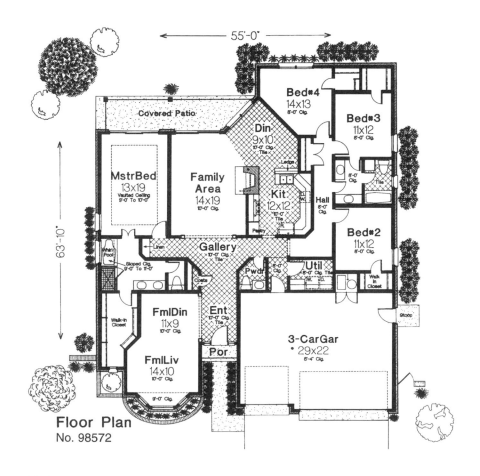

Floor Plan
No. 98572

To order your Blueprints, call 1-800-235-5700

Design by
Frank Betz Associates, Inc.

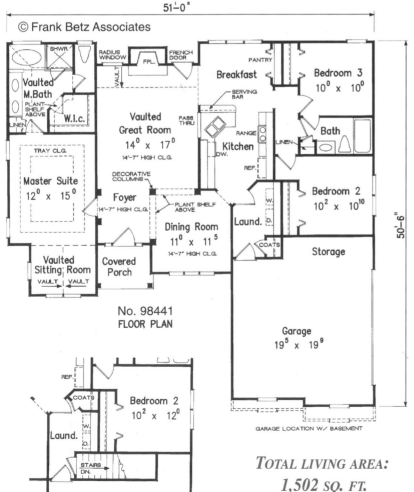

© Frank Betz Associates

51'-0"

50'-6"

Vaulted M.Bath

SHWR.

RADIUS WINDOW

FPL.

FRENCH DOOR

PANTRY

Breakfast

Bedroom 3
10⁰ x 10⁰

PLANT SHELF ABOVE

W.I.c.

LINEN

Vaulted Great Room
14⁰ x 17⁰
14'-7" HIGH CLG.

PASS THRU

SERVING BAR

Kitchen

RANGE

DW.

Bath

LINEN

REF.

TRAY CLG.

Master Suite
12⁰ x 15⁰

DECORATIVE COLUMNS

Foyer
14'-7" HIGH CLG.

PLANT SHELF ABOVE

Bedroom 2
10² x 10¹⁰

Dining Room
11⁰ x 11⁵
14'-7" HIGH CLG.

Laund.
W. D.

COATS

Vaulted Sitting Room
VAULT   VAULT

Covered Porch

Storage

No. 98441
FLOOR PLAN

Garage
19⁵ x 19⁹

REF.

COATS

Bedroom 2
10² x 12⁰

Laund.

W. D.

STAIRS DN.

GARAGE LOCATION W/ BASEMENT

OPT. BASEMENT STAIR LOCATION

TOTAL LIVING AREA:
1,502 SQ. FT.

High Ceilings and Arched Windows

■ This plan features:

— Three bedrooms

— Two full baths

■ Natural illumination streams into the Dining Room and Sitting Area through large, arched windows

■ Kitchen with pass through to the Great Room and a serving bar for the Breakfast Room

■ Great Room topped by a vaulted ceiling accented by a fireplace

■ Decorative columns accent the entrance of the Dining Room

■ Tray ceiling in the Master Suite and a vaulted ceiling over the sitting room and the Master Bath

■ No materials list is available for this plan

■ An optional basement or crawl space foundation — please specify when ordering

MAIN FLOOR — 1,502 SQ. FT.
GARAGE — 448 SQ. FT.
BASEMENT — 1,555 SQ. FT.

Design by
Sun-Tel

Refer to **Pricing Schedule B** on
the order form for pricing information

Carefree Comfort

■ This plan features:

— Three bedrooms

— Two full baths

■ A dramatic vaulted Foyer

■ A range top island Kitchen with a sunny eating Nook surrounded by a built-in planter

■ A vaulted ceiling in the Great Room with a built-in bar and corner fireplace

■ A bayed Dining Room that combines with the Great Room for a spacious feeling

■ A Master Bedroom with a private reading nook, vaulted ceiling, walk-in closet, and a well appointed private Bath

■ Two additional Bedrooms share a full hall Bath

■ An optional basement, slab or crawl space foundation— please specify when ordering

MAIN AREA — 1,665 SQ. FT.

TOTAL LIVING AREA:
1,665 SQ. FT.

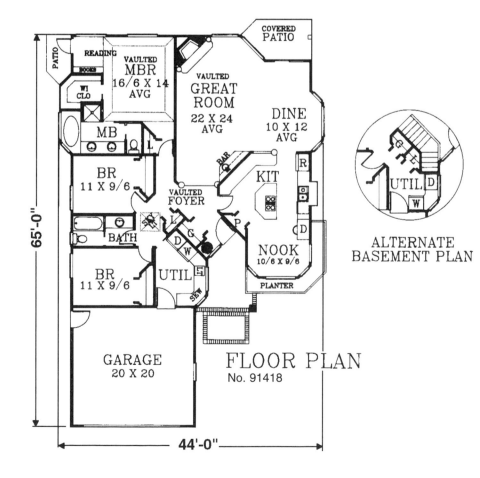

ALTERNATE
BASEMENT PLAN

FLOOR PLAN
No. 91418

Columns and Arches

- This plan features:
  — Three bedrooms
  — Two full and one half baths
- The open layout for Great Room and Kitchen provides a comfortable and relaxed living space
- Utility Room and Garage entry are convenient to the Kitchen
- The Dining Room is enhanced by a decorative ceiling
- Private Master Bedroom offers a vaulted ceiling, walk-in closet and comfortable Bath
- Two additional Bedrooms, a Home Office, Loft Area and full Bath share the second floor
- No materials list is available for this plan

FIRST FLOOR — 1,194 SQ. FT.
SECOND FLOOR — 876 SQ. FT.
BASEMENT — 1,194 SQ. FT.
GARAGE — 736 SQ. FT.

TOTAL LIVING AREA:
2,070 SQ. FT.

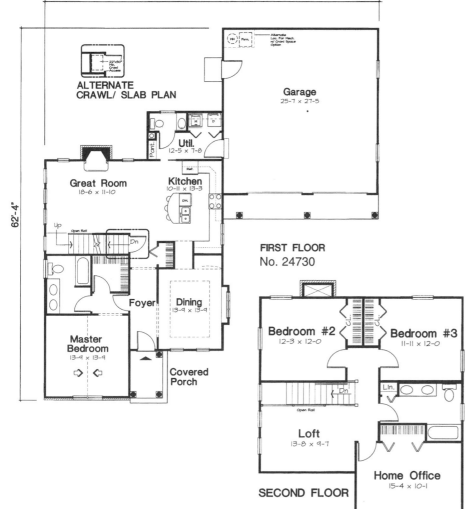

56'-0"

62'-4"

ALTERNATE CRAWL/ SLAB PLAN

Garage
25-7 x 27-5

Util.
12-5 x 7-8

Great Room
18-6 x 11-10

Kitchen
10-11 x 13-3

Up

Open Rail

Dn

FIRST FLOOR
No. 24730

Foyer

Dining
13-9 x 13-9

Master Bedroom
13-4 x 13-9

Covered Porch

Bedroom #2
12-3 x 12-0

Bedroom #3
11-11 x 12-0

Dn

Open Rail

Loft
13-8 x 9-7

Home Office
15-4 x 10-1

SECOND FLOOR

Design by
Donald A. Gardner Architects, Inc.

Refer to **Pricing Schedule D** on the order form for pricing information

© 1998 Donald A. Gardner, Inc.

Classic Cottage

■ This plan features:

— Three bedrooms

— Two full and one half baths

■ An economic design for a narrow lot

■ Twin dormers and a gabled Garage provide substantial curb appeal

■ Dramatic Great Room enhanced by two clerestory dormers and a balcony

■ Crowned in an elegant tray ceiling, the first floor Master Suite has a private Bath and a walk-in closet

FIRST FLOOR — 1,336 SQ. FT.
SECOND FLOOR — 523 SQ. FT.
GARAGE & STORAGE — 492 SQ. FT.
BONUS ROOM — 225 SQ. FT.

TOTAL LIVING AREA:
1,859 SQ. FT.

SECOND FLOOR

attic storage

great room below

railing

attic storage

BED RM.
13-0 x 11-0

down

lin.

bath

down

BED RM.
11-0 x 12-0

cl   cl

foyer below

cl   cl

attic storage

BONUS RM.
11-0 x 16-8

attic storage

PORCH

DINING
11-0 x 10-0

MASTER BED RM.
13-0 x 15-0

GREAT RM.
19-0 x 17-0

fireplace

(cathedral ceiling)

KIT.
11-0 x 13-0

pan.

master bath

lin.

pd. rm.

lin.

d

UTIL.
9-1 x 5-8

w

storage

FOYER
6-0 x 11-11

cl

up

walk-in closet

GARAGE
21-0 x 21-0

PORCH

53-0

FIRST FLOOR
No. 98014

45-0

© 1998 Donald A Gardner, Inc.

To order your Blueprints, call 1-800-235-5700

Design by
Garrell Associates, Inc.

P L A N   N O .   9 3 6 0 9

GRAND ROOM
BELOW

W.I.C.

M. BATH

MASTER
BEDROOM
13'-3" x 18'-9"

SITTING
9'-9" x 11'-11"

BEDROOM 4
10'-7" x 12'-0"

FOYER
BELOW

B#2

BEDROOM 3
11'-5" x 10'-6"

SECOND FLOOR PLAN

BEDROOM 2
13'-3" x 10'-40"

54'-0"

GRAND ROOM
19'-7" x 14'-11"

KITCHEN

BREAKFAST

KEEPING
ROOM
13'-3" x 18'-3"

45'-4"

STUDY OR
LIVING ROOM
12'-7" x 12'-0"

FOYER

DINING
11'-11" x 13'-0"

PWDR

LAUNDRY

KITCHEN

OPTION KITCHEN

FIRST FLOOR PLAN
No. 93609

TWO CAR GARAGE

Ideal Family Home

■ This plan features:

— Four bedrooms

— Two full and one half baths

■ Inside, from the two-story Foyer
enter either the Living Room or
the Dining Room

■ In the rear of the home there is
the Grand Room and the Keeping
Room, both with fireplaces

■ The L-shaped Kitchen has a
center island and is open to the
Breakfast Nook

■ Upstairs, the Master Bedroom has
a decorative ceiling and a huge
walk-in closet

■ An optional basement or slab
foundation — please specify
when ordering

■ No materials list is available for
this plan

FIRST FLOOR — 1,534 SQ. FT.
SECOND FLOOR — 1,236 SQ. FT.
GARAGE — 418 SQ. FT.

TOTAL LIVING AREA:
2,771 SQ. FT.

Design by
Fillmore Design Group

Essence of Style & Grace

■ This plan features:

— Four bedrooms

— Three full and one half baths

■ French doors introduce the Study

■ Columns define the Gallery and the formal areas

■ The expansive Family Room has an inviting fireplace

■ The first floor Master Bedroom offers a vaulted ceiling and a walk-in closet

■ No materials list is available for this plan

■ An optional basement or slab foundation — please specify when ordering

FIRST FLOOR — 2,036 SQ. FT.
SECOND FLOOR — 866 SQ. FT.
GARAGE — 720 SQ. FT.

TOTAL LIVING AREA:
2,902 SQ. FT.

SECOND FLOOR

Bed#4 12x15

Bed#3 12x12

Bed#2 12x10
SLOPE CLNG. TO 9'-0"

BALCONY

OPEN TO ENTRY BELOW

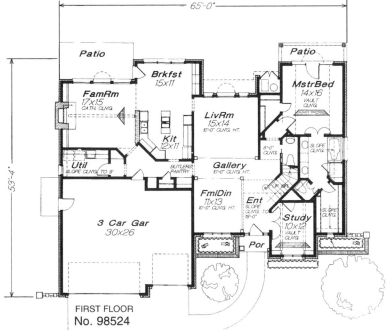

65'-0"

53'-4"

Patio

Brkfst 15x11

FamRm 17x15 CATH. CLNG.

Kit 12x11

Util SLOPE CLNG. TO 9'

3 Car Gar 30x26

LivRm 15x14 10'-0" CLNG. HT.

BUTLERS PANTRY

Gallery 10'-0" CLNG. HT.

FmlDin 11x13 10'-0" CLNG. HT.

Ent SLOPE CLNG. TO 9'-0"

Patio

MstrBed 14x16 VAULT CLNG.

Study 10x12 VAULT CLNG.

Por

FIRST FLOOR
No. 98524

Design by
James Fahy, P.E., P.C.

WIDTH 58'-0"
DEPTH 44'-0"

DIN RM
11'8 x 11'11

KIT
9'8 x 11'7

DIN
8'8 x 11'5

MBR
15'8 x 13'5

MBATH

PANTRY
REF

Dress'g

LIV RM
15' x 13'8

Two-Story
FOYER

Mud Rm/Entry

Lav

WI Closet

W
D
Laun

COUNTER

Covered Entry

GARAGE
21'4 x 21'8

FIRST FLOOR
No. 94105

BR3
11' x 11'7

BATH 2

Foyer Below

BR2
11'4 x 11'11

SECOND FLOOR

TOTAL LIVING AREA:
1,792 SQ. FT.

Classic Style and Comfort

■ This plan features:

— Three bedrooms

— Two full and one half bath

■ Covered Entry leads into two-story Foyer with a dramatic landing staircase brightened by a decorative window

■ Spacious Living/Dining Room combination with hearth fireplace and decorative windows

■ Hub Kitchen with built-in Pantry and informal Dining area with sliding glass door to rear yard

■ First floor Master Bedroom offers a walk-in closet, Dressing Area and a full Bath

■ Two additional Bedrooms on the second floor share a full Bath

■ No materials list is available for this plan

FIRST FLOOR — 1,281 SQ. FT.
SECOND FLOOR — 511 SQ. FT.
GARAGE — 481 SQ. FT.

Design by
Donald A. Gardner Architects, Inc.

Refer to **Pricing Schedule C** on the order form for pricing information

S. NATHAN

© 1990 Donald A. Gardner Architects, Inc.

Compact Three Bedroom

- This plan features:
— Three bedrooms
— Two full baths

- Contemporary interior punctuated by elegant columns

- Dormers above the covered Porch light the Foyer leading to the dramatic Great Room crowned in a cathedral ceiling and enhanced by a fireplace

- Great Room opens to the island Kitchen with Breakfast Area and access to a spacious rear Deck

- Tray ceilings adding interest to the Bedroom/Study, Dining Room and the Master Bedroom

- Luxurious Master Bedroom highlighted by a walk-in closet and a bath with dual vanity, separate shower and a pampering whirlpool tub

MAIN FLOOR — 1,452 SQ. FT.
GARAGE AND STORAGE — 427 SQ. FT.

TOTAL LIVING AREA:
1,452 SQ. FT.

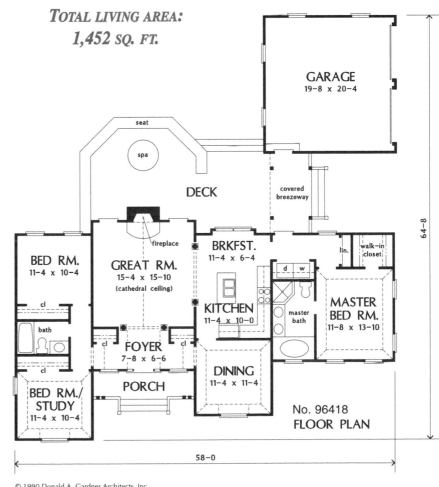

GARAGE
19-8 x 20-4

seat

spa

DECK

covered breezeway

64-8

fireplace

BED RM.
11-4 x 10-4

GREAT RM.
15-4 x 15-10
(cathedral ceiling)

BRKFST.
11-4 x 6-4

lin.   walk-in closet

cl

bath

cl

cl

FOYER
7-8 x 6-6

cl

KITCHEN
11-4 x 10-0

d w

master bath

MASTER BED RM.
11-8 x 13-10

cl

BED RM./ STUDY
11-4 x 10-4

PORCH

DINING
11-4 x 11-4

No. 96418
FLOOR PLAN

58-0

© 1990 Donald A. Gardner Architects, Inc.

To order your Blueprints, call 1-800-235-5700

Design by
Frank Betz Associates, Inc.

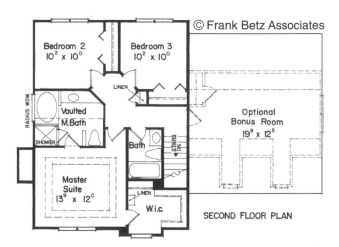

FIRST FLOOR PLAN
No. 98422

45'-10"

35'-6"

FRENCH DOOR

Breakfast

Dining Room
10³ x 10⁰

Kitchen
RANGE

D.W.

PASSTHRU

REF.

PANTRY

Garage
19⁵ x 23⁵

W.
D.

FPL.

Family Room
13⁹ x 18⁸

Pdr.

STAIRS DN.

COATS

Foyer

STAIRS UP

Porch

© Frank Betz Associates

Bedroom 2
10² x 10⁰

Bedroom 3
10² x 10⁰

LINEN

RADIUS WDW.

Vaulted M.Bath

SHOWER

Bath

LINEN

STAIRS DN.

Optional Bonus Room
19⁸ x 12⁵

Master Suite
13⁹ x 12⁰

W.i.c.

SECOND FLOOR PLAN

Covered Porch Shelters Entry

■ This plan features:

— Three bedrooms

— Two full and one half baths

■ There is a convenient pass-through from the Kitchen into the Family Room

■ An easy flow into the Dining Room enhances the interaction of the living spaces

■ A fireplace highlights the spacious Family Room

■ Decorative ceiling treatment in the Master Bedroom

■ An optional basement or crawl space foundation — please specify when ordering

FIRST FLOOR — 719 SQ. FT.
SECOND FLOOR — 717 SQ. FT.
BONUS — 290 SQ. FT.
BASEMENT — 719 SQ. FT.
GARAGE — 480 SQ. FT.

TOTAL LIVING AREA:
1,436 SQ. FT.

Design by
Design Basics, Inc.

Refer to **Pricing Schedule C** on the order form for pricing information

Comfort and Convenience

■ This plan features:

— Three bedrooms

— One full, one three-quarter and one half baths

■ A covered front Porch leads into the tiled Entry

■ The Dining Room features a front alcove with three windows

■ The Great Room is illuminated by a wall of windows

■ The Kitchen shares a snack bar with the Breakfast Nook

■ The Master Bedroom includes a high ceiling and a walk-in closet

FIRST FLOOR — 1,421 SQ. FT.
SECOND FLOOR — 448 SQ. FT.
BASEMENT — 1,421 SQ. FT.
GARAGE — 480 SQ. FT.

TOTAL LIVING AREA:
1,869 SQ. FT.

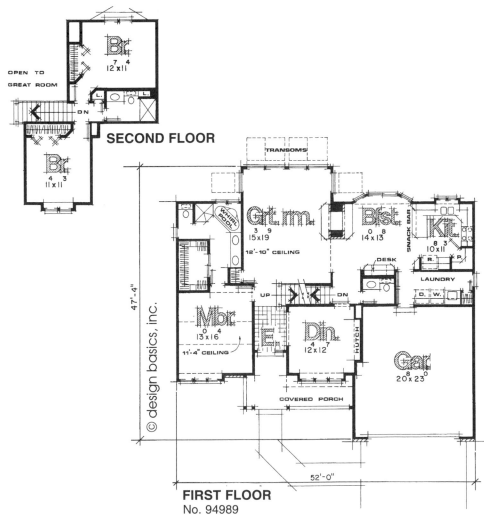

SECOND FLOOR

FIRST FLOOR
No. 94989

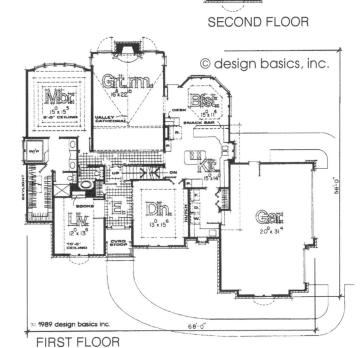

© design basics, inc.

SECOND FLOOR

Br.
11⁰ x 13⁷

Br.
12⁴ x 13¹⁰

Br.
12⁰ x 13³
10'-0"
CEILING

OPEN TO BELOW

VALLEY CATHEDRAL

BALCONY

OPEN TO BELOW

LIN.

TRANS.

Mbr.
15⁰ x 15⁵
9'-0" CEILING

Gt.rm.
16⁰ x 22⁰
VALLEY CATHEDRAL

Bfst.
15⁰ x 11⁶

Kit.
15⁰ x 14⁰

Dn.
13⁰ x 15⁶

Liv.
12⁰ x 13⁶
10'-0" CEILING

Gar.
20⁰ x 31⁴

DESK

SNACK BAR

SKYLIGHT

W/P

SOCKS

CVRD. STOOP

58'-0"

68'-0"

© 1989 design basics inc.

FIRST FLOOR
No. 99461

Magnificent Grandeur

■ This plan features:

— Four bedrooms

— Two full, one three-quarter and one half baths

■ Decorative ceilings and built-ins enhance the Living Room and the Dining Room

■ The island Kitchen serves the Dining Room and the Breakfast Area with equal ease

■ Great Room is topped by a valley cathedral ceiling and highlighted by a fireplace

■ The Master Suite includes a decorative ceiling, a whirlpool tub and separate shower and a walk-in closet

FIRST FLOOR — 1,972 SQ. FT.
SECOND FLOOR — 893 SQ. FT.
GARAGE — 658 SQ. FT.

TOTAL LIVING AREA:
2,865 SQ. FT.

Design by
Donald A. Gardner Architects, Inc.

Refer to **Pricing Schedule D** on the order form for pricing information

Casual Country Charmer

■ This plan features:

— Three bedrooms

— Two full baths

■ Columns and arches frame the front Porch

■ The open floor plan combines the Great Room, Kitchen and Dining Room

■ The Kitchen offers a convenient breakfast bar for meals on the run

■ The Master Suite features a private Bath oasis

■ Secondary Bedrooms share a full Bath with a dual vanity

MAIN FLOOR — 1,770 SQ. FT.
BONUS — 401 SQ. FT.
GARAGE — 630 SQ. FT.

TOTAL LIVING AREA:
1,770 SQ. FT.

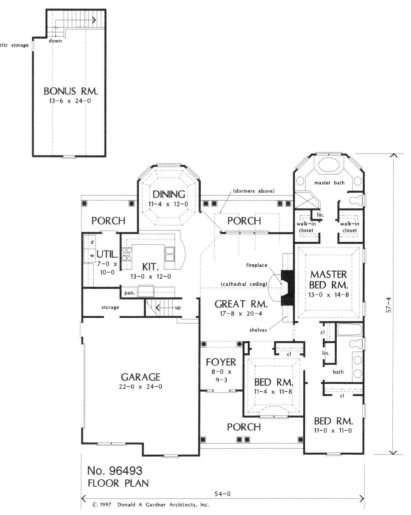

No. 96493
FLOOR PLAN

Refer to **Pricing Schedule E** on the order form for pricing information

Design by
The Garlinghouse Company

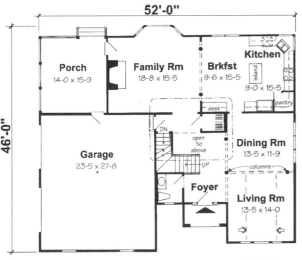

52'-0"

46'-0"

- Porch
  14-0 x 15-9
- Family Rm
  18-8 x 15-5
- Brkfst
  9-6 x 15-5
- Kitchen
  Island
  9-0 x 15-5
- pantry
- desk
- DN
- open to above
- UP
- Garage
  23-5 x 27-8
- Dining Rm
  13-5 x 11-9
- columns
- Foyer
- Living Rm
  13-5 x 14-0

First Floor
No. 24664

- crawl access
- w/h
- fum.

**Crawl Space/
Slab Option**

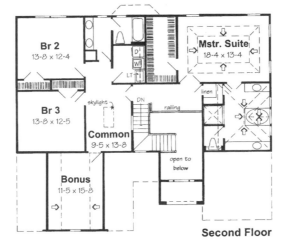

- Br 2
  13-8 x 12-4
- Mstr. Suite
  18-4 x 13-4
- D
- W
- LT
- skylight
- Br 3
  13-8 x 12-5
- DN
- railing
- linen
- Common
  9-5 x 13-8
- open to below
- Bonus
  11-5 x 15-8

Second Floor

Impressive Two-Story Entry

■ This plan features:

— Three bedrooms

— Two full and one half baths

■ Columns, a vaulted ceiling and decorative windows highlight the Living and Dining rooms

■ The open, efficient Kitchen has a corner Pantry and a work island

■ The comfortable Family Room is enhanced by a lovely bay window and a cozy fireplace

■ The private and plush Master Suite offers a walk-in closet, two vanities and a whirlpool tub

■ No materials list is available for this plan

FIRST FLOOR — 1,245 SQ. FT.
SECOND FLOOR — 1,383 SQ. FT.
BONUS — 192 SQ. FT.
BASEMENT — 1,229 SQ. FT.
GARAGE — 667 SQ. FT.

TOTAL LIVING AREA:
2,628 SQ. FT.

Handsome Detailing

■ This plan features:

— Three bedrooms

— Two full and one half baths

■ Handsome detailing unique windows are hallmarks of the front elevation of this design

■ In the entry, a U-shaped staircase with a window leads to a second floor balcony, two Bedrooms and a full Bath

■ Triple arch windows in the front and rear of the Great Room create an impressive view

■ Spacious secondary Bedrooms easily provide room for a desk or toy chest

FIRST FLOOR — 1,314 SQ. FT.
SECOND FLOOR — 458 SQ. FT.
GARAGE — 454 SQ. FT.

TOTAL LIVING AREA:
1,772 SQ. FT.

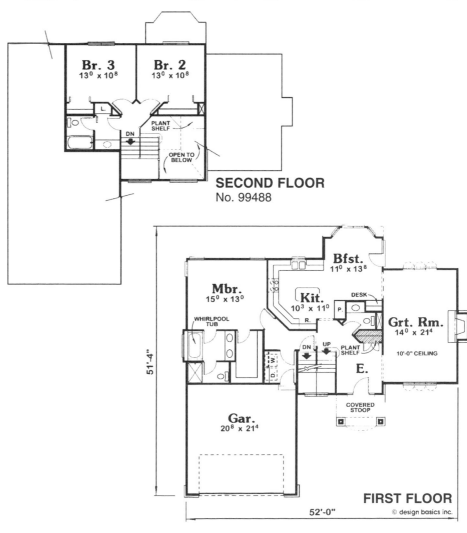

SECOND FLOOR
No. 99488

Br. 3
13^0 x 10^8

Br. 2
13^0 x 10^8

PLANT SHELF

DN

OPEN TO BELOW

FIRST FLOOR
© design basics inc.

Mbr.
15^0 x 13^0

WHIRLPOOL TUB

Bfst.
11^0 x 13^8

Kit.
10^3 x 11^0

DESK

Grt. Rm.
14^0 x 21^4

10'-0" CEILING

DN   UP

PLANT SHELF

E.

COVERED STOOP

Gar.
20^8 x 21^4

51'-4"

52'-0"

Design by
Design Basics, Inc.

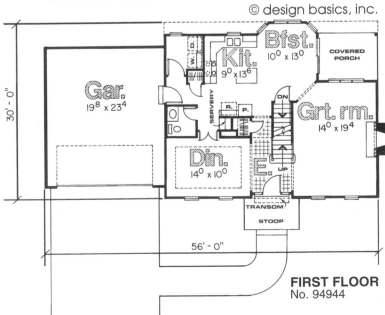

© design basics, inc.

SECOND FLOOR

FIRST FLOOR
No. 94944

Spectacular Sophistication

■ This plan features:

— Four bedrooms

— Two full and one half baths

■ Open Foyer with circular window and a plant shelf leads into the Dining Room

■ Great Room with an inviting fireplace and windows front and back

■ Open Kitchen has a work island and accesses the Breakfast Area

■ Master Bedroom features a nine-foot boxed ceiling, a walk-in closet and whirlpool bath

■ Three additional Bedrooms share a full Bath with a double vanity

FIRST FLOOR — 941 SQ. FT.
SECOND FLOOR — 992 SQ. FT.
BASEMENT — 941 SQ. FT.
GARAGE — 480 SQ. FT.

TOTAL LIVING AREA:
1,933 SQ. FT.

Design by
Larry E. Belk

Refer to **Pricing Schedule E**
on the order form for pricing information

A Classic Design

■ This plan features:

— Four bedrooms

— Two full and one half baths

■ The dramatic arch detail is repeated at the Dining Room entrance

■ The Kitchen, Breakfast Room and Family Room are open to one another

■ The Kitchen has amenities including a walk-in Pantry, double ovens and an eating bar

■ The Master Suite is designed apart from the other Bedrooms for privacy

■ Two Bedrooms share a Bath and have walk-in closets

■ No materials list is available for this plan

Main floor — 2,678 sq. ft
Garage — 474 sq. ft.

Total living area:
_2,678 sq. ft._

© Larry E. Belk

MAIN FLOOR
No. 96600

WIDTH 70–2

To order your Blueprints, call 1-800-235-5700

Refer to **Pricing Schedule C** on the order form for pricing information

Design by
Design Basics, Inc.

© design basics, inc.

FIRST FLOOR
No. 94906

SECOND FLOOR

Brick Accents and Dormer Windows

■ This plan features:

— Four bedrooms

— Two full and one half baths

■ A detailed Covered Porch leads into easy-care Entry

■ Formal Dining Room welcomes guests with decorative windows

■ A well integrated Family Room, Kitchen and Breakfast area accommodate many family activities

■ A private Master Bedroom accented by a transom window and plush Bath with a whirlpool tub

■ Three secondary Bedrooms share a full Bath and an unfinished Storage Room

FIRST FLOOR — 1,348 SQ. FT.
SECOND FLOOR — 609 SQ. FT.
STORAGE ROOM — 341 SQ. FT.
BASEMENT — 1,348 SQ. FT.
GARAGE — 566 SQ. FT.

TOTAL LIVING AREA:
1,957 SQ. FT.

Design by
Donald A. Gardner Architects, Inc.

ЯR

Refer to **Pricing Schedule C** on the order form for pricing information

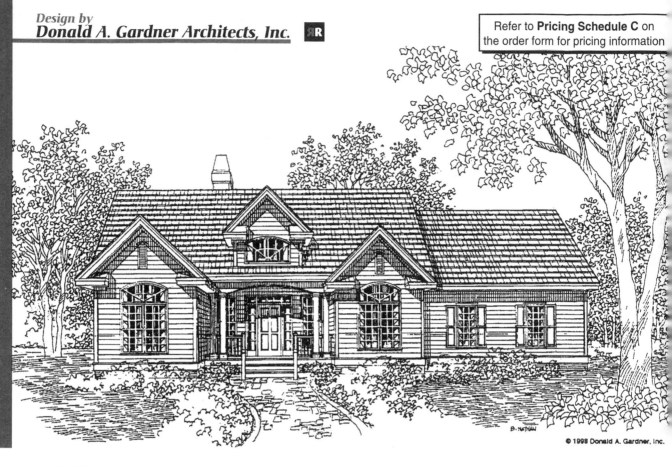

B. NATHAN

© 1998 Donald A. Gardner, Inc.

Economical Three Bedroom

■ This plan features:

— Three bedrooms

— Two full baths

■ Three bold gables, arched windows and columns frame the entrance to this home

■ From the covered Porch enter the Foyer that is brightened by windows beside the door

■ The Foyer is separated from the Great Room by columns

■ The Great Room has a fireplace and a cathedral ceiling with skylights

■ The Kitchen is conveniently arranged and has a vaulted ceiling

■ No materials list is available for this plan

MAIN FLOOR — 1,411 SQ. FT.
BONUS ROOM — 330 SQ. FT.
GARAGE — 481 SQ. FT.

TOTAL LIVING AREA:
1,411 SQ. FT.

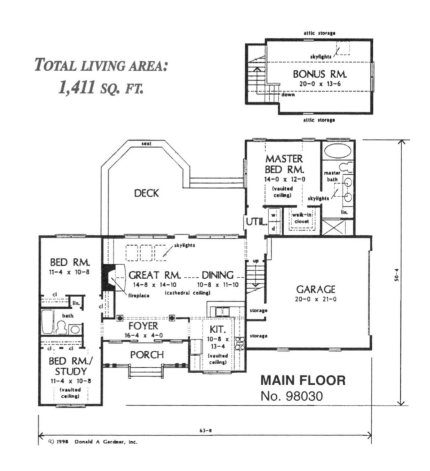

204

To order your Blueprints, call 1-800-235-5700

Design by
Frank Betz Associates, Inc.

© Frank Betz Associates

50'-0"
55'-4"

Master Suite
17⁵ x 14⁴
TRAY CEILING

Vaulted Great Room
19³ x 18⁷
16'-0" HIGH CEILING

VAULT

FPL.

FRENCH DOOR   RADIUS WDW.

ARCHED OPENING

Dining Room
11⁸ x 11⁰
VAULT   VAULT

SERVING BAR

DECORATIVE COLUMNS

DW.   RANGE

ISLAND

REF.

Kitchen

SHWR.

Vaulted M.Bath
K.S.

PLANT SHELF ABOVE

LINEN

W.i.c.

ARCHED OPENINGS

PAN.

Breakfast
TRAY CLG.

Bedroom 2
12⁰ x 11⁰

W.i.c.

COATS

Foyer
16'-0" HIGH CLG.

Pwdr. Laund.
W.
D.

Storage

LINEN

VLT.   VLT.

Bedroom 3
11¹⁰ x 10⁹

Garage
21⁵ x 20³

Bath

RADIUS WDW.

Main floor
No. 98430

GARAGE LOCATION W/ BASEMENT

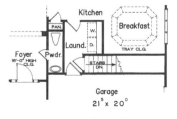

Kitchen

PAN.

W.
D.

Laund.

Breakfast
TRAY CLG.

Foyer
16'-0" HIGH CLG.

Pwdr.

STAIRS DN.

Garage
21⁵ x 20⁰

OPT. BASEMENT STAIRS LOCATION

MAIN FLOOR — 1,884 SQ. FT.
BASEMENT — 1,908 SQ. FT.
GARAGE — 495 SQ. FT.

TOTAL LIVING AREA:
1,884 SQ. FT.

With All the Amenities

■ This plan features:
— Three bedrooms
— Two full and one half baths

■ Sixteen foot high ceiling over the Foyer

■ Arched openings highlight the hallway accessing the fireplaced Great Room

■ French door to the rear yard and decorative columns at its arched entrance

■ Vaulted ceiling in Dining Room

■ Expansive Kitchen features a center work island, a built-in Pantry and a Breakfast Area defined by a tray ceiling

■ Master Suite has a tray ceiling, lavish Bath and a walk-in closet

■ Secondary Bedrooms have private access to a full Bath

■ An optional basement, slab or crawl space foundation — please specify when ordering

Design by
Donald A. Gardner Architects, Inc.

Refer to **Pricing Schedule D** on
the order form for pricing information

© 1997 Donald A. Gardner Architects, Inc.

Perfect Home for Narrow Lot

■ This plan features:

— Three bedrooms

— Two full and one half baths

■ Wraparound Porch and two-car Garage features unusual for narrow lot floor plan

■ Alcove of windows and columns add distinction to Dining Room

■ Cathedral ceiling above inviting fireplace accent spacious Great Room

■ Efficient Kitchen with peninsula counter accesses side Porch and Deck

■ Master suite on first floor and two additional Bedrooms and Bonus Room on second floor

FIRST FLOOR — 1,219 SQ. FT.
SECOND FLOOR — 450 SQ. FT.
BONUS ROOM — 406 SQ. FT.
GARAGE — 473 SQ. FT.

TOTAL LIVING AREA:
1,669 SQ. FT.

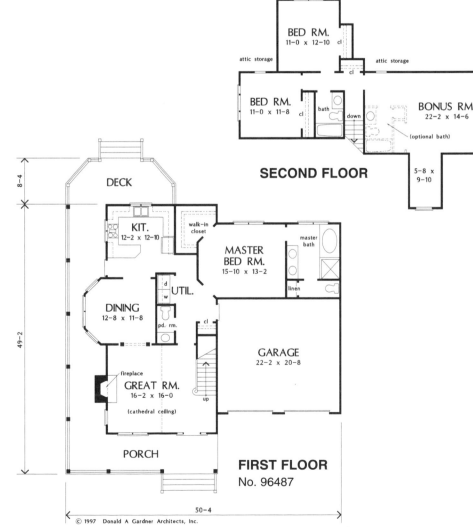

SECOND FLOOR

BED RM.
11-0 x 12-10

attic storage

BED RM.
11-0 x 11-8

bath

down

BONUS RM.
22-2 x 14-6

(optional bath)

attic storage

5-8 x 9-10

FIRST FLOOR
No. 96487

DECK

KIT.
12-2 x 12-10

walk-in closet

MASTER BED RM.
15-10 x 13-2

master bath

linen

DINING
12-8 x 11-8

UTIL.

pd. rm.

fireplace

GREAT RM.
16-2 x 16-0

(cathedral ceiling)

up

GARAGE
22-2 x 20-8

PORCH

8-4

49-2

50-4

© 1997 Donald A Gardner Architects, Inc.

To order your Blueprints, call 1-800-235-5700

Design by
Frank Betz Associates, Inc.

WIDTH 50'-4"
DEPTH 45'-0"

© Frank Betz Associates

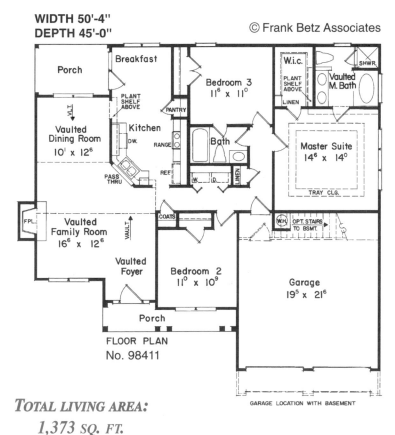

FLOOR PLAN
No. 98411

TOTAL LIVING AREA:
1,373 SQ. FT.

GARAGE LOCATION WITH BASEMENT

Style and Convenience

■ This plan features:

— Three bedrooms

— Two full baths

■ Large front windows, dormers and an old-fashioned Porch add a pleasing style

■ A vaulted ceiling tops the Foyer

■ A Formal Dining Room flows from the Family Room crowned in an elegant vaulted ceiling

■ The efficient Kitchen is enhanced by a pantry and direct access to the Dining Room and Breakfast Room

■ A decorative tray ceiling, a five-piece private Bath and a walk-in closet in the Master Suite

■ An optional basement or crawl space foundation — please specify when ordering

MAIN FLOOR — 1,373 SQ. FT.
BASEMENT — 1,386 SQ. FT.

Design by
Fillmore Design Group

Refer to **Pricing Schedule C** on the order form for pricing information

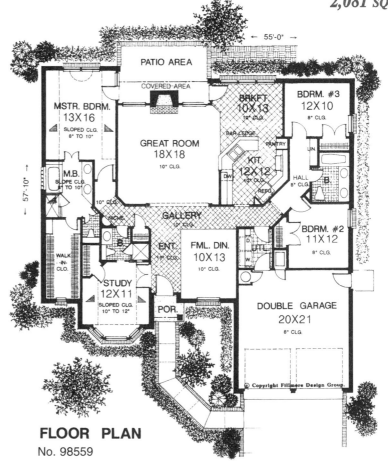

Packed with Options

■ This plan features:

— Three bedrooms

— Three full baths

■ This home has a tiled Entry and Gallery that connects the living space

■ The Great Room has a rear wall fireplace that is set between windows

■ Both Dining Areas are located steps away from the Kitchen

■ The Study has a sloped ceiling and a front bay of windows

■ The Master Bedroom has a private Bath and a galley-like walk- in closet

■ Two secondary Bedrooms are on the opposite side of the home

■ No materials list is available for this plan

MAIN FLOOR — 2,081 SQ. FT.
GARAGE — 422 SQ. FT.

TOTAL LIVING AREA:
2,081 SQ. FT.

FLOOR PLAN
No. 98559

To order your Blueprints, call 1-800-235-5700

Design by
Design Basics, Inc.

© design basics inc.

Stately Elevation

■ This plan features:

— Four bedrooms

— Three full and one half baths

■ The stateliness of this home is evident from the covered stoop with transom

■ Once inside the tiled entry turn right into the Dining Room which features a decorative ceiling

■ The Great Room is the center of the home and has a fireplace with windows beside it

■ The secluded Master Bedroom has a tray ceiling, a walk in closet, a private covered Porch, and a Bath

■ Three additional Bedrooms on the other side of the home share two full Baths

MAIN FLOOR — 2,655 SQ. FT.
BASEMENT — 2,655 SQ. FT.
GARAGE — 695 SQ. FT.

TOTAL LIVING AREA:
2,655 SQ. FT.

MAIN FLOOR

No. 99448

© design basics inc.

72' - 8"

66' - 8"

Bfst. 12⁰ x 13⁴
11'-0" CLG.

TRANSOMS

COVERED PORCH

Br. 2 12⁰ x 12⁰

Grt. rm. 16⁰ x 20⁰
11'-0" CEILING

SNACK BAR

Kit. 14⁰ x 13⁴

Mbr. 17⁰ x 16⁰
11'-0" CEILING

Br. 3 12⁰ x 12⁰

Din. 12⁰ x 16⁰
9'-6" CLG.

Br. 4 12⁰ x 14⁰
OPTIONAL DEN 10'-0" CEILING

COVERED STOOP

Gar. 22⁰ x 31⁰

Design by
Design Basics, Inc.

Refer to **Pricing Schedule F** on the order form for pricing information

A Streamlined Design

■ This plan features:

— Three bedrooms

— One full, one three-quarter and two half bath

■ Recessed, glass arched entrance leads into unique Entry and Living Room with alcove access to Covered Porch

■ Dining Room with triple arch window adjoins Living Room

■ Ideal Kitchen with a walk-in Pantry and work island

■ Open Family Room with a cozy fireplace and lots of windows

■ Master Bedroom wing offers an alcove of windows, two walk-in closets and a luxurious Bath

■ No materials list is available for this plan

MAIN FLOOR — 3,312 SQ. FT.
GARAGE — 752 SQ. FT.

TOTAL LIVING AREA:
3,312 SQ. FT.

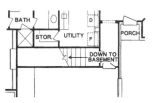

BASEMENT STAIR OPTION

© Carmichael & Dame

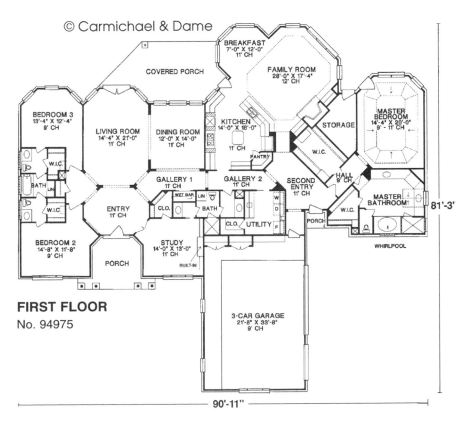

FIRST FLOOR
No. 94975

To order your Blueprints, call 1-800-235-5700

TOTAL LIVING AREA:
1,911 SQ. FT.

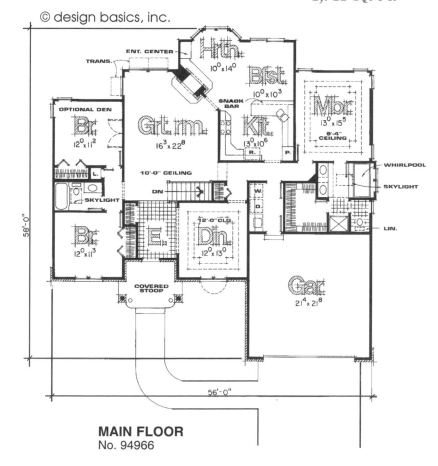

© design basics, inc.

MAIN FLOOR
No. 94966

Beautiful Arched Window

■ This plan features:

— Three bedrooms

— Two full baths

■ Ten foot ceilings top the Entry and the Great Room

■ Breakfast Room and Hearth Room are in an open layout and share a see-through fireplace

■ Built-in Pantry and corner sinks enhance efficiency in the Kitchen

■ Split bedroom plan assures home-owner's privacy in the Master Suite which includes a decorative ceiling, private Bath and large walk-in closet

■ Two additional Bedrooms at the opposite side of the home share a full, skylit Bath in the hall

MAIN FLOOR — 1,911 SQ. FT.
GARAGE — 481 SQ. FT.

Design by
Design Basics, Inc.

Refer to **Pricing Schedule F** on the order form for pricing information

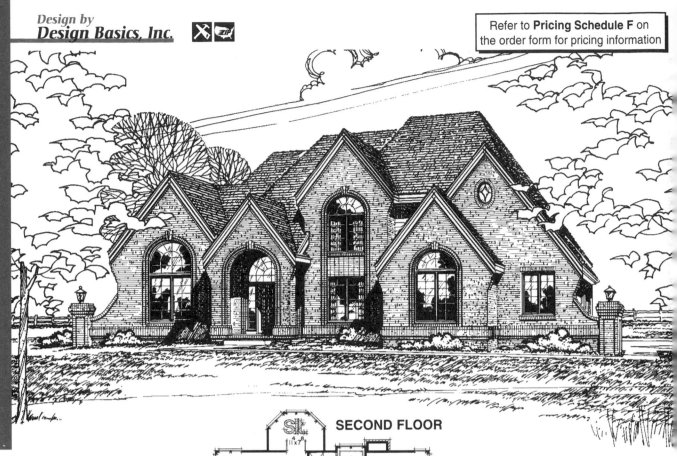

Glorious Gables

■ This plan features:

— Four bedrooms

— Two full, one three-quarter and one half baths

■ Arched windows and entry lead to tiled Entry with cascading staircase

■ Arched ceiling topping Living and Dining room

■ Double door leads into quiet Library with book shelves

■ Hub Kitchen with angled, work island/snackbar, built-in Pantry and desk

■ Comfortable Family Room with hearth fireplace

■ Private Master Bedroom suite offers a Sitting Area

FIRST FLOOR — 1,709 SQ. FT.
SECOND FLOOR — 1,597 SQ. FT.
GARAGE — 721 SQ. FT.
BASEMENT — 1,709 SQ. FT.

TOTAL LIVING AREA:
3,306 SQ. FT.

SECOND FLOOR

FIRST FLOOR
No. 94933

© design basics, inc.

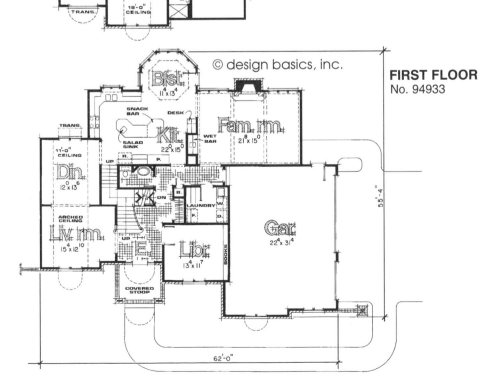

Design by
Studer Residential Design, Inc.

Master
Bedroom
12' x 15'4"

slope ceiling / slope ceiling

Bedroom
10' x 12'

Bedroom
10' x 12'

Dressing

Bath

wood rail   stairs dn   linen

Foyer
Below

Bedroom
11'10" x 10'3"

plant shelf

walk-in closet

SECOND FLOOR

hanging
space

Laun.
7'10"
x 9'3"

Breakfast
10'10" x 12' 3"

walk-in
closet

Kitchen
13'8" x 15'1"   wet bar

pantry

Bath

Great Room
13'10" x 19'8"

butler's
pantry

stairs dn   stairs up

wood rail

41'10"

Two-car Garage
23' x 21'10"

Dining Room
11'10" x 12'8"

Foyer

high ceiling

slope
ceiling

FIRST FLOOR
No. 92638

61'2"

Friendly Front Porch

■ This plan features:

— Four bedrooms

— Two full and one half baths

■ Central Foyer with a graceful
staircase, opens to formal Dining
Room and expansive Great Room

■ Inviting fireplace and front to
back windows in the Great Room

■ L-shaped Kitchen with work
island/snackbar and Butler's
Pantry easily serves Dining
Room and Breakfast Bay

■ Nearby Laundry Room, walk-in
closet and Garage entry add to
Kitchen efficiency

■ Corner Master Bedroom accented
by a slope ceiling, Dressing Area
and walk-in closet

■ No materials list is available for
this plan

FIRST FLOOR — 1,199 SQ. FT.
SECOND FLOOR — 1,060 SQ. FT.

TOTAL LIVING AREA:
2,259 SQ. FT.

Design by
Patrick Morabito A.I.A.

Refer to **Pricing Schedule C** on the order form for pricing information

Conventional and Classic Comfort

■ This plan features:

— Three bedrooms

— Two full and one half baths

■ Porch accesses two-story Foyer with decorative window and a landing staircase

■ Formal Dining Room accented by a recessed window

■ Spacious Family Room crowned by a vaulted ceiling over a hearth fireplace

■ Efficient Kitchen with an extended counter and bright Dinette area with bay window

■ First floor Master Bedroom has a walk-in closet and Master Bath

■ Two additional Bedrooms and a full Bath complete second floor

■ No materials list is available for this plan

FIRST FLOOR — 1,454 SQ. FT.
SECOND FLOOR — 507 SQ. FT.
BASEMENT — 1,454 SQ. FT.
GARAGE — 624 SQ. FT.

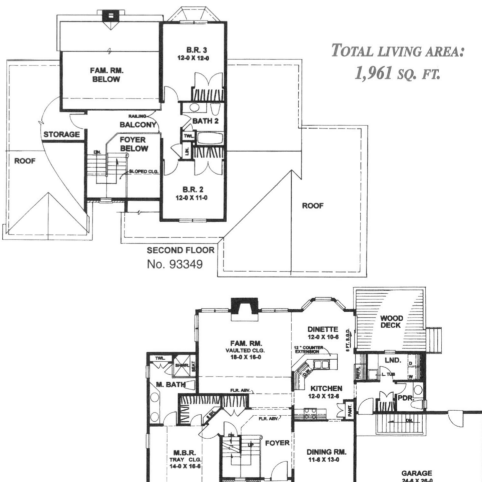

TOTAL LIVING AREA:
1,961 SQ. FT.

SECOND FLOOR
No. 93349

FIRST FLOOR
WIDTH= 63'-0"
DEPTH= 47'-0"

To order your Blueprints, call 1-800-235-5700

Design by
James Fahy, P.E., P.C.

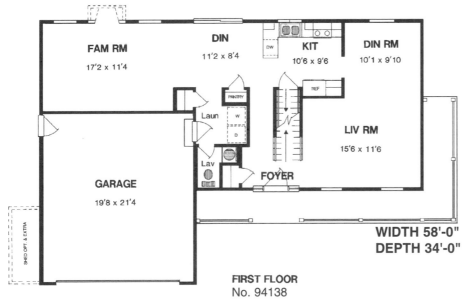

WIDTH 58'-0"
DEPTH 34'-0"

FIRST FLOOR
No. 94138

FAM RM
17'2 x 11'4

DIN
11'2 x 8'4

KIT
10'6 x 9'6

DIN RM
10'1 x 9'10

PANTRY

Laun

Lav

LIV RM
15'6 x 11'6

FOYER

GARAGE
19'8 x 21'4

SHED OPT. & EXTRA

Friendly Front Porch

■ This plan features:

— Three bedrooms

— One full and one half baths

■ Country, homey feeling with
wrap-around Porch

■ Adjoining Living Room and
Dining Room creates spacious
feeling

■ Efficient Kitchen easily serves
Dining Area with extended
counter and a built-in Pantry

■ Spacious Family Room with
optional fireplace and access to
Laundry/Garage entry

■ Large Master Bedroom with a
walk-in closet and access to a full
Bath, offers a private Bath option

■ Two additional Bedrooms with
ample closets and full Bath
access

■ No materials list is available for
this plan

BR 2
10' x 10'5

BATH

W I Closet

Hall

BR 3
10' x 11'5

MBR
12' x 17'

SECOND FLOOR

FIRST FLOOR — 900 SQ. FT.
SECOND FLOOR — 676 SQ. FT.
GARAGE — 448 SQ. FT.
BASEMENT — 900 SQ. FT.

TOTAL LIVING AREA:
1,576 SQ. FT.

Design by
Design Basics, Inc.

Refer to **Pricing Schedule C** on the order form for pricing information

© design basics inc.

Columns and Arched Windows

- This plan features:
  — Three bedrooms
  — Two full baths
- Ten-foot entry with views of the volume Dining Room and Great Room
- A brick fireplace and arched windows in the Great Room
- Large island Kitchen with an angled range and a built-in Pantry
- Master Suite with a whirlpool Bath and a sloped ceiling
- An optional basement or slab foundation — please specify when ordering

MAIN FLOOR — 1,806 SQ. FT.
GARAGE — 548 SQ. FT.

TOTAL LIVING AREA:
1,806 SQ. FT.

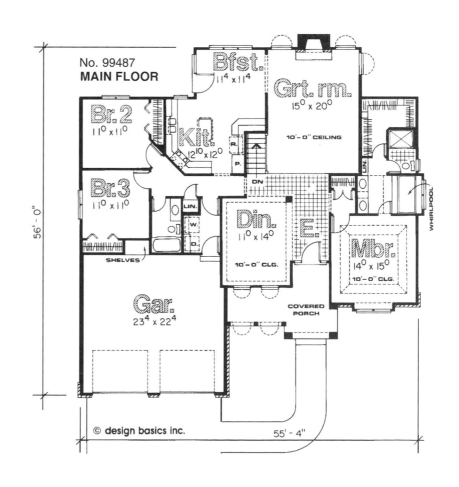

No. 99487
MAIN FLOOR

Bfst. 11⁴ x 11⁴

Grt. rm. 15⁰ x 20⁰
10'-0" CEILING

Br. 2 11⁰ x 11⁰

Kit. 12¹⁰ x 12⁰

Br. 3 11⁰ x 11⁰

LIN.

DN

Din. 11⁰ x 14⁰
10'-0" CLG.

Mbr. 14⁰ x 15⁰
10'-0" CLG.

WHIRLPOOL

SHELVES

Gar. 23⁴ x 22⁴

COVERED PORCH

© design basics inc.   55' - 4"

56' - 0"

To order your Blueprints, call 1-800-235-5700

Design by
Donald A. Gardner, Architects, Inc.

© 1997 Donald A. Gardner Architects, Inc.

B. NATHAN

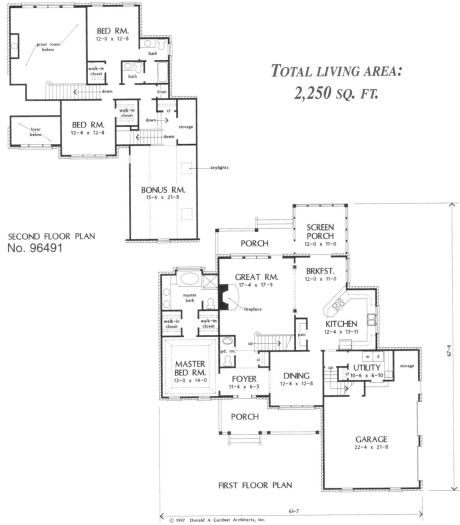

SECOND FLOOR PLAN
No. 96491

TOTAL LIVING AREA:
2,250 SQ. FT.

FIRST FLOOR PLAN

© 1997 Donald A Gardner Architects, Inc.

Traditional Two-Story Home

■ This plan features:

— Three bedrooms

— Two full and two half baths

■ Facade handsomely accented by multiple gables, keystone arches and transom windows

■ Arched clerestory window lights two-story Foyer for dramatic entrance

■ Two-story Great Room excites with inviting fireplace, wall of windows and back Porch access

■ Open Kitchen has easy access to Screen Porch and Dining Room

■ Private Master Bedroom offers two walk-in closets and a deluxe Bath

FIRST FLOOR — 1,644 SQ. FT.
SECOND FLOOR — 606 SQ. FT.
BONUS ROOM — 548 SQ. FT.
GARAGE & STORAGE — 657 SQ. FT.

Design by
Design Basics, Inc.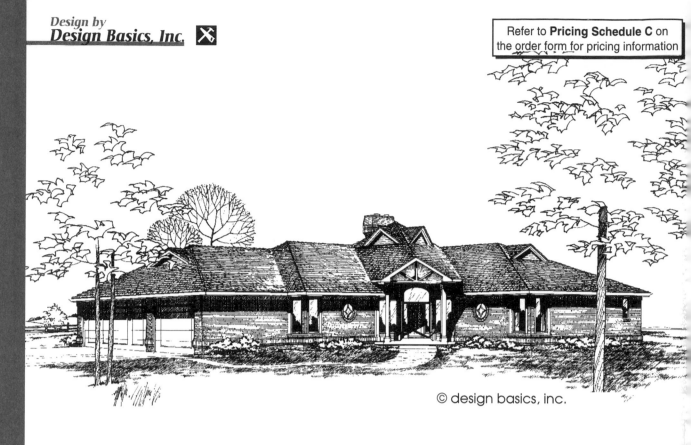

Refer to **Pricing Schedule C** on the order form for pricing information

© design basics, inc.

Visually Open Plan

■ This plan features:

— Three bedrooms

— Two full and one half baths

■ Diagonal views of this open plan give it an expansive look

■ The covered stoop opens into a Y-shaped tiled foyer

■ The Great Room has a high ceiling and a fireplace

■ The Kitchen/Breakfast Area is open and boasts an island with a snack bar

■ Diamond-shaped Dining Room

■ The Bedroom wing contains three large Bedrooms and two full Baths

■ A three-car Garage with storage rounds out this plan

MAIN FLOOR — 2,133 SQ. FT.
GARAGE — 656 SQ. FT.

TOTAL LIVING AREA:
2,133 SQ. FT.

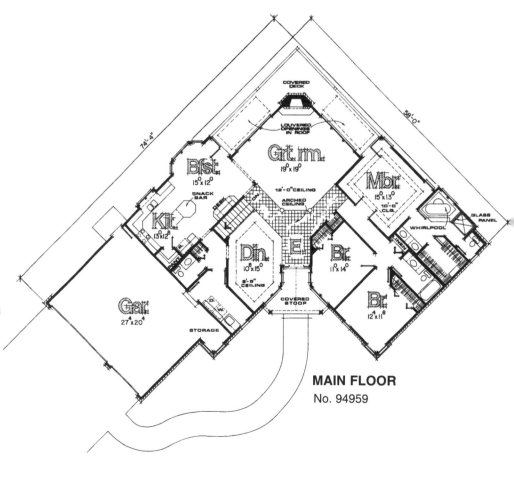

MAIN FLOOR
No. 94959

To order your Blueprints, call 1-800-235-5700

Design by
Building Science Associates

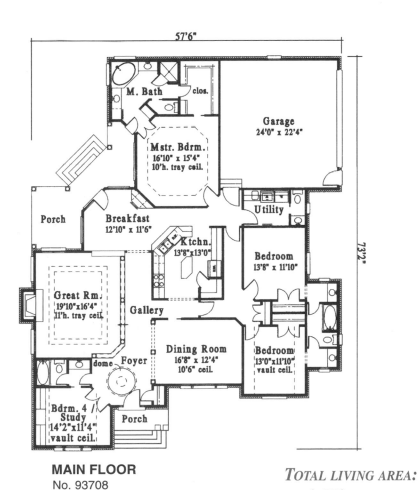

MAIN FLOOR
No. 93708

TOTAL LIVING AREA:
2,579 SQ. FT.

Tailored for a View to the Side

■ This plan features:

— Three/Four bedrooms

— Three full and one half baths

■ Entry Foyer highlighted by a ceiling dome and French doors leading to the private Study

■ Elegant formal Dining Room with a high ceiling, columns and arched entrance

■ Sunken Great Room with a high tray ceiling, arched openings with columns and a fireplace

■ An island and walk-in Pantry add to the Kitchen's efficiency

■ A tray ceiling and lavish Bath pamper the owner in the Master Suite

■ Two additional Bedrooms share a split vanity Bath

■ No materials list is available for this plan

MAIN FLOOR — 2,579 SQ. FT.
GARAGE — 536 SQ. FT.

Design by
Larry E. Belk

Refer to **Pricing Schedule E**
on the order form for pricing information

COPYRIGHT LARRY E. BELK

With A European Influence

■ This plan features:

— Four bedrooms

— Two full and one half baths

■ The Foyer opens to the well-proportioned Dining Room

■ Double French doors with transoms lead off the Living Room to the rear Porch

■ The spacious Kitchen is adjacent to the Breakfast and Family Room

■ The Master Bedroom features a tray ceiling and a luxurious Master Bath

■ An optional basement, slab or crawl space foundation — please specify when ordering

■ No materials list is available for this plan

MAIN FLOOR — 2,745 SQ. FT.
GARAGE — 525 SQ. FT.

TOTAL LIVING AREA:
2,745 SQ. FT.

WIDTH 69–6

MAIN FLOOR
No. 96602

© Larry E. Belk

To order your Blueprints, call 1-800-235-5700

Design by
Donald A. Gardner Architects, Inc.

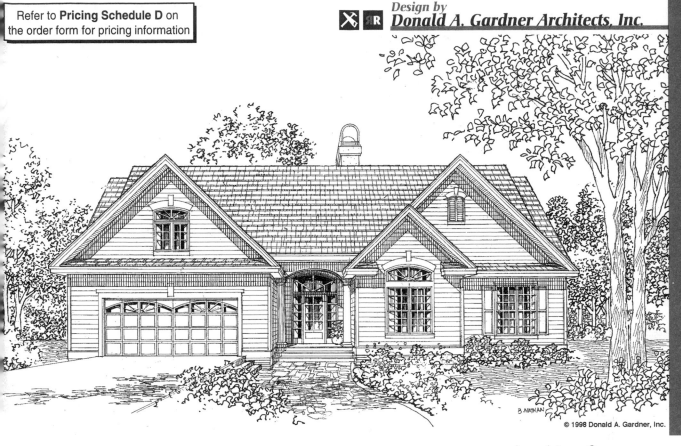

B. NATHAN

© 1998 Donald A. Gardner, Inc.

An Air of Sophistication

- This plan features:
— Three bedrooms
— Two full baths

- Gables with arch topped windows and keystone accents add and air of sophistication

- The covered Porch reveals the front door with a transom and sidelights

- Just beyond is the Great Room with a fireplace and a cathedral ceiling

- The U-shaped Kitchen has a counter that delineates it from the Dining Room

- The Master Bedroom has a cathedral ceiling and a walk-in closet

- Two other Bedrooms both have bright front wall windows

MAIN FLOOR — 1,629 SQ. FT.

TOTAL LIVING AREA:
1,629 SQ. FT.

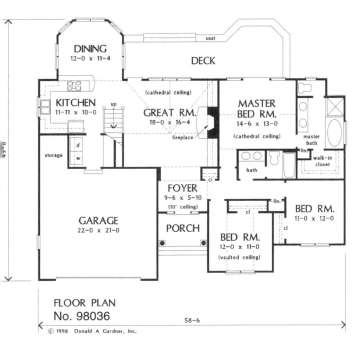

FLOOR PLAN
No. 98036
58-6
© 1998 Donald A Gardner, Inc.

Design by
Design Basics, Inc.

Refer to **Pricing Schedule E** on the order form for pricing information

Great Room Enhanced by Fireplace

- This plan features:
— Four bedrooms
— Two full and one half baths

- Formal Dining Room with a bay window and hutch space

- A see-through fireplace serves both the Hearth Room and the Great Room

- Arched windows and French doors in the Den

- Laid out in an open format, are the Kitchen, Hearth Room and the Breakfast Room

- The Kitchen has an island counter and a walk-in pantry

- There is a cathedral ceiling over the Breakfast Area

- Master Bedroom with an arched window and a whirlpool bath

FIRST FLOOR — 1,963 SQ. FT.
SECOND FLOOR — 778 SQ. FT.
BASEMENT — 1,963 SQ. FT
GARAGE — 658 SQ. FT.

TOTAL LIVING AREA:
2,741 SQ. FT.

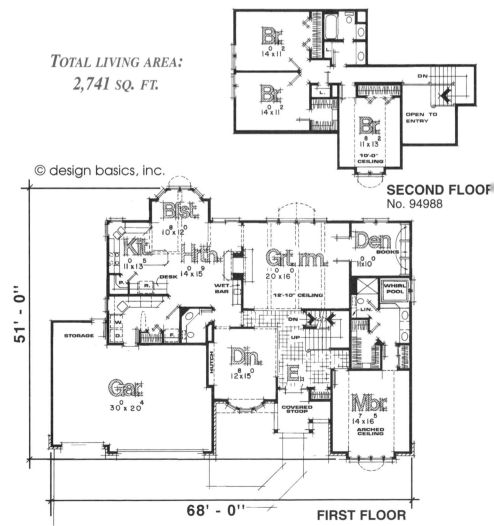

© design basics, inc.

SECOND FLOOR
No. 94988

FIRST FLOOR

222

Refer to **Pricing Schedule E** on the order form for pricing information

Design by
Donald A. Gardner Architects, Inc.

© 1990 Donald A. Gardner Architects, Inc.

B. NATHAN

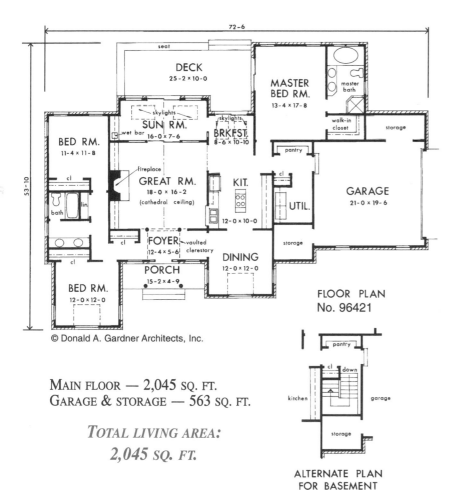

72-6

seat

DECK
25-2 × 10-0

MASTER BED RM.
13-4 × 17-8

master bath

skylights

SUN RM.
16-0 × 7-6
wet bar

skylights

BRKFST.
8-6 × 10-10

walk-in closet

storage

pantry

BED RM.
11-4 × 11-8

fireplace

GREAT RM.
18-0 × 16-2
(cathedral ceiling)

KIT.
12-0 × 10-0

cl

GARAGE
21-0 × 19-6

UTIL.

53-10

bath

FOYER
12-4 × 5-6
vaulted clerestory

storage

DINING
12-0 × 12-0

BED RM.
12-0 × 12-0

PORCH
15-2 × 4-9

© Donald A. Gardner Architects, Inc.

FLOOR PLAN
No. 96421

MAIN FLOOR — 2,045 SQ. FT.
GARAGE & STORAGE — 563 SQ. FT.

TOTAL LIVING AREA:
2,045 SQ. FT.

pantry

cl down

kitchen

garage

storage

ALTERNATE PLAN
FOR BASEMENT

French Influenced One-Story

■ This plan features:

— Three bedrooms

— Two full baths

■ Elegant details and arched windows, round columns and rich brick veneer

■ Arched clerestory window in the foyer introduces natural light to a large Great Room with cathedral ceiling and built-in cabinets

■ Great room adjoins a skylit Sun Room with a wetbar which opens onto a spacious Deck

■ Kitchen with cooking island located with easy access to a large Pantry and Utility Room

■ Large Master Bedroom with deck access and features a garden tub, separate shower, and dual vanity

■ An optional basement or crawl space foundation — please specify when ordering

Design by
James Fahy, P.E., P.C. ✕

Refer to **Pricing Schedule C** on the order form for pricing information

Small, But Not Lacking

■ This plan features:

— Three bedrooms

— One full and one three quarter baths

■ Great Room adjoins the Dining Room for ease in entertaining

■ Kitchen highlighted by a peninsula counter/snackbar extending work space and offering convenience in serving informal meals or snacks

■ Split-bedroom plan allows for privacy in the Master Bedroom with a Bath and a walk-in closet

■ Two additional Bedrooms share the full family Bath in the hall

■ Garage entry convenient to the Kitchen

MAIN AREA — 1,546 SQ. FT.
BASEMENT — 1,530 SQ. FT.
GARAGE — 440 SQ. FT.

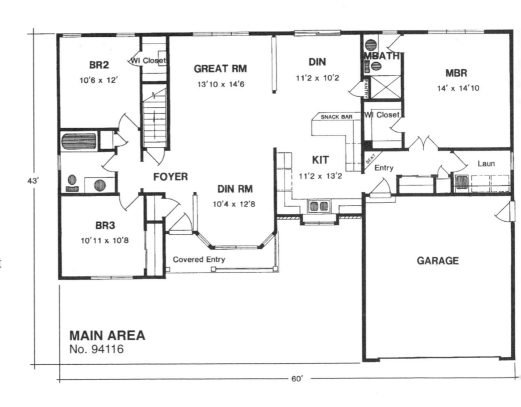

MAIN AREA
No. 94116

TOTAL LIVING AREA:
1,546 SQ. FT.

Design by
Donald A. Gardner Architects, Inc.

© 1994 Donald A. Gardner Architects, Inc.

Clever Use of Interior Space

- ■ This plan features:
- — Three bedrooms
- — Two full baths
- ■ Efficient interior with cathedral and tray ceilings create feeling of spaciousness
- ■ Great Room boasts cathedral ceiling, a cozy fireplace, built-in shelves and columns
- ■ Octagonal Dining Room and Breakfast alcove are bathed in light and accesses Porch
- ■ Open Kitchen features an island and Pantry
- ■ The Master Bedroom is enhanced by a tray ceiling and a plush bath

MAIN FLOOR — 1,737 SQ. FT.
GARAGE & STORAGE — 517 SQ. FT.

TOTAL LIVING AREA:
1,737 SQ. FT.

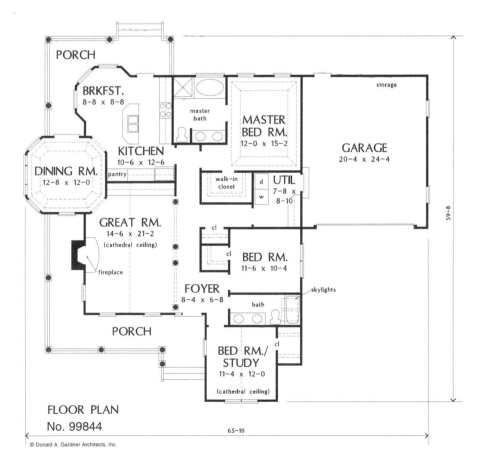

PORCH

BRKFST.
8-8 x 8-8

master bath

storage

MASTER BED RM.
12-0 x 15-2

GARAGE
20-4 x 24-4

KITCHEN
10-6 x 12-6

pantry

DINING RM.
12-8 x 12-0

walk-in closet

UTIL
7-8 x 8-10

d   w

59-8

GREAT RM.
14-6 x 21-2
(cathedral ceiling)

fireplace

cl

cl

BED RM.
11-6 x 10-4

FOYER
8-4 x 6-8

skylights

bath

PORCH

BED RM./ STUDY
11-4 x 12-0
(cathedral ceiling)

cl

FLOOR PLAN
No. 99844

65-10

© Donald A. Gardner Architects, Inc.

B. NATHAN

Design by
Design Basics, Inc.

Refer to **Pricing Schedule E** on the order form for pricing information

© 1990 design basics inc.

Executive Digs

■ This plan features:

— Four bedrooms

— Three full and one half baths

■ The Family Room features an elegant bowed widow and shares a three-sided fireplace with the Breakfast Room and Kitchen

■ The Master Suite features a tiered ceiling and an irresistible oval whirlpool tub in the bath

■ All secondary Bedrooms have access to a Hollywood Bath or a private Bath

■ Bedroom two is elegantly accented by a beautiful arched window

FIRST FLOOR — 1,583 SQ. FT.
SECOND FLOOR — 1,331 SQ. FT.
GARAGE — 676 SQ. FT.

TOTAL LIVING AREA:
2,914 SQ. FT.

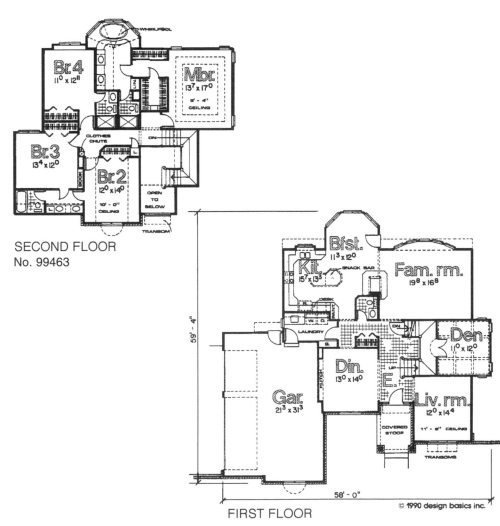

SECOND FLOOR
No. 99463

FIRST FLOOR

© 1990 design basics inc.

To order your Blueprints, call 1-800-235-5700

Design by
Frank Betz Associates, Inc.

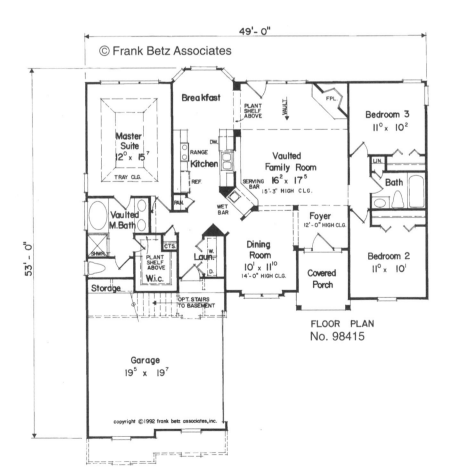

© Frank Betz Associates

49'-0"

53'-0"

Breakfast

PLANT SHELF ABOVE

VAULT

FPL.

Master Suite 12⁰ x 15⁷
TRAY CLG.

Kitchen
DW.
RANGE
REF.
PAN.

Bedroom 3 11⁰ x 10²

Vaulted Family Room 16² x 17⁵
15'-3" HIGH CLG.
SERVING BAR

LIN.

Bath

Vaulted M.Bath
SHWR.
CTS.
PLANT SHELF ABOVE
W.i.c.
WET BAR

Foyer 12'-0" HIGH CLG.

Laun. W. D.

Dining Room 10¹ x 11¹⁰
14'-0" HIGH CLG.

Storage

Covered Porch

Bedroom 2 11⁰ x 10¹

OPT. STAIRS TO BASEMENT

FLOOR PLAN
No. 98415

Garage 19⁵ x 19⁷

copyright ©1992 frank betz associates,inc.

Split Bedroom Plan

■ This plan features:
— Three bedrooms
— Two full baths

■ A tray ceiling gives a decorative touch to the Master Bedroom

■ A full Bath located between the secondary Bedrooms

■ A corner fireplace and a vaulted ceiling highlight the Family Room

■ A wetbar/serving bar and a built-in Pantry add to the convenience of the Kitchen

■ The formal Dining Room is crowned in an elegant high ceiling

■ An optional basement, crawl space or slab foundation — please specify when ordering

MAIN FLOOR — 1,429 SQ. FT.
BASEMENT — 1,472 SQ. FT.
GARAGE — 438 SQ. FT.

TOTAL LIVING AREA:
1,429 SQ. FT.

Design by
Studer Residential Design, Inc.

Refer to **Pricing Schedule C** on the order form for pricing information

Comfortable and Charming

■ This plan features:

— Three bedrooms

— Two full baths

■ Foyer flows into spacious Great Room with massive fireplace and lots of windows

■ Formal Dining Room with sloped ceiling has expansive view of back yard

■ Cooktop island and Pantry in Kitchen efficiently serves the Breakfast area and Dining Room

■ Corner Master Bedroom offers a sloped ceiling, huge walk-in closet and pampering Bath

■ Two additional Bedrooms, one with an arched window, share a full Bath

■ No materials list is available for this plan.

MAIN AREA — 1,964 SQ. FT.
GARAGE — 447 SQ. FT.
BASEMENT — 1,809 SQ. FT.

TOTAL LIVING AREA:
1,964 SQ. FT.

MAIN AREA
No. 92660

Design by
Fillmore Design Group

Attractive Exterior

■ This plan features:

— Three bedrooms

— Two full baths

■ In the Gallery, columns separate the space into the Great Room and the Dining Room

■ There is access to the backyard covered Patio from the bayed Breakfast Nook

■ The large Kitchen is a chef's dream with lots of counter space and a Pantry

■ The Master Bedroom is removed from traffic areas and contains a luxurious Master Bath

■ A hall connects the two secondary Bedrooms which share a full skylit Bath

■ No materials list is available for this plan

MAIN FLOOR — 2,167 SQ. FT.
GARAGE — 690 SQ. FT.

TOTAL LIVING AREA:
2,167 SQ. FT.

MAIN FLOOR
No. 98512

Design by
Larry E. Belk

Refer to **Pricing Schedule A** on the order form for pricing information

A Stylish, Open Concept Home

■ This plan features:

— Three bedrooms

— Two full baths

■ An angled Entry creates the illusion of space

■ Two square columns flank the bar and separate the Kitchen from the Living Room

■ The Dining Room may service both formal and informal occasions

■ The Master Bedroom has a large walk-in closet

■ The Master Bath has a dual vanity, linen closet and whirlpool tub/shower combination

■ Two additional Bedrooms share a full Bath

■ No materials list is available for this plan

MAIN FLOOR — 1,282 SQ. FT.
GARAGE — 501 SQ. FT.

TOTAL LIVING AREA:
1,282 SQ. FT.

WIDTH 48–10

OPTIONAL BAY WINDOW

LIN

MASTER BATH

DINING
9–8 X 9–6
10 FT CLG

LIVING ROOM
16–0 X 17–6
10 FT CLG

FP

BEDRM 3
10–0 X 10–0

SLOPE

MASTER BEDRM
11–0 X 14–0
10 FT CLG

10 FT CLG
KITCHEN
13–4 X 9–6

ARCH

FOYER

ARCH

BATH 2

LIN

BEDRM 2
10–0 X 12–0

DEPTH 52–6

PORCH

STORAGE

GARAGE

MAIN FLOOR
No. 93021

Design by
Larry E. Belk

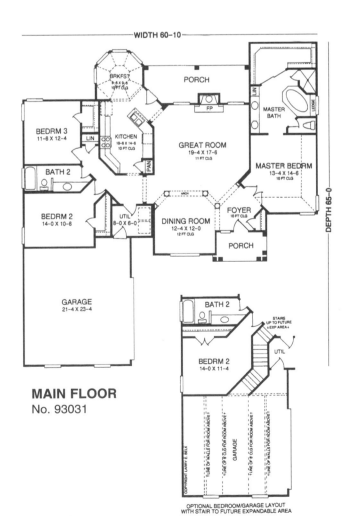

WIDTH 60-10

MAIN FLOOR
No. 93031

OPTIONAL BEDROOM/GARAGE LAYOUT
WITH STAIR TO FUTURE EXPANDABLE AREA

Elegant Entry Flanked by Columns

■ This plan features:

— Three bedrooms

— Two full baths

■ An angled Foyer opens to the large Great Room with a fireplace

■ The formal Dining Room is defined with columns

■ The master Suite is entered through double doors, and is located away from the other Bedrooms

■ The kitchen has Pantry plus plenty of cabinet and counter space

■ No materials list is available for this plan

MAIN FLOOR — 1,955 SQ. FT.
GARAGE — 561 SQ. FT.
BONUS — 240 SQ. FT.

TOTAL LIVING AREA:
1,955 SQ. FT.

Design by
Donald A. Gardner Architects, Inc.

Refer to **Pricing Schedule D** on the order form for pricing information

© 1998 Donald A. Gardner, Inc.

B. NATHAN

Style and Practicality

■ This plan features:

— Three bedrooms

— Two full baths

■ Slightly wrapping front and side porches

■ Plan easily fits onto a narrow lot

■ A cathedral ceiling enhances the Great Room with fireplace and built-ins

■ An optional Loft/Study above the Kitchen overlooks the Great Room

■ Columns frame the entry to the Dining Room which is topped by a tray ceiling

■ Complete Master Suite with tray ceiling, bay window, and bath with garden tub and separate shower

MAIN FLOOR — 1,795 SQ. FT.
BONUS ROOM — 368 SQ. FT.
GARAGE — 520 SQ. FT.

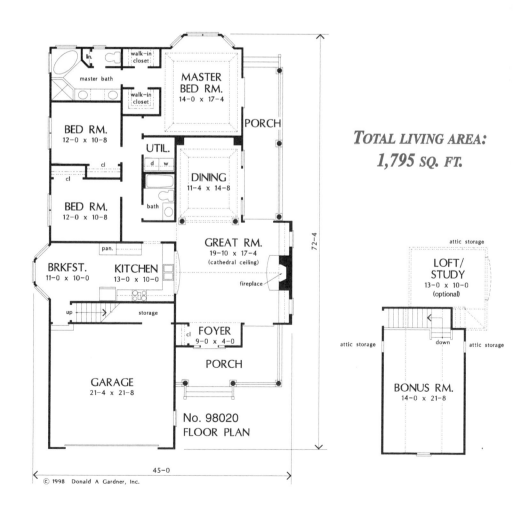

TOTAL LIVING AREA:
1,795 SQ. FT.

No. 98020
FLOOR PLAN

© 1998 Donald A Gardner, Inc.

To order your Blueprints, call 1-800-235-5700

Design by
Design Basics, Inc.

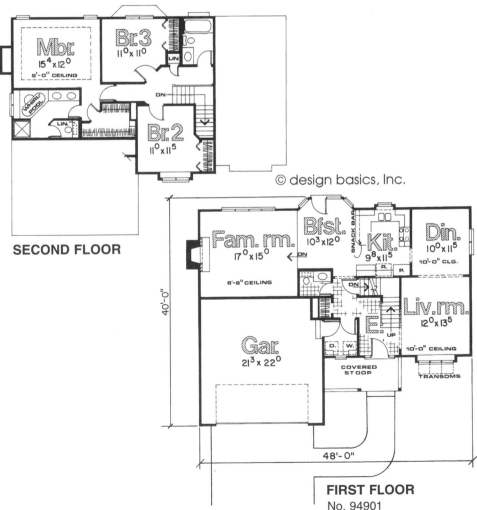

SECOND FLOOR

© design basics, inc.

FIRST FLOOR
No. 94901

Friendly Front Porch

■ This plan features:

— Three bedrooms

— Two full and one half baths

■ A lovely staircase and formal Living Room with transom

■ Dining Room is open to Living Room for entertaining ease

■ Efficient, U-shaped Kitchen with Pantry, snack bar counter and adjoining Breakfast bay

■ Step down into spacious Family Room with handsome fireplace and a wall of windows

■ Master Bedroom offers a boxed ceiling, walk-in closet and a pampering bath

■ Two additional bedrooms with ample closets share a full bath

FIRST FLOOR — 1,042 SQ. FT.
SECOND FLOOR — 803 SQ. FT.
BASEMENT — 1,042 SQ. FT.
GARAGE — 486 SQ. FT.

TOTAL LIVING AREA:
1,845 SQ. FT.

Design by
Design Basics, Inc.

Refer to **Pricing Schedule E** on the order form for pricing information

© design basics inc.

Visually Dramatic Exterior

- This plan features:
— Four bedrooms
— Three full and one half baths

- Multiple rooflines, brick and quoins meld to create a visually dramatic exterior

- The Living Room has a high ceiling and a large front window

- The Master Bedroom has a decorative ceiling and a private Bath

- Upstairs find three Bedrooms all with large closets

FIRST FLOOR — 2,098 SQ. FT.
SECOND FLOOR — 790 SQ. FT.
GARAGE — 739 SQ. FT.

TOTAL LIVING AREA:
2,888 SQ. FT.

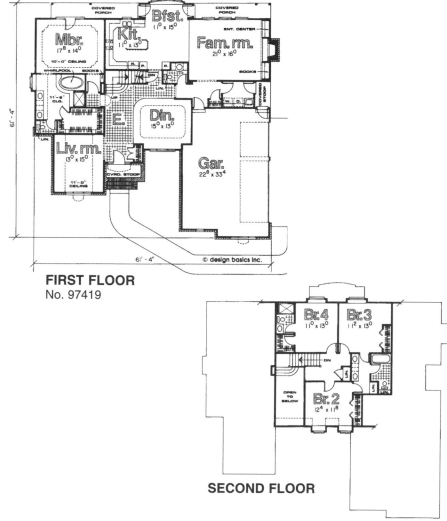

FIRST FLOOR
No. 97419

SECOND FLOOR

To order your Blueprints, call 1-800-235-5700

Design by
Design Basics, Inc.

FIRST FLOOR — 905 SQ. FT.
SECOND FLOOR — 863 SQ. FT.
BASEMENT — 905 SQ. FT.
GARAGE — 487 SQ. FT.

TOTAL LIVING AREA:
1,768 SQ. FT.

© design basics, inc.

SECOND FLOOR

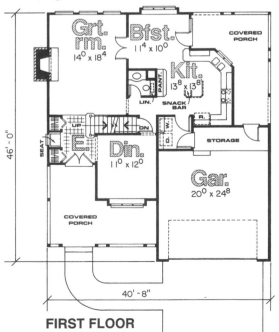

FIRST FLOOR
No. 94907

Victorian Accents

■ This plan features:

— Three bedrooms

— Two full and one half baths

■ Covered Porch and double doors lead into Entry accented by a window seat and curved banister staircase

■ Decorative windows overlooking the backyard and a large fireplace highlight the Great Room

■ A hub Kitchen with an island/snack bar and large Pantry acesses the formal Dining Room and Breakfast Area

■ Powder Room, Laundry Area, Garage entry and storage nearby to Kitchen

■ Cathedral ceiling crowns Master Bedroom with two walk-in closets, dual vanity and a whirlpool tub

■ Two additional Bedrooms, one with a vaulted ceiling above a window seat, share a full Bath

Design by
Design Basics, Inc.

Refer to **Pricing Schedule C** on
the order form for pricing information

Appealing Brick Elevation

■ This plan features:

— Three bedrooms

— Two full and one three-quarter baths

■ Formal Living and Dining Rooms flank the Entry

■ Impressive Great Room topped by an eleven-foot ceiling

■ Awing windows frame the raised hearth fireplace

■ Attractive Kitchen/Dinette Area includes an island, desk, wrapping counters, a walk-in Pantry and access to the covered Patio

■ Pampering Master Suite with a skylight Dressing Area

MAIN FLOOR — 2,172 SQ. FT.
GARAGE — 680 SQ. FT.

TOTAL LIVING AREA:

2,172 SQ. FT.

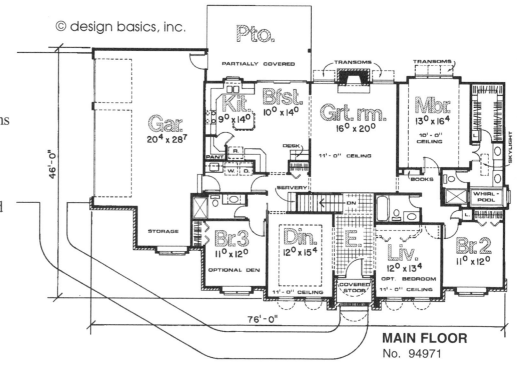

MAIN FLOOR
No. 94971

To order your Blueprints, call 1-800-235-5700

Turret Master Bedroom

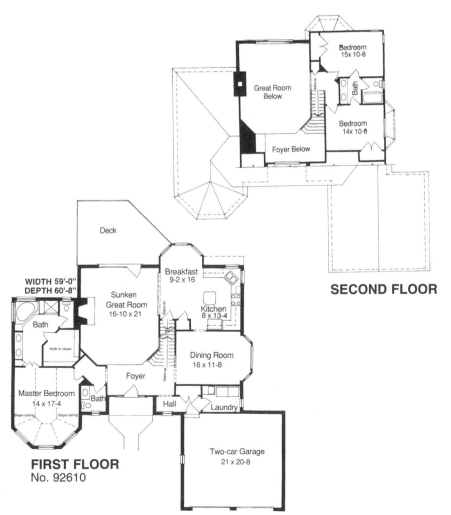

SECOND FLOOR

WIDTH 59'-0"
DEPTH 60'-8"

Deck

Sunken
Great Room
16-10 x 21

Breakfast
9-2 x 16

Kitchen
8 x 13-4

Bath

Walk-in closet

Master Bedroom
14 x 17-4

Slope ceiling   Slope ceiling

Foyer

Bath

Hall

Dining Room
16 x 11-8

Laundry

Two-car Garage
21 x 20-8

FIRST FLOOR
No. 92610

Bedroom
15 x 10-8

Great Room
Below

Bath

Bedroom
14 x 10-8

Foyer Below

■ This plan features:

— Three bedrooms

— Two full and one half baths

■ Curved glass entry into two-story
Foyer with graceful, apron
staircase

■ Sunken Great Room has a focal
point fireplace and atrium door

■ Efficient U-shaped Kitchen with
work island, built-in Pantry,
Breakfast alcove and adjoining
Dining Room with bay window

■ Sloped ceiling accents window
alcove in Master Bedroom offering a plush Bath

■ Two Bedrooms have private
access to a double vanity bath

■ No materials list is available for
this plan

FIRST FLOOR — 1,625 SQ. FT.
SECOND FLOOR — 475 SQ. FT.
GARAGE — 438 SQ. FT.
BASEMENT — 1,512 SQ. FT.

TOTAL LIVING AREA:
2,100 SQ. FT.

Design by
Frank Betz Associates, Inc.

Refer to **Pricing Schedule C** on the order form for pricing information

Split Bedroom Plan

■ This plan features:

— Three bedrooms

— Two full baths

■ Dining Room is crowned by a tray ceiling

■ Living Room/Den privatized by double doors at its entrance

■ The Kitchen includes a walk-in Pantry and a corner double sink

■ The vaulted Breakfast Room flows naturally from the Kitchen

■ The Master Suite is topped by a tray ceiling, and contains a compartmental Bath

■ An optional basement, slab or crawl space foundation — please specify when ordering

MAIN FLOOR — 2,051 SQ. FT.
BASEMENT — 2,051 SQ. FT.
GARAGE — 441 SQ. FT.

TOTAL LIVING AREA:
2,051 SQ. FT.

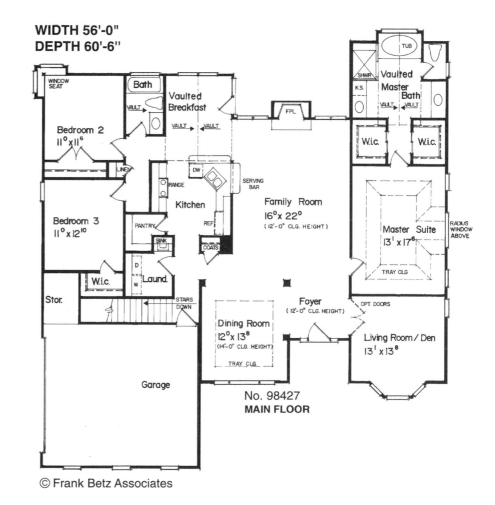

WIDTH 56'-0"
DEPTH 60'-6"

No. 98427
MAIN FLOOR

© Frank Betz Associates

238

Refer to **Pricing Schedule C** on the order form for pricing information

Design by
The Garlinghouse Company

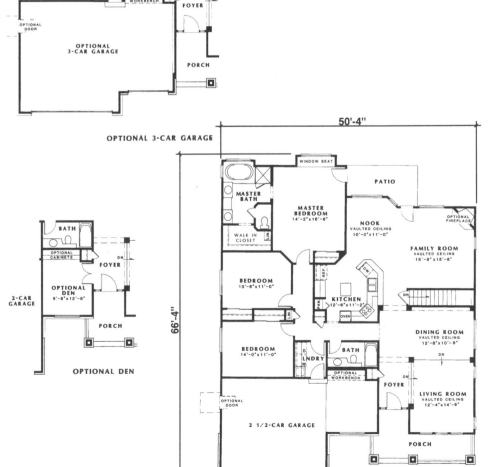

BEDROOM

BATH

LNDRY

OPTIONAL WORKBENCH

DN

FOYER

OPTIONAL DOOR

OPTIONAL 3-CAR GARAGE

PORCH

OPTIONAL 3-CAR GARAGE

BATH

OPTIONAL CABINETS

DN

FOYER

OPTIONAL DEN
9'-8"x12'-8"

2-CAR GARAGE

PORCH

OPTIONAL DEN

50'-4"

66'-4"

WINDOW SEAT

PATIO

MASTER BATH

MASTER BEDROOM
14'-2"x16'-6"

NOOK
VAULTED CEILING
10'-0"x11'-0"

OPTIONAL FIREPLACE

WALK IN CLOSET

FAMILY ROOM
VAULTED CEILING
18'-8"x15'-8"

BEDROOM
13'-8"x11'-0"

REF.

KITCHEN
12'-6"x11'-2"

PAN.

LIN.

DW

DN

OVEN

DINING ROOM
VAULTED CEILING
12'-8"x10'-0"

BEDROOM
14'-0"x11'-0"

D
W

LNDRY

BATH

OPTIONAL WORKBENCH

DN

FOYER

DN

LIVING ROOM
VAULTED CEILING
12'-4"x14'-6"

OPTIONAL DOOR

2 1/2-CAR GARAGE

PORCH

MAIN LEVEL No. 24257

Welcoming Porch Beckons You Inside

■ This plan features:

— Three bedrooms

— Two full baths

■ Vaulted ceilings in the Living Room, Dining Room, Family Room and Eating Nook

■ A U-shaped, Kitchen with an island, built-in Pantry and peninsula eating bar

■ A spacious, open layout between the Kitchen, Eating Nook and Family Room

■ A Master Suite with private Master Bath and access to the Patio

■ Two additional Bedrooms share a full hall Bath

FIRST FLOOR — 2,108 SQ. FT.
GARAGE — 462 SQ. FT.
BONUS — 121 SQ. FT.

TOTAL LIVING AREA:
2,108 SQ. FT.

Design by
Design Basics, Inc.

Refer to **Pricing Schedule C** on the order form for pricing information

Just Perfect

■ This plan features:

— Four bedrooms

— Two full and one half baths

■ The covered Porch leads into a tiled Entry

■ The Dining Room has a built-in hutch and a front window wall overlooking the Porch

■ The Great Room features a see-through fireplace and transom rear windows

■ The Breakfast Bay opens into U-shaped Kitchen with a snack bar

■ The Master Suite has a private Bath with a whirlpool tub

FIRST FLOOR — 1,421 SQ. FT.
SECOND FLOOR — 578 SQ. FT.

TOTAL LIVING AREA:
1,999 SQ. FT.

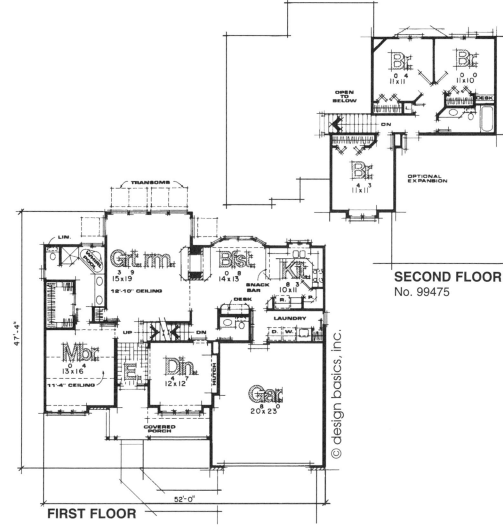

SECOND FLOOR
No. 99475

FIRST FLOOR

To order your Blueprints, call 1-800-235-5700

Design by
Fillmore Design Group

Fabulous Living Room

■ This plan features:

— Three bedrooms

— Two full and one half baths

■ The Living Room has a beautiful hip ceiling adorning it as well as a fireplace

■ It is your choice to create either a Study or a formal Dining Room

■ A center island complements the L-shaped Kitchen

■ The large Master Bedroom includes a pullman ceiling, a five-piece Bath, and a walk-in closet

■ A three-car Garage has ample space in it for storage or a workshop

■ No materials list is available for this plan

MAIN LEVEL — 2,132 SQ. FT.
UPPER LEVEL — 983 SQ. FT.
GARAGE — 660 SQ. FT.

TOTAL LIVING AREA:
3,115 SQ. FT.

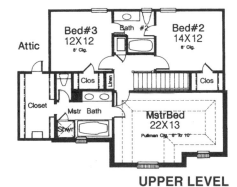

UPPER LEVEL

MAIN LEVEL

Design by
Frank Betz Associates, Inc.

Refer to **Pricing Schedule C** on the order form for pricing information

© Frank Betz Associates

FIRST FLOOR PLAN

54'–0"

46'–10"

Master Suite
13⁰ x 17³

TRAY CEILING

FPL.

FRENCH DOOR

Vaulted Great Room
16⁰ x 18⁵

Vaulted Breakfast

PLANT SHELF ABOVE

FPL.

Vaulted Keeping Room
12⁶ x 15⁰

SERVING BAR

DW.

Laund.

Kitchen

RANGE

PANTRY

REF.

W. D.

RADIUS WINDOW

Vaulted M.Bath

FRENCH DOOR

SHWR.

COATS

OPEN RAIL

STAIRS DN.

Garage
19⁵ x 21⁹

LINEN
PLANT SHELF ABOVE

Pwdr.

Two Story Foyer

STAIRS

OPEN RAIL

W.i.c.

COVERED PORCH

Dining Room
11⁰ x 12³

Details, Details, Details

■ This plan features:

— Three bedrooms

— Two full and one half baths

■ This elevation is highlighted by stucco, stone arched windows

■ The two-story Foyer allows access to the Dining Room and the Great Room

■ A vaulted ceiling and a fireplace can be found in the Great Room

■ The Breakfast Room has a vaulted ceiling and flows into the Kitchen and Keeping Room

■ The Master Suite has a tray ceiling, a huge walk-in closet and a compartmental bath

■ An optional basement or crawl space foundation — please specify when ordering

FIRST FLOOR — 1,628 SQ. FT.
SECOND FLOOR — 527 SQ. FT.
BONUS ROOM — 207 SQ. FT.
BASEMENT — 1,628 SQ. FT.
GARAGE — 440 SQ. FT.

SECOND FLOOR PLAN
No. 98447

Breakfast Below

VAULT

Keeping Room Below

PLANT SHELF

VAULT

Great Room Below

Bath

LINEN

W.i.c.

VAULT

OPEN RAIL

STAIRS DN.

Bedroom 3
12⁰ x 12⁸

Foyer Below

PLANT SHELF BELOW

Bedroom 2
11⁰ x 12³

LINEN

W.i.c.

W.i.c.

Opt. Bonus Room
11⁵ x 15⁹

TOTAL LIVING AREA:
2,155 SQ. FT.

To order your Blueprints, call 1-800-235-5700

Design by
Studer Residential Design, Inc.

Master Bedroom 12' x 14'11"

walk-in closet

Bath

Bath

Bedroom 10'6" x 11'2"

computer desk

Great Room Below

Balcony

stairs dn

Bedroom 11' x 12'

window seat

SECOND FLOOR

TOTAL LIVING AREA:
1,897 SQ. FT.

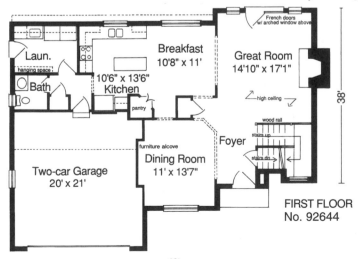

Laun.

hanging space

Bath

Kitchen 10'6" x 13'6"

pantry

Breakfast 10'8" x 11'

French doors w/ arched window above

Great Room 14'10" x 17'1"

high ceiling

wood rail

Two-car Garage 20' x 21'

furniture alcove

Dining Room 11' x 13'7"

Foyer

stairs up

stairs dn

38'

48'

FIRST FLOOR
No. 92644

Distinctive Detail and Design

■ This plan features:

— Three bedrooms

— Two full and one half baths

■ Impressive pilaster entry into open Foyer with landing staircase enhanced by decorative windows

■ Great Room with a hearth fireplace, French doors, arched window and a high ceiling

■ Dining Room enhanced by a furniture alcove

■ L-shaped Kitchen with work island, walk-in Pantry, Breakfast Area, adjoining Laundry, half Bath and Garage entry

■ Master Bedroom offers a walk-in closet, and plush Bath with two vanities and whirlpool tub

■ Two additional Bedrooms share a full Bath and computer desk

■ No materials list is available for this plan

FIRST FLOOR — 1,036 SQ. FT.
SECOND FLOOR — 861 SQ. FT.
GARAGE — 420 SQ. FT.

Design by
Design Basics, Inc.

Refer to **Pricing Schedule B** on the order form for pricing information

Charming Country Style

■ This plan features:

— Three bedrooms

— Two full and one half baths

■ Specious Great Room enhanced by a fireplace and transom windows

■ Breakfast Room with a bay window and direct access to the Kitchen

■ Snack bar extends work space in the Kitchen

■ Master Suite enhanced by a boxed nine-foot ceiling

■ Second floor balcony overlooks the U-shaped stairs and entry

FIRST FLOOR — 1,191 SQ. FT.
SECOND FLOOR — 405 SQ. FT.
BASEMENT — 1,191 SQ. FT.
GARAGE — 454 SQ. FT.

TOTAL LIVING AREA:
1,596 SQ. FT.

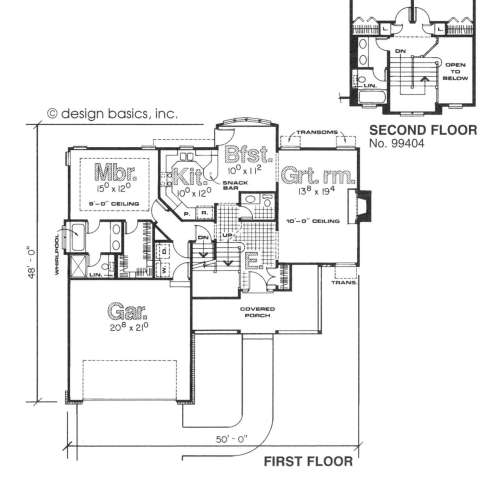

SECOND FLOOR
No. 99404

FIRST FLOOR

To order your Blueprints, call 1-800-235-5700

Design by
Design Basics, Inc.

SECOND FLOOR

Br. 3
10⁰ x 11⁰

Br. 4
10⁰ x 11⁰

DN

OPEN TO BELOW

LIN.

Mbr.
14⁸ x 13⁵

9' - 0" CEILING

10' - 0" CEILING

L.

W/P

Br. 2
11⁰ x 11³

10' - 0" CEILING

TRANSOM

© design basics, inc.

TOTAL LIVING AREA:
1,931 SQ. FT.

TRANSOMS

Bfst.
12⁰ x 13⁰

Kit.
12⁰ x 11⁰

Grt. rm.
14⁰ x 18⁰

DESK

SNACK BAR

10' - 0" CEILING

PANT.

42' - 0"

DN

UP

STORAGE

Din.
11⁰ x 12⁰

Gar.
20⁸ x 28⁰

TRANSOMS

TRANS.

COVERED PORCH

54' - 0"

FIRST FLOOR
No. 94902

Abundance of Windows for Natural Lighting

■ This plan features:

— Four bedrooms

— Two full and one half baths

■ Ten foot ceiling, transom windows and hearth fireplace accent the Great Room

■ Island counter/snack bar, Pantry and desk featured in Kitchen/Breakfast Area

■ Kitchen conveniently accesses Laundry Area and Garage

■ Beautiful arched window under volume ceiling in Bedroom two

■ Master Bedroom features decorative ceilings, walk-in closets and double vanity Bath with a whirlpool tub

■ Two additional Bedrooms with ample closets share a full Bath

FIRST FLOOR — 944 SQ. FT.
SECOND FLOOR — 987 SQ. FT.
BASEMENT — 944 SQ. FT.
GARAGE — 557 SQ. FT.

Everything You Need...
...to Make Your Dream Come True!

You pay only a fraction of the original cost for home designs by respected professionals.

You've Picked Your Dream Home!

You can already see it standing on your lot... you can see yourselves in your new home... enjoying family, entertaining guests, celebrating holidays. All that remains ahead are the details. That's where we can help. Whether you plan to build-it-yourself, be your own contractor, or hand your plans over to an outside contractor, your Garlinghouse blueprints provide the perfect beginning for putting yourself in your dream home right away.

We even make it simple for you to make professional design modifications. We can also provide a materials list for greater economy.

My grandfather, L.F. Garlinghouse, started a tradition of quality when he founded this company in 1907. For over 90 years, homeowners and builders have relied on us for accurate, complete, professional blueprints. Our plans help you get results fast... and save money, too! These pages will give you all the information you need to order. So get started now... I know you'll love your new Garlinghouse home!

Sincerely,

EXTERIOR ELEVATIONS

Elevations are scaled drawings of the front, rear, left and right sides of a home. All of the necessary information pertaining to the exterior finish materials, roof pitches and exterior height dimensions of your home are defined.

CABINET PLANS

These plans, or in some cases elevations, will detail the layout of the kitchen and bathroom cabinets at a larger scale. This gives you an accurate layout for your cabinets or an ideal starting point for a modified custom cabinet design. Available for most plans in our collection. You may also show the floor plan without a cabinet layout. This will allow you to start from scratch and design your own dream kitchen.

TYPICAL WALL SECTION

This section is provided to help your builder understand the structural components and materials used to construct the exterior walls of your home. This section will address insulation, roof components, and interior and exterior wall finishes. Your plans will be designed with either 2x4 or 2x6 exterior walls, but most professional contractors can easily adapt the plans to the wall thickness you require. Available for most plans in our collection.

FIREPLACE DETAILS

If the home you have chosen includes a fireplace, the fireplace detail will show typical methods to construct the firebox, hearth and flue chase for masonry units, or a wood frame chase for a zero-clearance unit. Available for most plans in our collection.

FOUNDATION PLAN

These plans will accurately dimension the footprint of your home including load bearing points and beam placement if applicable. The foundation style will vary from plan to plan. Your local climatic conditions will dictate whether a basement, slab or crawlspace is best suited for your area. In most cases, if your plan comes with one foundation style, a professional contractor can easily adapt the foundation plan to an alternate style.

ROOF PLAN

The information necessary to construct the roof will be included with your home plans. Some plans will reference roof trusses, while many others contain schematic framing plans. These framing plans will indicate the lumber sizes necessary for the rafters and ridgeboards based on the designated roof loads.

TYPICAL CROSS SECTION

A cut-away cross-section through the entire home shows your building contractor the exact correlation of construction components at all levels of the house. It will help to clarify the load bearing points from the roof all the way down to the basement.

DETAILED FLOOR PLANS

The floor plans of your home accurately dimension the positioning of all walls, doors, windows, stairs and permanent fixtures. They will show you the relationship and dimensions of rooms, closets and traffic patterns. The schematic of the electrical layout may be included in the plan. This layout is clearly represented and does not hinder the clarity of other pertinent information shown. All these details will help your builder properly construct your new home.

STAIR DETAILS

If stairs are an element of the design you have chosen, the plans will show the necessary information to build these, either through a stair cross section, or on the floor plans. Either way, the information provides your builders the essential reference points that they need to build the stairs.

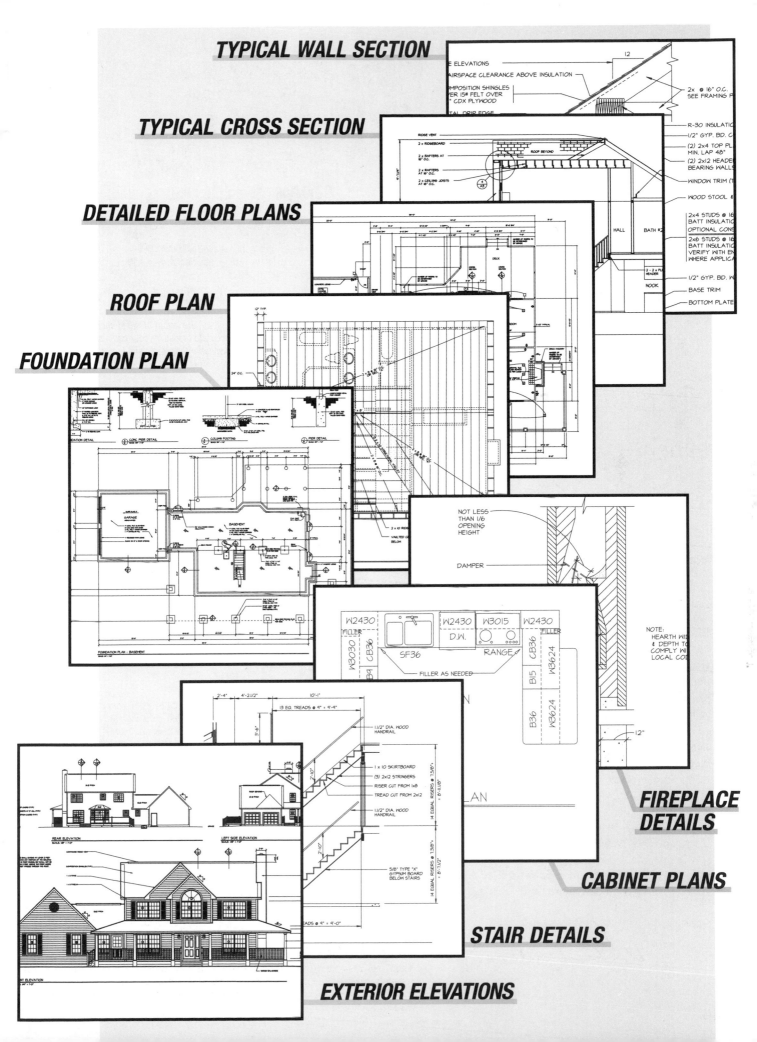

TYPICAL WALL SECTION

TYPICAL CROSS SECTION

DETAILED FLOOR PLANS

ROOF PLAN

FOUNDATION PLAN

FIREPLACE DETAILS

CABINET PLANS

STAIR DETAILS

EXTERIOR ELEVATIONS

Garlinghouse Options & Extras
...Make Your Dream A Home

Reversed Plans Can Make Your Dream Home Just Right!

"That's our dream home...if only the garage were on the other side!"

You could have exactly the home you want by flipping it end-for-end. Check it out by holding your dream home page of this book up to a mirror. Then simply order your plans "reversed." We'll send you one full set of mirror-image plans (with the writing backwards) as a master guide for you and your builder.

The remaining sets of your order will come as shown in this book so the dimensions and specifications are easily read on the job site...but most plans in our collection come stamped "REVERSED" so there is no construction confusion.

As Shown   Reversed

We can only send reversed plans with multiple-set orders. There is a $50 charge for this service.

Some plans in our collection are available in *Right Reading Reverse*. Right Reading Reverse plans will show your home in reverse, with the writing on the plan being readable. This easy-to-read format will save you valuable time and money. Please contact our Customer Service Department at (860) 343-5977 to check for Right Reading Reverse availability. (For this service there is a $165 charge for plan series 998', 964', 980' and $125 for all other plans.)

Specifications & Contract Form

We send this form to you free of charge with your home plan order. The form is designed to be filled in by you or your contractor with the exact materials to use in the construction of your new home. Once signed by you and your contractor it will provide you with peace of mind throughout the construction process.

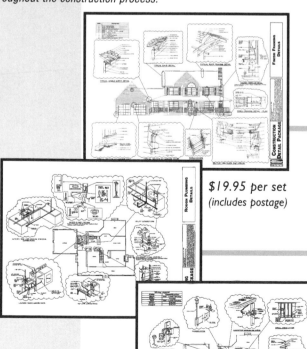

$19.95 per set
(includes postage)

Remember To Order Your Materials List

It'll help you save money. Available at a modest additional charge, the Materials List gives the quantity, dimensions, and specifications for the major materials needed to build your home. You will get faster, more accurate bids from your contractors and building suppliers — and avoid paying for unused materials and waste. Materials Lists are available for all home plans except as otherwise indicated, but can only be ordered with a set of home plans. Due to differences in regional requirements and homeowner or builder preferences... electrical, plumbing and heating/air conditioning equipment specifications are not designed specifically for each plan. However, non-plan specific detailed typical prints of residential electrical, plumbing and construction guidelines can be provided. Please see below for additional information. If you need a detailed materials cost you might need to purchase a Zip Quote. (Details follow)

Detail Plans Provide Valuable Information About Construction Techniques

Because local codes and requirements vary greatly, we recommend that you obtain drawings and bids from licensed contractors to do your mechanical plans. However, if you want to know more about techniques — and deal more confidently with subcontractors — we offer these remarkably useful detail sheets. These detail sheets will aid in your understanding of these technical subjects. **The detail sheets are not specific to any one home plan and should be used only as a general reference guide.**

RESIDENTIAL CONSTRUCTION DETAILS

Ten sheets that cover the essentials of stick-built residential home construction. Details foundation options — poured concrete basement, concrete block, or monolithic concrete slab. Shows all aspects of floor, wall and roof framing. Provides details for roof dormers, overhangs, chimneys and skylights. Conforms to requirements of Uniform Building code or BOCA code. Includes a quick index and a glossary of terms.

RESIDENTIAL PLUMBING DETAILS

Eight sheets packed with information detailing pipe installation methods, fittings, and sized. Details plumbing hook-ups for toilets, sinks, washers, sump pumps, and septic system construction. Conforms to requirements of National Plumbing code. Color coded with a glossary of terms and quick index.

RESIDENTIAL ELECTRICAL DETAILS

Eight sheets that cover all aspects of residential wiring, from simple switch wiring to service entrance connections. Details distribution panel layout with outlet and switch schematics, circuit breaker and wiring installation methods, and ground fault interrupter specifications. Conforms to requirements of National Electrical Code. Color coded with a glossary of terms.

Modifying Your Favorite Design, Made *EASY*!

OPTION #1

Modifying Your Garlinghouse Home Plan

Simple modifications to your dream home, including minor non-structural changes and material substitutions, can be made between you and your builder by marking the changes directly on your blueprints. However, if you are considering making significant changes to your chosen design, we recommend that you use the services of The Garlinghouse Co. Design Staff. We will help take your ideas and turn them into a reality, just the way you want. Here's our procedure!

When you place your Vellum order, you may also request a free Garlinghouse Modification Kit. In this kit, you will receive a red marking pencil, furniture cut-out sheet, ruler, a self addressed mailing label and a form for specifying any additional notes or drawings that will help us understand your design ideas. Mark your desired changes directly on the Vellum drawings. NOTE: Please use only a **red pencil** to mark your desired changes on the Vellum. Then, return the redlined Vellum set in the original box to The Garlinghouse Company at, 282 Main Street Extension, Middletown, CT 06457. **IMPORTANT:** Please **roll** the Vellums for shipping, **do not fold** the Vellums for shipping.

We also offer modification estimates. We will provide you with an estimate to draft your changes based on your specific modifications before you purchase the vellums, for a $50 fee. After you receive your estimate, if you decide to have The Garlinghouse Company Design Staff do the changes, the $50 estimate fee will be deducted from the cost of your modifications. If, however, you choose to use a different service, the $50 estimate fee is non-refundable. (Note: Personal checks cannot be accepted for the estimate.)

Within 5 days of receipt of your plans, you will be contacted by a member of The Garlinghouse Co. Design Staff with an estimate for the design services to draw those changes. A 50% deposit is required before we begin making the actual modifications to your plans.

Once the design changes have been completed to your vellum plan, a representative from The Garlinghouse Co. Design Staff will call to inform you that your modified Vellum plan is complete and will be shipped as soon as the final payment has been made. For additional information call us at 1-860-343-5977. Please refer to the Modification Pricing Guide for estimated modification costs. Please call for Vellum modification availability for plan numbers 85,000 and above.

OPTION #2

Reproducible Vellums for Local Modification Ease

If you decide not to use the Garlinghouse Co. Design Staff for your modifications, we recommend that you follow our same procedure of purchasing our Vellums. You then have the option of using the services of the original designer of the plan, a local professional designer, or architect to make the modifications to your plan.

With a Vellum copy of our plans, a design professional can alter the drawings just the way you want, then you can print as many copies of the modified plans as you need to build your house. And, since you have already started with our complete detailed plans, the cost of those expensive professional services will be significantly less than starting from scratch. Refer to the price schedule for Vellum costs. Again, please call for Vellum availability for plan numbers 85,000 and above.

IMPORTANT RETURN POLICY: Upon receipt of your Vellums, if for some reason you decide you do not want a modified plan, then simply return the Kit and the unopened Vellums. Reproducible Vellum copies of our home plans are copyright protected and only sold under the terms of a license agreement that you will receive with your order. Should you not agree to the terms, then the Vellums may be returned, **unopened,** for a full refund less the shipping and handling charges, plus a 15% restocking fee. For any additional information, please call us at 1-860-343-5977.

MODIFICATION PRICING GUIDE

CATEGORIES	ESTIMATED COST
KITCHEN LAYOUT — PLAN AND ELEVATION	$175.00
BATHROOM LAYOUT — PLAN AND ELEVATION	$175.00
FIREPLACE PLAN AND DETAILS	$200.00
INTERIOR ELEVATION	$125.00
EXTERIOR ELEVATION — MATERIAL CHANGE	$140.00
EXTERIOR ELEVATION — ADD BRICK OR STONE	$400.00
EXTERIOR ELEVATION — STYLE CHANGE	$450.00
NON BEARING WALLS (INTERIOR)	$200.00
BEARING AND/OR EXTERIOR WALLS	$325.00
WALL FRAMING CHANGE — 2X4 TO 2X6 OR 2X6 TO 2X4	$240.00
ADD/REDUCE LIVING SPACE — SQUARE FOOTAGE	QUOTE REQUIRED
NEW MATERIALS LIST	QUOTE REQUIRED
CHANGE TRUSSES TO RAFTERS OR CHANGE ROOF PITCH	$300.00
FRAMING PLAN CHANGES	$325.00
GARAGE CHANGES	$325.00
ADD A FOUNDATION OPTION	$300.00
FOUNDATION CHANGES	$250.00
RIGHT READING PLAN REVERSE	$575.00
ARCHITECTS SEAL (Available for most states)	$300.00
ENERGY CERTIFICATE	$150.00
LIGHT AND VENTILATION SCHEDULE	$150.00

Questions?

Call our customer service department at **1-860-343-5977**

"How to obtain a construction cost calculation based on labor rates and building material costs in <u>your</u> Zip Code area!"

ZIP-QUOTE!
HOME COST CALCULATOR

WHY?

Do you wish you could quickly find out the building cost for your new home without waiting for a contractor to compile hundreds of bids? Would you like to have a benchmark to compare your contractor(s) bids against? *Well, Now You Can!!,* with **Zip-Quote** Home Cost Calculator. Zip-Quote is only available for zip code areas within the United States.

HOW?

Our new **Zip-Quote** Home Cost Calculator will enable you to obtain the calculated building cost to construct your new home, based on labor rates and building material costs within your zip code area, without the normal delays or hassles usually associated with the bidding process. Zip-Quote can be purchased in two separate formats, an itemized or a bottom line format.

"How does **Zip-Quote** actually work?" When you call to order, you must choose from the options available, for your specific home, in order for us to process your order. Once we receive your **Zip-Quote** order, we process your specific home plan building materials list through our Home Cost Calculator which contains up-to-date rates for all residential labor trades and building material costs in your zip code area. "The result?" A calculated cost to build your dream home in your zip code area. This calculation will help you (as a consumer or a builder) evaluate your building budget. This is a valuable tool for anyone considering building a new home.

All database information for our calculations is furnished by Marshall & Swift, L.P. For over 60 years, Marshall & Swift L.P. has been a leading provider of cost data to professionals in all aspects of the construction and remodeling industries.

OPTION 1

The **Itemized Zip-Quote** is a detailed building material list. Each building material list line item will separately state the labor cost, material cost and equipment cost (if applicable) for the use of that building material in the construction process. Each category within the building material list will be subtotaled and the entire Itemized cost calculation totaled at the end. This building materials list will be summarized by the individual building categories and will have additional columns where you can enter data from your contractor's estimates for a cost comparison between the different suppliers and contractors who will actually quote you their products and services.

OPTION 2

The **Bottom Line Zip-Quote** is a one line summarized total cost for the home plan of your choice. This cost calculation is also based on the labor cost, material cost and equipment cost (if applicable) within your local zip code area.

COST

The price of your **Itemized Zip-Quote** is based upon the pricing schedule of the plan you have selected, in addition to the price of the materials list. Please refer to the pricing schedule on our order form. The price of your initial **Bottom Line Zip-Quote** is $29.95. Each additional **Bottom Line Zip-Quote** ordered in conjunction with the initial order is only $14.95. **Bottom Line Zip-Quote** may be purchased separately and does NOT have to be purchased in conjunction with a home plan order.

FYI

An **Itemized Zip-Quote** Home Cost Calculation can ONLY be purchased in conjunction with a Home Plan order. The **Itemized Zip-Quote** can not be purchased separately. The **Bottom Line Zip-Quote** can be purchased separately and doesn't have to be purchased in conjunction with a home plan order. Please consult with a sales representative for current availability. If you find within 60 days of your order date that you will be unable to build this home, then you may exchange the plans and the materials list towards the price of a new set of plans (see order info pages for plan exchange policy). The **Itemized Zip-Quote** and the **Bottom Line Zip-Quote** are NOT returnable. The price of the initial **Bottom Line Zip-Quote** order can be credited towards the purchase of an **Itemized Zip-Quote** order only. Additional **Bottom Line Zip-Quote** orders, within the same order can not be credited. Please call our Customer Service Department for more information.

Zip-Quote is available for plans where you see this symbol. Please call for current availability.

SOME MORE INFORMATION

The Itemized and Bottom Line Zip-Quotes give you approximated costs for constructing the particular house in your area. These costs are not exact and are only intended to be used as a preliminary estimate to help determine the affordability of a new home and/or as a guide to evaluate the general competitiveness of actual price quotes obtained through local suppliers and contractors. However, Zip-Quote cost figures should never be relied upon as the only source of information in either case. Land, sewer systems, site work, landscaping and other expenses are not included in our building cost figures. The Garlinghouse Company and Marshall & Swift L.P. can not guarantee any level of data accuracy or correctness in a Zip-Quote and disclaim all liability for loss with respect to the same, in excess of the original purchase price of the Zip-Quote product. All Zip-Quote calculations are based upon the actual blueprint materials list with options as selected by customer and do not reflect any differences that may be shown on the published house renderings, floor plans, or photographs.

Ignoring Copyright Laws Can Be
A $1,000,000 Mistake

Recent changes in the US copyright laws allow for statutory penalties of up to **$100,000** per incident for copyright infringement involving any of the copyrighted plans found in this publication. The law can be confusing. So, for your own protection, take the time to understand what you can and cannot do when it comes to home plans.

···WHAT YOU CANNOT DO···

You Cannot Duplicate Home Plans

Purchasing a set of blueprints and making additional sets by reproducing the original is **illegal**. If you need multiple sets of a particular home plan, then you must purchase them.

You Cannot Copy Any Part of a Home Plan to Create Another

Creating your own plan by copying even part of a home design found in this publication is called "creating a derivative work" and is **illegal** unless you have permission to do so.

You Cannot Build a Home Without a License

You must have specific permission or license to build a home from a copyrighted design, even if the finished home has been changed from the original plan. It is **illegal** to build one of the homes found in this publication without a license.

What Garlinghouse Offers

Home Plan Blueprint Package

By purchasing a multiple set package of blueprints or a vellum from Garlinghouse, you not only receive the physical blueprint documents necessary for construction, but you are also granted a license to build one, and only one, home. You can also make simple modifications, including minor non-structural changes and material substitutions, to our design, as long as these changes are made directly on the blueprints purchased from Garlinghouse and no additional copies are made.

Home Plan Vellums

By purchasing vellums for one of our home plans, you receive the same construction drawings found in the blueprints, but printed on vellum paper. Vellums can be erased and are perfect for making design changes. They are also semi-transparent making them easy to duplicate. But most importantly, the purchase of home plan vellums comes with a broader license that allows you to make changes to the design (ie, create a hand drawn or CAD derivative work), to make copies of the plan, and to build one home from the plan.

License To Build Additional Homes

With the purchase of a blueprint package or vellums you automatically receive a license to build one home and only one home, respectively. If you want to build more homes than you are licensed to build through your purchase of a plan, then additional licenses may be purchased at reasonable costs from Garlinghouse. Inquire for more information.

Order Form

Order Code No. H9TF1

Plan prices guaranteed until 06/01/00 — After this date call for updated pricing

____ set(s) of blueprints for plan #_____ $_____

____ Vellum & Modification kit for plan #_____ $_____

____ Additional set(s) @ $35 each for plan #_____ $_____

____ Mirror Image Reverse @ $50 each $_____

____ Right Reading Reverse @ $165 each for plan series 998', 964', 980', and $125 for all other plans $_____

____ Materials list for plan #_____ $_____

____ Detail Plans @ $19.95 each

     ❑ Construction   ❑ Plumbing   ❑ Electrical $_____

____ Bottom line ZIP Quote@$29.95 for plan #_____ $_____

____ Additional Bottom Line Zip Quote

     @ $14.95 for plan(s) #_____

_____ $_____

____ Itemized ZIP Quote for plan(s) #_____ $_____

Shipping (see charts on opposite page) $_____

Subtotal $_____

Sales Tax (CT residents add 6% sales tax, KS residents add 6.15% sales tax) (Not required for other states) $_____

TOTAL AMOUNT ENCLOSED $_____

Send your check, money order or credit card information to:
(No C.O.D.'s Please)

Please submit all United States & Other Nations orders to:

Garlinghouse Company
P.O. Box 1717
Middletown, CT. 06457

Please Submit all Canadian plan orders to:

Garlinghouse Company
60 Baffin Place, Unit #5
Waterloo, Ontario N2V 1Z7

ADDRESS INFORMATION:

NAME:_____

STREET:_____

CITY:_____

STATE:_____ ZIP:_____

DAYTIME PHONE:_____

Credit Card Information

Charge To: ❑ Visa   ❑ Mastercard

Card # |__|__|__|__|__|__|__|__|__|__|__|__|__|__|__|__|

Signature _____ Exp. _____/_____

IMPORTANT INFORMATION TO READ BEFORE YOU PLACE YOUR ORDER

How Many Sets Of Plans Will You Need?

The Standard 8-Set Construction Package

Our experience shows that you'll speed every step of construction and avoid costly building errors by ordering enough sets to go around. Each tradesperson wants a set — the general contractor and all subcontractors; foundation, electrical, plumbing, heating/air conditioning and framers. Don't forget your lending institution, building department and, of course, a set for yourself. * Recommended For Construction *

The Minimum 4-Set Construction Package

If you're comfortable with arduous follow-up, this package can save you a few dollars by giving you the option of passing down plan sets as work progresses. You might have enough copies to go around if work goes exactly as scheduled and no plans are lost or damaged by subcontractors. But for only $50 more, the 8-set package eliminates these worries.
* Recommended For Bidding *

The Single Study Set

We offer this set so you can study the blueprints to plan your dream home in detail. They are stamped "study set only-not for construction", and you cannot build a home from them. In pursuant to copyright laws, it is _illegal_ to reproduce any blueprint.

Our Reorder and Exchange Policies:

If you find after your initial purchase that you require additional sets of plans you may purchase them from us at special reorder prices (please call for pricing details) provided that you reorder within 6 months of your original order date. There is a $28 reorder processing fee that is charged on all reorders. For more information on reordering plans please contact our Customer Service Department at (860) 343-5977.

We want you to find your dream home from our wide selection of home plans. However, if for some reason you find that the plan you have purchased from us does not meet your needs, then you may exchange that plan for any other plan in our collection. We allow you sixty days from your original invoice date to make an exchange. At the time of the exchange you will be charged a processing fee of 15% of the total amount of your original order plus the difference in price between the plans (if applicable) plus the cost to ship the new plans to you. Call our Customer Service Department at (860) 343-5977 for more information. Please Note: Reproducible vellums can only be exchanged if they are unopened.

Important Shipping Information

Please refer to the shipping charts on the order form for service availability for your specific plan number. Our delivery service must have a street address or Rural Route Box number — never a post office box. (PLEASE NOTE: Supplying a P.O. Box number _only_ will delay the shipping of your order.) Use a work address if no one is home during the day.

Orders being shipped to APO or FPO must go via First Class Mail. Please include the proper postage.

For our International Customers, only Certified bank checks and money orders are accepted and must be payable in U.S. currency. For speed, we ship international orders Air Parcel Post. Please refer to the chart for the correct shipping cost.

Important Canadian Shipping Information

To our friends in Canada, we have a plan design affiliate in Kitchener, Ontario. This relationship will help you avoid the delays and charges associated with shipments from the United States. Moreover, our affiliate is familiar with the building requirements in your community and country. We prefer payments in U.S. Currency. If you, however, are sending Canadian funds please add 40% to the prices of the plans and shipping fees.

An Important Note About Building Code Requirements:

All plans are drawn to conform to one or more of the industry's major national building standards. However, due to the variety of local building regulations, your plan may need to be modified to comply with local requirements — snow loads, energy loads, seismic zones, etc. Do check them fully and consult your local building officials.

A few states require that all building plans used be drawn by an architect registered in that state. While having your plans reviewed and stamped by such an architect may be prudent, laws requiring non-conforming plans like ours to be completely redrawn forces you to unnecessarily pay very large fees. If your state has such a law, we strongly recommend you contact your state representative to protest.

The rendering, floor plans, and technical information contained within this publication are not guaranteed to be totally accurate. Consequently, no information from this publication should be used either as a guide to constructing a home or for estimating the cost of building a home. Complete blueprints must be purchased for such purposes.

Garlinghouse 1999 Blueprint Price Code Schedule

Additional sets with original order $35

PRICE CODE	A	B	C	D	E	F	G	H
SETS OF SAME PLAN	$405	$445	$490	$530	$570	$615	$655	$695
4 SETS OF SAME PLAN	$355	$395	$440	$480	$520	$565	$605	$645
1 SINGLE SET OF PLANS	$305	$345	$390	$430	$470	$515	$555	$595
VELLUMS	$515	$560	$610	$655	$700	$750	$795	$840
MATERIALS LIST	$60	$60	$65	$65	$70	$70	$75	$75
ITEMIZED ZIP QUOTE	$75	$80	$85	$85	$90	$90	$95	$95

Shipping — (Plans 1-84999)

	1-3 Sets	4-6 Sets	7+ & Vellums
Standard Delivery (UPS 2-Day)	$25.00	$30.00	$35.00
Overnight Delivery	$35.00	$40.00	$45.00

Shipping — (Plans 85000-99999)

	1-3 Sets	4-6 Sets	7+ & Vellums
Ground Delivery (7-10 Days)	$15.00	$20.00	$25.00
Express Delivery (3-5 Days)	$20.00	$25.00	$30.00

International Shipping & Handling

	1-3 Sets	4-6 Sets	7+ & Vellums
Regular Delivery Canada (7-10 Days)	$25.00	$30.00	$35.00
Express Delivery Canada (5-6 Days)	$40.00	$45.00	$50.00
Overseas Delivery Airmail (2-3 Weeks)	$50.00	$60.00	$65.00

Option Key

- **Zip** Zip Quote Available
- **Right Reading Reverse**
- **Duplex Plan**
- **Materials List Available**

Index

TOP SELLING
GARAGE PLANS

Save money by Doing-It-Yourself using our Easy-To-Follow plans. Whether you intend to build your own garage or contract it out to a building professional, the Garlinghouse garage plans provide you with everything you need to price out your project and get started. Put our 90+ years of experience to work for you. Order now!!

No. 06016C $86.00

Apartment Garage With One Bedroom

No. 06015C $86.00

Apartment Garage With Two Bedrooms

- 24' x 28' Overall Dimensions
- 544 Square Foot Apartment
- 12/12 Gable Roof with Dormers
- Slab or Stem Wall Foundation Options

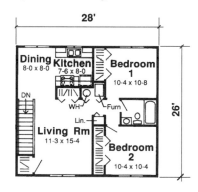

- 26' x 28' Overall Dimensions
- 728 Square Foot Apartment
- 4/12 Pitch Gable Roof
- Slab or Stem Wall Foundation Options

No. 06012C $54.00

30' Deep Gable &/or Eave Jumbo Garages

- 4/12 Pitch Gable Roof
- Available Options for Extra Tall Walls, Garage & Personnel Doors, Foundation, Window, & Sidings
- Package contains 4 Different Sizes
- 30' x 28'   • 30' x 32'   • 30' x 36'   • 30' x 40'

No. 06013C $68.00

Two-Car Garage With Mudroom/Breezeway

- Attaches to Any House
- 24' x 24' Eave Entry
- Available Options for Utility Room with Bath, Mudroom, Screened-In Breezeway, Roof, Foundation, Garage & Personnel Doors, Window, & Sidings

No. 06001C   **$48.00**

12', 14' & 16' Wide-Gable 1-Car Garages

- Available Options for Roof, Foundation, Window, Door, & Sidings
- Package contains 8 Different Sizes
- 12' x 20' Mini-Garage   • 14' x 22'   • 16' x 20'   • 16' x 24'
- 14' x 20'   • 14' x 24'   • 16' x 22'   º • 16' x 26'

No. 06003C   **$48.00**

24' Wide-Gable 2-Car Garages

- Available Options for Side Shed, Roof, Foundation, Garage & Personnel Doors, Window, & Sidings
- Package contains 5 Different Sizes
- 24' x 22'   • 24' x 24'   • 24' x 26'
- 24' x 28'   • 24' x 32'

No. 06007C   **$60.00**

Gable 2-Car Gambrel Roof Garages

- Interior Rear Stairs to Loft Workshop
- Front Loft Cargo Door With Pulley Lift
- Available Options for Foundation, Garage & Personnel Doors, Window, & Sidings
- Package contains 5 Different Sizes
- 22' x 26' • 22' x 28' • 24' x 28' • 24' x 30' • 24' x 32'

No. 06006C   **$48.00**

22' & 24' Deep Eave 2 & 3-Car Garages

- Can Be Built Stand-Alone or Attached to House
- Available Options for Roof, Foundation, Garage & Personnel Doors, Window, & Sidings
- Package contains 6 Different Sizes
- 22' x 28'   • 22' x 32'   • 24' x 32'
- 22' x 30'   • 24' x 30'   • 24' x 36'

No. 06002C   **$48.00**

20' & 22' Wide-Gable 2-Car Garages

- Available Options for Roof, Foundation, Garage & Personnel Doors, Window, & Sidings
- Package contains 7 Different Sizes
- 20' x 20'   • 20' x 24'   • 22' x 22'   • 22' x 28'
- 20' x 22'   • 20' x 28'   • 22' x 24'

No. 06008C   **$60.00**

Eave 2 & 3-Car Clerestory Roof Garages

- Interior Side Stairs to Loft Workshop
- Available Options for Engine Lift, Foundation, Garage & Personnel Doors, Window, & Sidings
- Package contains 4 Different Sizes
- 24' x 26'   • 24' x 28'   • 24' x 32'   • 24' x 36'

Order Code No: **G9TF1**

Garage Order Form

Please send me 3 complete sets of the following GARAGE PLANS:

Item no. & description		Price
Additional Sets	$	_____
(@ $10.00 EACH)	$	_____
Shipping Charges: UPS-$3.75, First Class-$4.50	$	_____
Subtotal:	$	_____
Resident sales tax: KS-6.15%, CT-6%	$	_____
(NOT REQUIRED FOR OTHER STATES)		

Total Enclosed:
$ _____

My Billing Address is:

Name: _____

Address: _____

City: _____

State: _____ Zip: _____

Daytime Phone No. (_____) _____

My Shipping Address is:

Name: _____

Address: _____
(UPS will not ship to P.O. Boxes)

City: _____

State: _____ Zip: _____

For Faster Service...Charge It!
U.S. & Canada Call
1(800)235-5700

All foreign residents call 1(860)343-5977

MASTERCARD, VISA

Card # | | | | | | | | | | | | | | |

Signature _____ Exp. ___/___

If paying by credit card, to avoid delays:
billing address must be as it appears on credit card statement

or FAX us at (860) 343-5984

Here's What You Get

- Three complete sets of drawings for each plan ordered
- Detailed step-by-step instructions with easy-to-follow diagrams on how to build your garage (not available with apartment garages)
- For each garage style, a variety of size and garage door configuration options
- Variety of roof styles and/or pitch options for most garages
- Complete materials list
- Choice between three foundation options: Monolithic Slab, Concrete Stem Wall or Concrete Block Stem Wall
- Full framing plans, elevations and cross-sectionals for each garage size and configuration

Build-It-Yourself PROJECT PLAN

Order Information For Garage Plans:
All garage plan orders contain three complete sets of drawings with instructions and are priced as listed next to the illustration. Additional sets of plans may be obtained for $10.00 each with your original order. UPS shipping is used unless otherwise requested. Please include the proper amount for shipping.

GARLINGHOUSE

Send your order to:
(With check or money order payable in U.S. funds only)
The Garlinghouse Company
P.O. Box 1717
Middletown, CT 06457

No C.O.D. orders accepted; U.S. funds only. UPS will not ship to Post Office boxes, FPO boxes, APO boxes, Alaska or Hawaii.
Canadian orders must be shipped First Class.
Prices subject to change without notice.